Mrs. Homeschool

— A NOVEL —

Karen Louise Peters

◆ FriesenPress

Suite 300 - 990 Fort St
Victoria, BC, V8V 3K2
Canada

www.friesenpress.com

Copyright © 2021 by Karen Louise Peters
First Edition — 2021

The human condition is pretty universal. By both observing others and delving within, my imagination has been sparked for the telling of this story. This is, however, entirely a work of fiction. Any resemblance to real persons, living or dead, is entirely coincidental. All persons, events, places, settings, and organizations are either used fictitiously, or are the product of my imagination, though I wish "Helen" were real—I could have used her in my own homeschool journey.

Leaf artwork: Vecteezy.com

ISBN
978-1-03-910583-6 (Hardcover)
978-1-03-910582-9 (Paperback)
978-1-03-910584-3 (eBook)

1. EDUCATION, HOME SCHOOLING

Distributed to the trade by The Ingram Book Company

Chapter One

April 2008

I sometimes wonder where I was when I changed my mind.

Like, I remember the farm auction when I was twelve years old where I changed my mind in a millisecond about Benny Painchaud after having a crush on him for three years. Embarrassment can do that. And I recall clearly the Grade 9 classroom where pumpkin pie tasted good for the first time. Apparently gloating affects the taste buds. As a young adult, I even know the words I said before I had a chance to think them, right there in front of my non-functioning, powered parking stall that changed my career path from dental hygienist to electrician.

Oh, I know that sometimes you are confronted with a realization such as that you no longer believe you can lose your salvation and could not pinpoint for the life of you when the scale tipped.

And, as much as I couldn't relate, some people claimed that they even couldn't remember their own moment of salvation. What was with that? How could anyone not remember what it felt like to go from the Kingdom of Darkness to the Kingdom of Light. That moment, above all things, I hoped I would never forget.

But I had been put in a position where, as much as I tried to ignore the inevitable, a decision had to be made, and I just don't remember making it. In fact, there were many times I felt like I didn't have a choice.

My husband, on the other hand, appeared to realign his educational convictions during a two-hour phone call. I suspect it wouldn't have been so sudden if he hadn't been out of work for almost two months and the offer hadn't so perfectly met the current need of a full-time job to start almost immediately.

"Ainslee," he appealed to me after being contacted out of the blue by his former high school teacher, "it'll be an adventure. I need to be able to provide for us and I think this can do that." I saw hope, a spark ignited in his eyes that I hadn't seen in several months. Of course I wanted him to succeed. It didn't take much convincing really. I have my faults, but I love him. And I love adventure.

"You're okay if I pursue this?" he clarified, reaching a tentative hand to cover my shoulder.

Every thought in my head at that moment confirmed the need for some kind of change in our lives. What could be harder than the current state of stressing about providing groceries for our five- and four-year-old sons. I recalled just last Sunday in church the class teacher asking, "Is physical change necessary for spiritual growth?" It was my introspective, discouraged Lyndon himself who answered with, "Physical change is not *necessary* for spiritual growth, but it's almost always the *impetus* for growth."

And even more than I wanted financial security, I wanted us to grow spiritually.

Chapter Two

June 2008

The Garmin GPS directed us only so far. After eight-hundred-fifty-nine kilometers of driving west by computer-generated voice directions, we reached Tracey, Alberta. I couldn't help but think of the Biblical Patriarchs who had escaped famine by heading to Egypt. It struck me as humorous, given the economy of the last several years. These days, we flee famine by going to Alberta.

Excitement prevented us from making a final stop at either of Tracey's service stations easily visible from the highway, which became the town's main thoroughfare. Part of the town of Tracey sprawled to our left, and the rest on the right. I clicked to a recent text message. "Ken says to continue to the west end of town, then turn right at the Farm and Ranch Supply," I directed Lyndon.

Other than *Mark's Work Wearhouse*, which carried my favourite Carhartt overalls, I hadn't seen any business of particular attraction to me, but I did easily notice the large sign for the Farm and Ranch Supply right next to the John Deere dealer. "Follow the blacktop for one and a half miles, turn east at range road 245. First right. House behind row of trees."

"Slow down," Lyndon laughed. "Range road what?"

Ken Berry, Lyndon's previous high school teacher, had not only worked hard to get Lyndon into his new position with the Christian Boundless Home School Board, but had also saved us the expense of a scouting trip with his e-mailed video tour of an old farmhouse for rent. Our quick agreement really had nothing to do with its location outside the town limits, or that it had more of a yard for the boys than we could've had in town, or the fact that the only other rental options in Tracey at the time were an apartment or a basement suite, but rather, the price. After paying $900 plus utilities for our trendy, small-town new-build in Manitoba, the price tag of less than half of that made financial recovery seem possible.

Turning south beside an impressive country yard, I gaped at the huge, newly-constructed, two-story with its triple-car garage facing the road. Mud-coloured siding and sections of square faux stone, white trim, multiple gables, three-car, front-facing garage. Even though I understood that we would be renting the old farmhouse not yet visible behind the trees, excitement surged. Momentarily.

Rounding the corner just south of the new "big house" squatted the original farmhouse. Much smaller and more neglected than viewed on a computer screen. The yard, which had appeared nostalgic with its ancient garage in barnboard siding, the weed flowers and a few genuinely beautiful perennials, threatened to be my emotional undoing before ever seeing the inside of this forlorn house. Lyndon breathed deep as he shifted the Ford Edge into park and peered at me, craving my affirmation, willing me not to reject him now in front of this lifeless house. Determination kicked in. This would be our adventure. This would be our home. If behind every successful man stands a good woman, my man would not find me sitting when he most needed me to stand. I swallowed the lump in my throat, ignored my racing heartbeat, and undid my seatbelt.

Lyndon stretched his legs before unbuckling Arnold's car seat, helping our child out onto the gravel drive overgrown with Russian chamomile. While I worked at releasing Brewster's seat, Arnold immediately spied the long-haired, grey-and-white cat sitting on the window ledge of the ancient garage. He took off in that direction, with Lyndon following at a bit of a distance, but it only took the cat a second to realize they were heading its direction before jumping off the ledge and into the tall weeds.

For the moment I chose to keep my eyes on Brewster and Arnold rather than taking in more of my new home. I couldn't help but smile again at our choices of Brewster's and Arnold's names. "We're not going with a soft, girlie-sounding name!" Lyndon proclaimed the first time around.

He'd confided in me only once his dislike for his own name and the locker room jeers all through eighth grade that especially backed his resolve. Thankfully, I'd had the wisdom not to remind him of these insults. However, recommending names to a man who'd taught high school Phys Ed for eight years also proved futile.

"How about Ashton?"

"Really, Ainslee? 'Go Ash!' Try saying that forty times a day and keeping a straight face."

"Forty times a day, Lyndon?" I chided.

"Let's see. Ashton Knight, Ashley Zielsberg, Ashley Howard, oh and don't let me forget Ash dash L-e-i-g-h Smith. I guess when your last name is Smith you have to try to get creative. And that's just Phys Ed 10."

"Okay fine," I laughed. "I get your point. There are other names. Do you like Devin?"

"Devin, Alex, Jordyn, Cameron," he paused. "Sue? Get it? I thought we wanted a boy's name."

"Oh dear," I sighed. "You're worried that Matt and Dave will be next on the girls' list?"

"You never know. So we're going to pick something tough and kind of ugly."

"Like?" I prompted.

"Like Brewster," Lyndon supplied. "Try shortening that."

"Brews?" I attempted. "Oh yeah, that's manly," dripping with sarcasm I pictured my baby making coffee.

"Ainslee. Not Brews. Brewster. Like Bruce. Still a man even when you're in a hurry."

So Brewster grew on me. And it reminded me to walk gently around my husband's somewhat irrational pain. Even if I was by nature too pragmatic to be gentle.

After exploring the old farm yard and finding asparagus, raspberries, a rose bush, and an old wagon wheel as treasures among the dumping ground of someone else's life, we found ourselves walking the perimeter of the house. We commented on everything from the old storm windows, to the inevitability of the boys skinning themselves on the sharpness of the old bottle-glass stucco. But all was said lightly, carefully, choosing to see the rose bush and wagon wheel adorning the old structure, making the empty house too, a treasure. Finally, seeing Lyndon grimace slightly as he bent to accept the dandelion from Brewster, I realized we would have to go in, hoping to find a chair. It was annoying that Lyndon's simple injury from six months ago refused to heal as it should have.

The landlords from the McMansion north of the treeline had let us know they frequently travelled and would not be available to meet us but that they would have the house open. The front door with its oval, floral-etched glass insert was definitely newer than the house. As soon as we opened it, funky smell, just that unlived-in, closed-up-too-long smell greeted us. A short but wide front hall with open closet space led immediately on the left to the kitchen and eating area. A pale green wooden bench was the only piece of furniture in the kitchen. Lyndon headed for it and the boys stayed right beside him.

Dead flies lined dark-brown window ledges and spotted the bowls of patterned-glass light shades. The kitchen cabinets stretched in a straight run for about eight feet overlooking the yard where we'd just parked, and were probably built out of fir plywood in the 1940s or 50s. I opened an upper door. Sturdy doors and shelves. Purple gingham, vinyl shelf-liner made me smile. I loved it when people put the pretty where it was purposeful. It certainly wasn't fashionable anymore but it made me resonate with those who previously lived here, as did the bent cup hooks and chipped plate rail. I closed the door gently, caressing the bronze handle with fingernail grooves beneath which told a story that this house had not always felt abandoned the way it did now. I ran my hand over the speckled Formica countertop. A large once-white single sink was centered beneath a window equally speckled with fly droppings. I recalled seeing what had looked like hollyhocks growing outside under this window. Another smile as I envisioned washing dishes with the tall trumpet-shaped flower reaching up over the window ledge. Of the few plants I recognized, fancy that the one that would keep me company while I washed dishes was this Hollyhock which shared a name with my childhood doll friend Holly Hobbie.

I quickly took in the dusty avocado green stove and fridge, one on either side of the kitchen creating a U-shaped work space, and thought only that I sure hoped they worked, before finding Lyndon watching me from his spot on the long bench placed against the paneled north kitchen wall.

Vaguely, I noticed the boys scurrying around upstairs. I peeked into the panelled living room and master bedroom off the kitchen, opened another door which led to a storage cellar by the look of it, then turned down the hall to the back of the house. Lyndon had moved from the bench and sat on the steps, taking pressure off what had become a very sore leg. We hoped that one advantage to switching out of teaching Phys Ed would be relief for that leg, but so far, with preparing to move, it hadn't improved.

"What do you think of that bathroom?" Lyndon asked after I poked my head into a small bedroom and then the bathroom next to it.

"Oh wow," I smiled around the corner at him. "Pretty cute hey?"

"Seriously, or you're joking?"

"Seriously! That blue tile is so sweet. I love the black trim!"

"You like the blue tub and sink too?"

"At least it's not pink! But yeah, I really like it. And it's in great shape for the age. They must have a good water supply."

"Pretty sure Ken said there's a bountiful well, cuz I remember thinking it's one less bill to pay," Lyndon grinned. "The boys are exploring the bedrooms upstairs."

"What's to explore? Aren't the rooms empty?"

"There's crawl spaces under the eaves," Lyndon raised an eyebrow at me.

"Nice. They'll never need toys!"

"You want to quickly see the laundry room before I go back up with you?" Lyndon asked.

"For sure," I answered, turning to the left across from the bathroom.

"No washer or dryer?" I observed sadly.

"We'll have to ask the landlord about that," Lyndon replied. "I guess we might need to buy those ourselves."

"Might be some room on the credit card," I responded.

Chapter Three

Lyndon texted Ken to let him know we had arrived, and, as promised, Ken Berry and his wife, Helen, arrived a short while later as our first guests, bringing supper with them.

"Well, now, Lyndon, look at you all grown up!" Mr. Berry exclaimed, opening his car door and stepping out onto the weed-covered gravel.

"It's good to see you too, Mr. Berry," Lyndon answered as we stepped out of the house reaching out with a smile to shake his former teacher's hand.

"And that's the last time you get to call me *Mr. Berry*, Lyndon. From now on, it's Ken." The older man reached toward his wife. "Did you ever get to meet Helen?"

"Sure did!" Lyndon responded, wrapping an arm around the petite lady's shoulders. "Got that brownie recipe from you, Helen, and you'll never believe what I managed to do with it!"

"You did not fall for him simply because of the brownies, did you dear?" she asked, turning her attention fully to me.

"Um, it sure helped," I laughed. "I'm Ainslee."

"Ainslee. Lyndon's treasure. It's so nice to meet you. Now, where are those young men I've been hearing about?"

"Good question! They've been occupied with the crawl space in the eaves of the bedrooms upstairs."

"Why don't I come meet them?" She turned to her husband. "Would you set up that folding table and lawn chairs in the house? Ainslee and I will be down to join you shortly."

And with that same cheery spirit, she engaged the boys so that by the time we settled on the lawn chairs, using the bench instead of the folding table for our drinks, and the kids on the picnic blanket Ken had spread on the floor, they ate with abandon in spite of the broccoli in with the chicken and pasta.

"So you said your household items are arriving tomorrow?" Ken asked Lyndon while we enjoyed a brownie served on a piece of paper towel, and coffee poured from Helen's thermos. The brownies tasted exactly the way Lyndon had always made them for me.

"Yeah, it couldn't have worked out better. Klassen Transport will drop our things off here and pick up a load of baby potatoes to take back to Manitoba with them. They would have been coming this way with extra space behind their pallets of Spitz, so they're not charging a whole lot to bring our things and it saved us using a U-haul. This way Ainslee and I could drive together." Lyndon grinned at me as though I really was his treasure. He seemed to be relaxing.

"Are you sure you don't want to sleep over at our place?" Helen asked again.

"I think we're going to camp out here tonight," Lyndon winked at the boys. "Mom put our sleeping bags and pillows in the back of the van so we've got those, and we might have to find some breakfast at McDonald's."

This announcement was met with grins.

"I've got some kids from the church youth group coming to help you when that truck arrives tomorrow morning. You're expecting it around 9?" Ken clarified.

"Yeah, that's what he was thinking."

"Alright, then, you guys sleep tight. We are sure glad to have you folks here. The school division families are looking forward to some more help."

And with that, we helped them load their folding chairs and supper dishes back in their car and said our goodnights.

* * * * *

As promised, the next morning by shortly after 9:00 we heard a semi-tractor rumbling on the asphalt-coated road toward our little rental. Ken Berry had driven up twenty minutes prior and, as they arrived, engaged the sleepy youth in drinks and donuts and a game of hacky sack. Although Lyndon was in a fair bit of pain from our night of sleeping on the air mattress, he'd taken some pain meds and appeared to be his usual teacher self, putting the ten or so youth and a few of their parents at ease with his gentle, charming personality. And I, also being my usual self, hung back a bit, trying to be friendly from a distance while getting the boys to finish their McDonald's eggers. The hashbrowns went down easily enough but the boys were devastated to discover that McDonalds didn't serve chicken nuggets for breakfast.

However, I knew the breakfast would be entirely forgotten when we heard that eighteen-wheeler purr, and I gave up, stuffing the breakfast aside, and our sleeping bags back in their packs.

"Ainslee, keep the boys inside while we move vehicles alright?" Lyndon called from the open front door. "Boys, you cannot come outside until Mom says, alright?" Lyndon commanded Brewster and Arnold.

"Yep. Thanks, Lyndon," I looked up from letting the air out of the flocked mattress. "You doing okay?" I looked up and met Lyndon's eyes.

"Doing good," he answered. "I just didn't think about how that semi would make it onto the yard so now Ken and I need to get everyone to move their vehicles and then the trucker is going to have to back up the driveway since he won't be able to turn around in this space." He paused, reading my need to have him connect with us, came inside and took a moment to communicate with the boys. "If you boys stand at this window, you'll be able to see the big truck first." He pointed them to the lower window on the west living room wall. "You don't have to rush with that, Ainslee," Lyndon encouraged me. "It could be twenty minutes yet before anything is ready to leave that truck."

As it turned out, Lyndon was right. By the time Ken had directed each of the youth vehicles to pull off the yard and park on the main gravel road, and the trucker had expertly backed his big rig the 300 feet up our narrow driveway and rounded the curve to land with the back of the trailer in place to unload our furniture and boxes, Brewster and Arnold and I had joined the group outside to watch the truck.

At this point, Lyndon changed places with me, keeping the boys occupied while I directed the youth to place furniture and boxes in the correct rooms. It was a good thing we still had only toddler beds for the boys I observed, as their little beds were maneuvered up the steep staircase to the attic bedrooms. In the future, we may have to resort to the foam mattresses that came compressed in a box like I'd seen on a TV advertisement.

The almost-new leather couch fit on the longer west living room wall under the biggest window. Beds and dressers were easy to place. Boxes were marked with their contents only because of the organized friend who had helped me pack, which made things much easier now. I would have thought we didn't have a lot of things and I had worked hard to get rid of the unnecessary, including the motorcycle helmets and jackets we had been storing in our garage in the Manitoba property. However, as the boxes kept getting carried in, it became obvious that even an intentionally compact home has a lot of things.

When we rolled up the moving straps an hour later, the trucker started his semi, to the delight of my boys, and we saw the Klassen Transport logo disappear around the bend, off to deliver his remaining load of sunflower seeds and exchange it for potatoes for the return to Manitoba.

A couple of the youth offered to help Lyndon put together the bed frames and some of the girls had shown enough interest in Brewster and Arnold to head upstairs with the boys and get the tour of their empty forts in the eaves of the bedrooms.

Ken Berry had waited until this moment of relative calm to make an introduction. "Ainslee, I was wanting you to meet Annaliese. She's the mom of a couple of these handsome young people. She is *Mrs. Homeschool* and can help you navigate."

Annaliese pulled me down and in for the hug then. But unlike Helen's touch which felt welcome and full of acceptance, I found myself bristling toward Annaliese. And after a couple of minutes of her gushing about home-schooling and how beautiful to have Lyndon setting an example for all these precious families, I felt stifled. Stifled and overwhelmed. Why couldn't she have admired the hollyhocks, given me a restaurant recommendation and waved goodbye while inviting us for a backyard wiener roast a week from Sunday.

Instead, I nodded dumbly while she explained the history of Alberta's first homeschool families. On another day I think I would have cared. On this day, it was too much information too soon. My breakfast was long gone, I worried that Lyndon had overworked his leg and would be in extra pain for the next week. I knew little about Lyndon's new job and didn't really care that *Natural Life* magazine had been influential in the modern-day Canadian homeschool movement. I needed to check in with Brewster and Arnold by now. I assumed they would be wanting a snack and drink as much as I did.

But I tried valiantly to be polite, even as I looked forward to sharing the rest of the day with Lyndon and the boys, learning about our new town.

So it was with mixed feelings that I heard Ken expertly usher Annaliese and her two kids with their adult-sized bodies out the door, wish the rest of the youth well with their upcoming exams and assignments or congratulate them on projects they'd completed, while he bade them goodbye. Because as soon as our little house was quiet, Ken invited Lyndon to come for a tour of the Home School division office after lunch. "Maybe while the kids are napping you can meet me there and we can go over some details. Does 1:00 work?" It was clear his 'you' was singular. Directed only at Lyndon.

This wasn't what I had expected. It was Saturday after all. Surely it could've waited until Monday?

But I suppose with our short night and early morning, it was true that the boys would need to nap. Still, in spite of all the lovely help Ken had rounded up for us, did Ken need Lyndon today more than I did? I'd left my life 859 kilometers away. Could I not have Lyndon until Monday?

Chapter Four

Over those first few weeks, while I unpacked, Helen Berry dropped by the house like an angel. Sometimes with a little bit of extra baking, sometimes to take the boys for a walk or examine a new batch of kittens. She asked for my vehicle keys a few times, buckled them into their car seats and drove them into town for a popsicle or to play at the park. It seemed she knew precisely when I needed a break from the boys, and when to suggest that I join as her guest for an evening aquasize class. When to slip me a Bible verse written on an index card with a butterfly sticker in one corner, and when to suggest that she would host a couple of other moms with young kids for a picnic at a park close to her house if I would come up with some games to keep them entertained.

Before I had children, I probably would have gone so far as to say I didn't really like kids. I managed to hide that detail reasonably well while I worked as a dental hygienist by turning their attention to the TV screen on the ceiling. In that regard, technology was a wonderful thing and I was glad every day that the dentist I worked for was progressive enough to have those screens installed. Kids kind of scared me. They certainly annoyed me. And absolutely grossed me out. I had no desire to babysit my friends' little ones. I figured, *you* brought them into the world, *you* keep them alive and well. If I'd have wanted kids, I'd have had them. However, as any mother knows, that was before I met Brewster. Before his screams quieted by being laid against my chest. Before Lyndon's Aunt Bonnie came to see us and commented that Brewster's ears looked just like Uncle Nick's and I had to fight the urge to cover those baby ears from hearing her nasty words. I wasn't quite sure what normal baby ears looked like, and maybe Brewster's did stick a little far from his head, but comparing them to Uncle Nick's? I knew then that as much as I had liked Aunt Bonnie, my allegiance had shifted. And if there was ever a side to be picked, Brewster and I would be on the same side. So I pushed away my insecurity, checked the internet for some children's games, bought the supplies, and enjoyed meeting the other moms Helen invited.

Four weeks after we arrived in Tracey, Lyndon got his first pay cheque. It wasn't huge, but it was probably the most welcome piece of paper we'd seen since our baptismal certificates eleven months prior. And because this paycheque represented God's answer to our prayers for work, for meaningful work, for learning how to grow in faithful obedience as a couple, we did the right thing. We paid our $400 rent and an amount on the credit card which included the rental damage deposit, moving costs to Klassen Transport, and payment on our gorgeous leather couch. We wrote a small cheque to a child sponsorship ministry. It was the first time since Lyndon had not been called back to substitute teach that we'd donated money, something we had actually rarely done, and it felt good and right. And then? We ordered pizza and drove to a little park in a valley we'd been told about and celebrated with the boys.

That whole first summer felt like a celebration. Like a fresh start. I enjoyed mowing the grass around the old buildings with a rusty push mower left beside the garage. There wasn't actually much grass to mow by the time I went around the junk piles. I was proud of myself for the tweaking I was able to do to get the antiquated machine running. The boys enjoyed the spray park in Tracey, and of course endless hours in their attic eave forts upstairs in their small bedrooms when it was too hot to play outside and almost as hot inside. I explored the local library and enjoyed meeting other moms while bringing the boys to story time. Then we'd bring books and videos home and learn about *How It's Made* while slurping the two-ingredient yogurt pops I was proud of myself for producing in our small kitchen.

In the evenings, Lyndon joined us in trying to tame the long-haired grey cat we'd encountered within the first few minutes of our arrival—the cat who then surprised us by leaving a batch of kittens under a pile of scrap metal and long grasses very shortly after. We drove to neighbouring towns and tasted ice cream from their snack shacks. Our favourite place brought us bumping down the pothole-filled roads in Grassy Lake where the boys chose birthday-cake-flavoured ice cream that came with a little candy on top that looked like a candle on a confetti-covered cake. We let Arnold and Brewster play at the Grassy Lake School park on brand-new playground equipment which they pretended was a spaceship.

With all the play in our days, along with finding space in our little home to best fit everything from the winter coats to the Ichiban noodles, and on the weekends attending a few different churches to see what felt like the best fit for our family, Lyndon and I talked constantly about how much the boys were growing and thriving. We talked about how worry-free we felt, sometimes about the new people we had met. And, though Lyndon's work took more time than I expected, especially when Ken had something he wanted to run by Lyndon, we talked very little about his new job.

* * * * *

I had been living in blissful ignorance until the day Lyndon and I took the boys and drove into Medicine Hat to purchase a pair of specialty shoes, hoping that, along with the chiropractic appointments, the strain in Lyndon's leg would heal. It was the very end of August and I also wanted to check for some new clothes for Brewster and Arnold. On a cool day the week before, we had pulled out the long pants and realized how much both boys had grown over the summer. Short pants are not truth-tellers the way long pants are. Lyndon dropped us off in front of the store while he found a spot to park before joining us.

Right there, right as I walked through the front doors, there in the front of Walmart, it hit me.

School supply lists.

They were posted prominently by grade and by school. School supplies. I panicked. I know normal mothers would have started thinking about their kid's first backpack by the time the child was three. But that wasn't me. I had bought them new toothbrushes and taught them how to floss in spite of the stress of our last year. Being a dental hygienist had, after all, left some mark on me. I had tested all the plugs in our rental house for safety. But I just didn't once think of school supply lists. Suddenly Lyndon was beside us.

"You like your new shoes, Daddy?" Brewster asked.

"Does they make your leg feel good?" Arnold chimed in.

"Maybe with these new shoes I'll be able to walk all the way back to Winnipeg for a Blue Bombers football game," Lyndon winked at the boys.

"Yeah, Dad, do it," Brewster smiled.

"I wanna watch Bombers too. I need new shoes," Arnold whined.

"I think you're right," Lyndon picked him up and set him in the cart. "You think you'll need some new pants to cheer for the Blue Bombers too?"

Lyndon had managed with a couple of sentences to get the boys excited about looking for some new clothes, but my heart was pounding. I felt nauseous.

Thankfully, Lyndon took over and we left the store with three new pants, several shirts, new shoes, socks, and underwear for each of them. Nearby was a fast-food restaurant with a play place, and it was after some fries and a trip back to the vehicle to open the packs of new socks so they could slip out of their sandals and play with covered feet, that Lyndon handed me an iced drink and moved his chair so he had a good view of the boys playing, that he asked, "What's going on?"

I searched for words. I didn't bother unfolding the school supply list I'd tucked in my purse for kindergarten at Tracey Public School.

"I think I'm a really bad mom," I finally managed to summarize.

"Okaaay," Lyndon couldn't suppress a little smile.

"Lyndon! Don't mock me. What kind of mom forgets about school!"

"The school supply lists, huh?" He rubbed a hand over his eyes and grinned. "Yep. Totally threw me for a loop too," he confided.

"Did not." I looked at him, incredulous.

"Not even kidding, Ainslee."

Our eyes met. We laughed then. It kind of started as a cautious giggle that grew to draw the looks of some folks down the room.

We laughed. We shook our heads. We held hands across the table and I asked, "Are we the world's worst parents?"

"I don't know. Maybe."

"It was just so stressful trying to decide what to do, and then the move and then feeling like it's going to be okay and finally having fun with the boys again...I, I just didn't think about kindergarten and, like, are we too late to register or what? How does that even work?"

Lyndon thought for a bit. "Well, kids don't have to be registered for school until they're six so, no, we're not too late."

"Do you think he's ready?" I whispered.

"The boys have been getting along so well," Lyndon mused.

"Okay, I know this is going to sound dumb, but can we just wait?" I asked.

"Well, you've been teaching him all kinds of things this summer just by being with him. With all the change we've had over the year, maybe letting him have a bit more time is just what he needs. It sure won't hurt."

"So are we really going to do that then?" I clarified. "Is that our decision? To wait until next year for Brewster's kindergarten or grade one?"

"Actually, I just read this research article about oldest boys in a family. According to statistics they tend to be a bit behind socially and academically so it might just be what's best for him. I'd feel great about that," Lyndon said. "It seems much better than rushing now to get us all geared up for the changes school would bring."

"Okay." I nodded at him.

"Okay," he repeated, squeezing my hand.

In that moment, the Blue Bombers had nothing on us. I felt like Lyndon and I were a pretty solid team.

Chapter Five

Later that fall was my initial foray into actual homeschool territory. Ken Berry and Lyndon had arranged a barbeque as an opportunity to socialize with all the homeschool families in the school division. Seventy-three families! Seventy-three families who would not only need two evaluations per year, but many of those students would require facilitating exams, driver education, and help selecting appropriate curriculum.

I was beginning to understand how Lyndon had managed to keep busy all summer. It was a little strange meeting all those people. I felt like I imagined a pastor's wife must feel arriving in church the first Sunday after moving: her husband's first sermon, the genuiness of her smile, and the children's clothing all to be laid on the parishioner's dinner table for equal dissection.

All I had, even after the summer of my husband working for Boundless, were stereotypes of homeschoolers. And here they were, all in one place! When we drove home after it was all done, I still couldn't scrub out of my mind the picture of Janeice nursing her four-year-old twins.

I don't know why it hadn't occurred to me until then that I didn't really have a choice about homeschooling Brewster and Arnold. It was a quiet drive back to Tracey. Dread loomed. What I had come to see as our cozy nest, our town to explore, to raise and nurture our kids, a place for me to grow myself, to get to know people through my electrical trade—this place suddenly felt tight and oppressive, and with every mile on the road that dark autumn night, we were careening toward a neglected house I thought I had been learning to love.

I have dreams for my life, I raged inwardly! Not crazy dreams. Not dreams that stood in conflict with raising a family. I had dreams of bringing my full self home to share with my family, teaching my kids the things I'd learned throughout my day working, filling their needs from a full self. I had zero desire ever to be one of those women who found a conversation about home remedies for diaper rash stimulating. I didn't want to bake bran muffins. I would not sit around at Pampered Chef parties. I would not. None of those things felt like they would fuel me, but rather that my life would be drained by them.

In what I felt was stark opposition to what I had imagined for our life here, I shuddered with all that I'd seen: the Kellers with their eleven children whose names all began with the letter 'E'; Janeice nursing her 4-year-olds; Susanna

Neudorf with her girls in their long denim skirts: home-made out of thrift store jeans judging by the seams; trying to have a conversation with Brenna while she allowed her eight-year-old, Chasyn, to interrupt no less than six times sharing his feats with the tether ball which he was attempting to play by himself. "I see, Chasyn! You *are* amazing. The ball almost hit your chin and you kept going. Great determination!" Then there was the slight annoyance of the Peters twins trying to sell their hemp and bead jewelry. Did I look like I was interested in bead jewelry?

I stole a look at Lyndon's face illuminated by lights on the dash. His contented silence fueled my indignant anger. I'm not sure which of us was more shocked when I suddenly burst into tears. "How long have you been planning this, Lyndon?"

My husband took a second to compose his shock at my question. "Um, Ken does this every fall, Ainslee. It's probably been on the calendar since last year..."

"I don't mean the stupid barbeque. I mean forcing us to homeschool. You never asked me. I can't believe you just planned my whole life. I just never thought you'd take advantage of me like this. It's like you're married to Ken, making plans for life with him, and I'm just an appliance you'll use to make your life with him look good! I am not about to be the next Mrs. Homeschool!"

I could tell immediately the way I'd questioned his motives wounded him. I didn't care. In that moment I was so thankful for my electrician papers. If Lyndon wanted to pursue this stupid, cultic homeschooling thing then let him. It would be hard, but I'd find a way to take care of myself and the kids. Was I angrier at him for duping me, or myself for being so blind. So trusting. So stupidly, blindly trusting.

Angry exhaustion took over, and when our headlights reflected against the bits of glass in the stucco on our house, I sat in the vehicle and allowed Lyndon to carry both sleeping boys up the steep stairs and tuck them into bed. I didn't care if it was hard on his leg. Maybe it would help him think about the pain he put me through tonight!

* * * * *

Lyndon was gone by the time Brewster woke me up by climbing in our bed the next morning. He smelled like campfire and told me new knock-knock jokes. We laughed together until he complained about being hungry. The autumn sun cast a glow in the kitchen as I microwaved us each a bowl of porridge.

I was halfway through my cereal before I remembered my ire from the night before. Oddly, what came to mind were slightly different images than I'd had the night before on our strained drive home.

Then, and throughout the rest of the day, I replayed new images:

Older siblings helping younger ones dish up bulgur salad. Ken Berry leading families to stand together and little children bowing their heads to pray. Dads and moms playing games of dodgeball with toddlers to teens.

My favourite memory was a group of teenagers sitting around a campfire singing *Jesus, Hope of the Nations* and other praise songs. The strum of guitars, a violin, clarinet, and flute. Jesse Hogan on the djembe drum. The kids would occasionally stop between songs to share musical instruction with each other. The result: haunting harmony seemingly rising from the smoke and sparks of the campfire. Praise. Worship. I had stopped and listened. Watched. Forgotten about quirks, and my incessant critiquing, while my spirit joined in blessing our Lord, wishing I could sing, thankful that they could and did. And sure, maybe they weren't actually all worshiping, maybe some of them were entirely insincere. Maybe they were loving the atmosphere, the sensuousness of rhythm and harmony, the joy of belonging and creating together, rather than loving the Lord. But whatever their motivation, their investment led me to worship.

* * * * *

A month passed. A month of normalcy. Lyndon went to work in the mornings and was out doing home visits a couple of evenings a week with Ken Berry. The boys needed to be fed and entertained. The grey cat started to rub against our legs when we went outside. I heard about a women's soccer league, and tried a new kind of motor oil when I changed the filter in the vehicle. We had decided to try a small-group fellowship evening with a group from the church we were leaning toward attending, and it so happened that Lyndon had already met at least two of them through the Boundless Homeschool Board. I also remembered one of the ladies from the homeschool barbeque, though I'd been trying to forget that evening ever happened. I checked job ads online, but realized with our decision to keep Brewster home for another year, by the time I paid childcare for both boys I wouldn't be making any money working away from home. Instead, even though I kept looking, I decided the best way to help us financially at this point would be to cut back our spending and do what I could myself. So besides changing the oil on the Edge and the Honda civic we'd bought for Lyndon to get to work, I put on the winter tires and learned to make homemade pizza.

*****

I don't think it was only because she had so endeared herself to me that I responded with cautious optimism to Lyndon's announcement that Saturday night. "Helen is speaking at the Ladies' Homeschool meeting later this month. Would you like to go?" So casual. Helen.

"Helen Berry?"

"Yep." He said no more. Played it cool.

How could I not want to hear what she had to say? Her visits had not been as frequent as the leaves changed to gold and dropped in the wind, but I knew her part-time job with a catering company was getting busier with the Christmas season approaching.

"Well, I'm not homeschooling, Lyndon."

"You can still go. Anyone can." He sounded slightly defensive. "I just thought you might want an evening out."

It was true. With the weather turning colder, I was finding it more of a challenge to be home with Brewster and Arnold. I hadn't found many other women who stayed home with their older pre-schoolers, especially when their kid actually was old enough to have gone to school, and it would be good for me to get out for an evening. Besides, two of the women from our church fellowship group homeschooled and I was starting to enjoy both of them. It was just that I had managed to ignore the homeschool pressure I felt after the fall barbeque and dismiss my anger at Lyndon. I'd even chalked my uncharacteristic outburst up to hormones and apologized to him. I didn't want that all getting stirred up again.

"I would like an evening out, Lyndon. Thanks for letting me know about it."

Lyndon must have relayed to Helen that I was planning to attend, and the night before the homeschool moms' meeting she texted to see if I would give her a ride, as her vehicle was at the garage getting a wheel bearing repaired. If I hadn't already developed a trust for Helen, I would have thought her downright conniving on that one. As it was, I felt relieved that she asked and I didn't have to find my way to Charlotte's country home by myself in the dark or show up alone and explain my presence. After all, I had made no declaration of homeschooling, or admission of mine and Lyndon's oversight regarding Brewster's school year, we were simply postponing kindergarten for a year.

Throughout the day, I had mentally prepared myself for this evening. Nothing could shock me about the group I was about to meet. I had been thoroughly shocked at the barbeque several months previous after all, and reminded myself that this would be a mostly conservative group. Modest, out-dated clothing, possibly hair coverings, mothball-like smells from the charcoal in their natural deodorant, hemp hearts in the snacks, and no knowledge of *Desperate Housewives* even though that's pretty much how I saw them.

So imagine, even before I shut off the vehicle, as I took in Charlotte's home illuminated by the latest in outdoor lighting technology, the surprise of seeing shipping containers stacked and staggered in a modern graphic with large, uncovered windows that allowed me to see that this really was a family home.

Helen was gathering together her purse and a book bag and a pair of slippers she'd set on the floor mat beside her feet.

"Not. Even. Kidding," I muttered to myself.

Helen looked up at me. She smirked.

"Open mind, Ainslee." And I was pretty sure she wasn't referring merely to the architecture.

Charlotte greeted us warmly at the modern door with its five horizontal window inserts, and I realized I recognized her from the TV series, *Training Designers*. Things collided in my brain. *Training Designers*, I get it, because her house is made of shipping containers which are hauled around the country by train, oh and she teaches people about design! She's shorter in real life than I thought she'd be. I'm in her house, please Ainslee, don't be stupid tonight. That window in the living room is actually a garage door! I wonder how you run wires and insulate a shipping-container house. Hang on, I'm here for a home-school meeting! She must homeschool! Is that what the *Training Designers* title actually means? I'm going to have to watch the show again...

And, somehow, I found myself without my winter coat and boots sitting on Charlotte's couch that had the look and feel of the leather on a well-worn, favourite saddle. It was even nicer than mine. A sleek gas fireplace with its sparkly glass stones at the bottom juxtaposed with the aged look of the couch and a shaggy, cream rug at my feet. A mug of sweet apple cider warmed my hands and sloshed a bit when a vivacious woman plopped herself down beside me.

"Nice to see you at Martha Stewart's. I came for the snacks," she mock whispered.

I laughed and turned my head to see I recognized Misty from our church small-group meeting. She's the one who had told me about the women's soccer league.

"Okay, so this house? Her husband is a scrap metal dealer."

I looked at her dumbly.

"You do know shipping containers are made out of metal, right?" Misty poked fun at me.

"So really, it's no different than how we drink lots of milk because my husband works at a dairy, or Susanna has a finished basement where she gets a sewing room cuz her husband works for a builder, or you, I dunno, I guess you homeschool cuz your husband is the guy—"

"I actually don't—"

But she didn't stop to let me in. "—the homeschooler guy, and, like, oh whatever, you know what I'm saying. Except," Misty paused dramatically, "except the difference is Charlotte is magic." Misty rolled her fingertips together. "She takes a bunch of metal boxes and turns it into, well, this." Misty gestured around the room and beyond the glass walls to the rooms jutting out from this space.

There were other pleasantries then. A few introductions. An explanation of Annaliese's unusual absence. Personally, I was relieved. I couldn't remember a thing she'd told me about Alberta's history of homeschooling after we'd unloaded the Klassen Transport truck the day of our move and I wasn't prepared for a pop quiz today. And the next thing I knew, Helen was reading what she'd written about her experience of teaching her two girls. Within a few minutes, her unfolded paper, as well as her voice, stopped shaking and I sensed passion as she shared.

"Homeschooling became for me a way of mentorship. A way of sharing life with my girls for the purpose of knowing Jesus. We had time in our day to memorize scripture verses rather than cramming for them in the car on the way to Sunday School. Chloe and Casey did not learn evolution as fact in school and then have to *unlearn* it at home. They learned math in the grocery store, composition by writing letters to our Compassion children, science through Fluffy the hairless cat, and social studies by visiting my mom and her friends in the senior's home. I do not ever recall my children asking, 'why do we need to learn this?'"

When Charlotte, TV personality by day and homeschool meeting hostess by night, asked if I was joining them for snacks, I tried to cover that I was lost in a spell. Helen had managed to stir my heart to resonate with, as she put it, the *heart of homeschooling*. I almost wanted to get home to Brewster and Arnold instead of socializing with these adults. I wanted to sit on the floor with them and build a block wall and tell them about Joshua's faith and obedience in leading the Israelites around Jericho. I wanted to kick a soccer ball together and have them enjoy how miraculously their bodies had been put together by God and point out the self-control they could learn through sport. A sense of urgency to pass the baton of faith well overwhelmed me.

For once, I felt that God had saved me from my broken family *for* something. Not just saved me *from brokeness,* but saved me *for* something.

Chapter Six

The church service started before any of us sitting in the pews realized it. Interrupting our visiting, came the sound of little voices. Angelic little voices, singing. The visiting stopped. We craned our necks to the increasing sound of music. Little voices, high and clear, now joined by bigger ones. And then they came down the aisle starting from the back, music swelling with the addition of harmony without any instruments. Boys and girls making such beautiful music I was beyond intrigued. I was caught up in the moment. The children kept marching to the front of the church. My only thought was reverent worship. I was suddenly aware of Lyndon nudging my leg and shaking beside me. "What?" I felt irritated. He held out the morning bulletin which I hadn't looked at yet. I followed his finger.

Special Music: E-Harmony

A warm welcome to the Keller family musicians –

Evangeline, Ethan, Eliza, Edyn, Ezekiel, Emanuel, Elias, Eva, Easton, Egypt, Eternity

I looked back up at the children now standing in perfect formation on the stage steps. Keller family. I quickly counted. Eleven. Back down at the bulletin which confirmed the eleven. E-harmony. Well, this family was nothing if not quick-witted.

And that kind of broke my spirit of worship for the morning service.

How does a couple do that? I had only met Eric and Evelyn Keller briefly at the fall family homeschool bar-beque a few months ago. Now I was curious about them. If you're a man named Eric and you meet a woman named Evelyn, do you assume it's meant to be for the two of you? Do you immediately ask her if she wants eleven kids whose names will all start with 'E'? If she says *yes! That's what I've always dreamed of,* you're in luck, but if she says *no,* how long before you meet another gal whose name starts with E, and who's available and who wants eleven kids. Like, what started all this? Or maybe he only asked for eight kids, whose names started with E of course, but then number nine took them by surprise and they just decided to go with it. But then you'd need an amazing urologist after number eleven or you'd have to aim for eighteen.

What kind of people do this, I wondered, again? *And what kind of people does it take to make eleven children who can sing like that? Or get eleven children to comply to perform together and appear to be enjoying it?* I sized up the youngest one. She looked to be about four. *Well, it's still possible that they're going for eighteen*, I imagined. If the names in the bulletin were in order of age, then she was Eternity. *Nope*, I concluded. *They saw a good urologist.*

* * * * *

Sharing cups of coffee at my wooden harvest table one evening when Ken and Lyndon had gone to visit home-school families in the Cardston area, I was filling Helen in on the Easter service at church, which they'd missed since they had been away seeing their adult daughter, Chloe, in North Dakota.

"Ainslee," Helen queried, "what part of the Keller's music ministry bothers you?" She could tell that my summary of E-harmony's performance in our church wasn't merely factual—that behind the words I thought I was choosing carefully and speaking lightly, was criticism. I would have thought that, at worst, I was making observations about choices another family made that I would want to make differently. Where the values that I observed in them, okay possibly assigned to them, were not the values I held, or at least were not expressed in ways that were acceptable to me.

"You mean beyond the fact of having *eleven* kids just to reach a goal?" I hated that I could hear the sarcasm in my own voice. "Do those kids feel wanted? Each one? As individuals? Does number ten believe she was truly wanted, or will she believe she was just a means to number *eleven*? Helen, what if those kids don't all actually love music? What if most of them do but even one or two would rather pursue a different interest, or hate being in the spotlight? That kind of wrecks the E-harmony, doesn't it? Is there individual freedom or do they feel forced to conform? And what are the consequences if they don't? I'm just not sure I can believe that a whole family of children willingly participates in such a broad family plan."

"They sure create beautiful music," Helen mused. She had been to several of E-harmony's concerts over the years.

I thought back to the opening song, the acapella one with the carefully rehearsed march into the church that stirred worship in me, amazement that God would gift an entire family of children with this ability to inspire praise for Himself. I recalled the instruments that came out after that and the talent and commitment required for them to be mastered. Yes. Beautiful music, no denying. But I couldn't shake the nagging thoughts of what went on behind the scenes in order for this music machine to keep running.

"Ainslee, you might be right," Helen spoke softly, as though she could read my thoughts. "And you don't have to emulate them in any way. Allow your observations and reactions to inform you about your own parenting goals and style. In some ways, we all put our kids on stages they never asked to be on, to conform to groups they never chose to be part of, to question whether we really wanted them. Don't paint all of homeschooling one colour because of what you're observing in one family. Let homeschool families speak for themselves as much as you felt the eleven should have a right to express their individuality."

Chapter Seven

By early summer, I'd been to exactly five homeschool support group meetings. We weren't officially home-schoolers, of course, but since we were taking the year to adjust to our new town—well, our new life I suppose—the monthly parent meetings and activities in-between made me feel connected. Brewster and Arnold loved to go play with the other kids, and be involved in the learning activities. It gave me an understanding of Lyndon's job which would help me offer support to him. And honestly, it just gave me something to do in this time before I went back to work. I never stopped to value that I was welcome even though I didn't claim to belong.

I'd also offered to help with the sound system at the small church we'd chosen to attend—the one where I'd experienced the Keller family share their devotion to music. My background as an electrician was helpful in navigating the system, and I genuinely found it fulfilling to help the message get heard. Maybe at this stage in my life it was as missional as I could get.

On this early summer evening though, I arrived at the church after supper to prepare for a wedding rehearsal later that evening. Sounds and smells of meal preparation for the next day's celebration wafted up from the dingy basement kitchen. I could hear the folding tables and stackable wooden chairs with their chipped edges being set out on the painted concrete floor. Well, a concrete floor that after years of scraping those wooden chairs across it for wedding meals and funeral gatherings, and Sunday School meetings, had some paint flecks left on it. It wasn't a glamourous building, but to many Tracey locals, it had been the centre of their spiritual training for almost a century. I had run a couple of cords across the worn main-floor carpet for the mics, but was at a bit of a standstill until I had more information on the bridal couple's plans for their ceremony. I sat alone in the sound booth at the back of the church scrolling through my phone while I waited, when two young people entered the church sanctuary. "I know, right," a young female voice said. "Honestly, she didn't even know what a bachelorette is."

"What? That's crazy!" a second voice chimed in. "She's always been so backward. Angela told me she got Karalee some lingerie for the shower, and Karalee was so embarrassed she just got all red and quick hid it right back in the bag. I don't know what's she's thinking getting married."

"So why are you even being a bridesmaid for her then?"

"Well, I like her and everything. She's super nice. I just think she doesn't know anything about the real world. She didn't even date anyone else. Well, she kind of didn't even date Darryl. It's so weird. Apparently, they can hang out in groups and maybe they got to be alone a bit after they got engaged but I don't know if she's ever even kissed him."

"I don't think her parents are mean like that though. It's like she wants to be so prim. I remember her saying in youth group once that one of our youth activities should be visiting at a seniors' home. And I think that was her own for-real idea. She's kinda from another planet. Honestly, what youth are going to come if we do stale stuff like hang out at a seniors' home. She just doesn't get it."

"I know. She was super homeschooled—"

"Shh, I think they're here now.. ."

And with that the gossip ended as the bride and groom arrived with the pastor to begin the evening rehearsal.

I was surprised to realize that I recognized the bride. She was one of the youth who had come last summer to help unload our boxes and furniture from the Klassen Transport truck. It was she who had stayed to the end playing in the eave forts upstairs in our house with Brewster and Arnold.

She couldn't be older than eighteen or nineteen at the most.

Homeschooled. That figured.

I'd been around the group long enough now to believe that some of them were raising girls to be keepers of the home and nothing more. It was probably a joy for their parents to see these girls marry young and bear their own offspring before they could be tempted by anything the world had to offer. So naïve.

From that point on, over the next hour, I made both mental and actual notes about the service plans, where mics needed to be placed, music that needed to be cued, a mic on the left side of the stage where the bride and groom would wash each other's feet to show their intent was to serve one another.

Their excitement about the next days' nuptials was obvious and contagious. They didn't seem like two teenagers. There seemed to be a well of depth to their character in spite of their ages.

Over the next week, Karalee and Darryl's wedding took up a fair bit of my mental space. Part of me felt disgusted by them marrying so young. What kind of parents had even allowed that? All kinds of statistics pointed to the brevity of marriages started too young. And though I knew I wasn't a great parent—Brewster's kindergarten year, after all—I did know better than to raise kids who couldn't connect with the world around them.

I did know better than that, didn't I?

Because part of raising kids is preparing them to show others how to love Jesus.

And how could they show others what loving Jesus was like if they thought teenagers would want to visit seniors' homes? I didn't want to raise my boys to be so out of touch.

What would Karalee and her new husband do when they realized most couples have lived together before getting married? How would their extreme commitment to purity by not even kissing before the wedding help them relate to other couples in the real world?

I mean, I knew that Christians should be living by a different standard. But how different was different enough?

Round and round these thoughts raced. And rather than focussing on the wedding and the question of raising kids who could connect with the real world, I became increasingly uncomfortable with myself. What made me value being able to converse in a sinful world with its sinful habits as greater than a naïve purity that sometimes reacted with shock to the sins of the world? Should it not be a great honour for me to raise kids who approached their twenties and had aspired to such a godly innocence that they were capable of being shocked by sin? Should I really be valuing the concept of connecting with the "real world" as highly as I did, or did I need to re-evaluate my priorities in my own heart and in raising boys who loved Jesus enough to reach the world He loved?

Chapter Eight

When June Thiessen found out that first winter that I was an electrician, and that my sons were similar in age to her youngest, she had the boys and me come out to her farm several times. The first time, she'd asked if I could let her know if her incubator would be protected from power surges. I was flattered. Her six children ranged in age from the two in post-secondary, three finishing their high school courses at home, to little Conan, who attended the Learning Centre three mornings a week while the older kids did their online schooling, and had hit it off with my Brewster and tolerated Arnold as payload on his wagon. June was everything a part of me wanted to be. She was a vet who chose to limit her practice currently to the three mornings Conan went to The Learning Centre and two Saturdays a month. The rest of the time she bred dogs. And incubated rare breeds of chicks. And sold life insurance and helped clients with investments for a well-known financial company. But I didn't know all of that when I met her, only that she was a family-minded vet, fitting her work schedule around their surprise blessing.

The first thing I found refreshing about June was that she broke every stereotype I'd absorbed about June Cleaver, even though I'd never actually watched *Leave it to Beaver*. Well, maybe not every stereotype now that I gave it a bit more thought. June from this generation didn't wear pumps and pearls to do her housework, and as I would discover soon, didn't obsess about housework at all, but she did her work looking as stylish as a modern-day woman could. June's J Brand jeans looked equally great left out or tucked in to her brown leather, mid-heeled boots. I noticed the brand when she bent over to carefully tuck those hems into her boots before stepping into the duck enclosure to check for their pastel blue and green eggs. I found myself mesmerized, caught between her pragmatically doing chores, the cute boots in the duck pen which looked suspiciously like the pair she'd worn to church last week, and the J Brand jeans which I would know nothing about except for a magazine I'd signed out from the library just last week when I took the boys for story time. The article touted the pants as one of the hottest trends of the year and had a price tag to match.

But other than the trendy appearance, June lived in her modest split-level house with her family like a normal person. Her home's entry had shoes lying exactly where they'd been kicked off, rather than neatly lined up or invisible because they were tucked into perfect custom shelving systems. The worn entry carpet was definitely there to catch pebbles and dirt from the shoes strewn across it, and apparently even a little straw from the barn. The dusty-rose kitchen counter had just enough cleared space to prepare tea for us and snacks for the boys.

That summer day, our second summer in Tracey, with our year of adjusting and indecision about Brewster's schooling drawing to a close, I packed up the tools I'd used to install a timer on the lights necessary for good egg production in the hen house. June had never yet paid me for the little jobs I'd done for her. I'd never left her a bill either. I supposed it was a relatively inexpensive way of giving the boys a fun afternoon.

Yes, I ruminated, securing the tool box behind the back seats, June had a large family and was already done raising a few of them. A lot of her work centered around her home, yet she didn't obsess over the things that didn't matter to her. June Thiessen had bucked the homeschool system and had a name. She wasn't just Mrs. Thiessen. Or Howard Thiessen's wife. She definitely wasn't Mrs. Homeschool. She was Dr. June Thiessen. Owner of June's Dog Breeding. She had a business card with the emblem of a financial company's logo and, more than that, had clients! Clients. The word itself created this air of importance. June was somebody. And as I left her house with my dirty, happy, tired boys and headed back to our rental south of the big house with the beautiful stonework and its three-car garage, I felt just like our home appeared behind the new-build: sweet but mightily overshadowed. Insignificant.

Chapter Nine

Our church small group was meeting at the Neudorf's that evening. I had learned so many things about and from Susanna since our initial meeting at the homeschool barbeque when we'd first arrived at Tracey. Like, I'd learned that I could cut my own pork chops from a pork loin for a fraction of the cost, and if I cut Lyndon and the boys' hair myself, I would save a minimum of $480 each year, perhaps closer to $1000! *That* I didn't do, but it was still good to know, and once in a while I wished both Lyndon and I had the courage to at least try it. I'd learned Susanna could both chop the head off a chicken and fillet a fish, though she'd rather chop the head off a chicken as she didn't love to eat fish. I learned that I knew almost nothing of the commitment required to memorize scripture. Oh, I could recite a handful of Bible verses in the years since I'd been introduced to Jesus, but Susanna *loved* God's Word.

She had memorized not only hundreds of individual verses, but the whole gospel of Mark.

I remembered with shame how my first thoughts about her last fall had been a disdain regarding the jean skirts her little girls wore. *"...made from thrift store jeans, judging by the seams..."* I think those were my exact thoughts. *"...judging by the seams..."* Judging. Why couldn't I have seen then what a thrifty, frugal, tenacious woman this little Susanna was. She was one of the most petite women I'd ever met, and one who worked the hardest. She and her husband had come to Canada from Bolivia arriving shortly before I'd met her.

This evening at their small home with the finished basement where Susanna was able to sew modest skirts for herself and her daughters from two-dollar jeans, Peter and Susanna continued sharing with us their salvation story.

By now we knew that at age sixteen, after listening to a Christian radio program on her older brother's forbidden radio, she had come to understand and accept salvation through Jesus Christ. Unfortunately, by then she'd been secretly pregnant with Peter's baby. And so when she was found out, not for being pregnant but for having her hope in Jesus because of listening to the radio, she was called in by the church elders. Susanna refused to renounce the assurance of her salvation. She had the audacity to quote 1 John 5:13 to the black-garbed men surrounding her: *"These things have I written unto you that believe on the name of the Son of God; that ye may **know** that you have* *eternal life...*" This earned Susanna a beating and banishment from the colony without the luxury of so much as a goodbye to her mother. Her older brother was rebuked for the radio, but because he also supplied the community with cocaine, it was more a formality than anything. Eighteen-year-old Peter, however, discovered from Susanna's sister the reason for Susanna's disappearance from the colony.

"I'd seen that light coming from Susanna's face," Peter shared. "She told me about what she'd heard from that radio preacher—that we didn't have to just work all the time to do more good things than sins. And that God would really forgive us and we could come to God and know we were washed and would be forgiven. Because before that we were always taught that *maybe* we could get to heaven but we had to keep doing whatever the church said and then maybe. And she said that we couldn't keep being together," and here Peter motioned awkwardly with his hands and cleared his throat, "but we could ask God to make us clean from that sin and wait until we could get married."

"But I didn't know then about Anna," Susanna interrupted.

"Yeah, and then what the elders did to you with a beating yet," Peter's eyes got glassy and he cleared his throat again, unable to finish his sentence. "Anna is our little miracle. She always shows us every day about grace—grace from God that He really does forgive our sin and give us good gifts."

Lyndon asked the question that was on all our minds then. "Where did you go when you were beaten and forced to leave, Susanna? And how did you find her Peter?"

"I guess you could say there was some compassion even in that," Susanna responded. "One of the elders, he brought me then to an empty granary away from where anyone lived. He told me he would be back in the morning to see if I had changed my mind. So that night was hard but yet glorious too," she smiled. "Then the next day that man and his wife came in a vehicle they had hired to take them to the city because his wife had cancer and he was going to take her to see the doctor. When I said I would not take it back, that I had said the Bible told us we could know we were forgiven, he said I must go to the city with them and if I wanted to believe what they said on the radio then I could be left there. That radio building was close to where the woman's doctor's office was. So when I got dropped off there I was so terrified because well, I didn't even know anything about the city. But it was like God guided me in there, and would you believe that place was like a house with these missionaries from Canada who worked there! Well, with many others working there too, of course. But the people from Canada who lived there, it was like they saw my bruises and they knew what had happened to me and they fed me and gave me a bed and even let me work so I had some money. But that lady could see after a few weeks that I needed a doctor and that's when I found out about Anna."

Peter picked up the story then. "Yeah, well, I was very young but I knew I wanted her for my life. I wanted Susanna. And I had been thinking about what she said she heard on the radio about Jesus forgiving our sin so far it is gone like the east from the west. Well, and that had been on my mind since I was a very young boy. I did not want to lay in my bed every night and wonder what I could do so I would not go to hell or every time there was a thunder storm and lightening try to think of all the bad things I had done that I should try to make right so I would not be condemned to hell. I thought, could it really be true that we could be at peace that our sins were really forgiven? For a few days I was afraid that the elders would beat me too because of her. But then I was worried about her and I missed her and I just decided I would go to that one elder and find out what they did with her no matter what happened to me. So I went to talk to him at his barn that one day and I expected a fight maybe even. No, instead when he saw me and I said Susanna's name, like I asked what happened to her he just turned his back and said he couldn't talk to me. I didn't leave though. I just stood there beside him the whole time while he milked three cows," Peter and Susanna looked at each other and shared a smile about his tenacity. "Yeah, he didn't look at me, but then he just said the name of a Bolivian guy who I knew drove people from our colony to the city." Peter raised his eyebrows at Susanna then.

"So then I knew that was the guy who knew where she was, or at least knew where she'd gone. As soon as I had some money I found that driver and it cost me pretty much all I had but I got to the city as soon as I could and sure enough she was still there at that radio station."

"But I was a little bit bigger when he saw me then because that was maybe almost three months before he came," Susanna shared. "And so he knew about the baby and then we had to decide what to do. But those missionaries they were so good to us. They helped Peter get saved too."

"Like parents," Peter added. "So they got us married and helped us find a place to live and a job for me."

"Yeah, and then we lived there for maybe eight years but even though those missionaries were so good to us we were so lonely and we didn't know if we could raise our girls there in that city and we had been learning English there so then we had a chance to come to Canada and it is like a dream come true," Susanna glowed.

Our small group sat there, stunned by their story. I'd never heard of anything like this. Had I ever met anyone with such a courageous faith? Did I love Jesus enough to cherish my relationship with Him above all things? Enough to travel however far it took so I could teach my kids to value God, His Word and find fellowship with His people?

Chapter Ten

Misty waited around on the parking lot until I changed out of the runners I'd worn for the mile-long walk from my house to the soccer pitches, and into my cleats for the first soccer practice. I'd found shin pads at the second-hand store and soccer socks and cleats that already hurt my feet at Canadian Tire. Thinking of the price tag on the only other option in the store and trying to tell myself these cheaper shoes would conform to my feet by the end of the first game, I'd worn them around the house for two days.

"How long since you've played soccer?" Misty asked.

"Before Arnold," I laughed nervously. "I don't know what will happen out there today, but I can't wait."

"Well, I'm glad to have company," Misty assured me kindly.

We started off the practice session with a few laps around the field. I forgot about the shoes rubbing against my heels and across the fronts of my feet. Breathing deep, in and out, focussing on changing my stride to help stretch my legs, I felt strong and powerful. With each warm-up exercise I gained confidence in kicking the ball with accuracy, keeping my hands out of the way while making full use of the rest of my body in stopping and redirecting each shot that came my way. It seemed so long since I'd felt this measure of freedom and joy. I didn't once think about my tall, solid frame, or my crooked nose or unruly, auburn curls and how red my face got when I exercised. Lyndon or the boys didn't cross my mind. I wasn't struggling with the idea of Brewster needing to be registered for Grade 1, or the continuing awkwardness of being new to the community and without friends and connections. I was just Ainslee: the soccer player, the team member, the nature lover.

Most of the team went to Tim Horton's after the practice. We ordered iced coffees, chatted about the practice and the upcoming fall season, noting how far we would need to travel for some of the games. With the shortage of women's teams, our league covered a large portion of the southeastern part of Alberta and would mean travelling at least once as far north as Provost. Could life get any better? I'd been somewhat envying Lyndon and his opportunity to visit the homeschool families, exploring Alberta for the first time. Now I had a chance to do the same.

* * * * *

Before we'd left Manitoba, I did dream of what life could be. Lyndon and I had left the boys with church friends for the day and borrowed a motor bike from an acquaintance who'd mentioned the option once and probably didn't mean it, but we were young and craving excitement and feeling nostalgic, so we reminded him of the offer anyway.

The fall after Arnold was born, we realized we hadn't had time to take our Kawasaki out for more than a grand total of about four and a half hours that whole summer season and, despite Lyndon's summer job putting up fences, we needed the money from the bike to replace our unreliable Chevy Malibu car before winter. As if parting with the bike were merely a temporary measure, Lyndon and I had both hung on to our helmets, riding boots, gloves, and leather jackets. Although, when I'd pulled the Rubbermaid bin off the shelf in the garage to make sure we were prepared for our adventure, I discovered there was no way I could fit my arms into those leather sleeves and bend them without cutting off circulation. Peeling the jacket off, assuming if the arms were that tight there'd be no way to zip it up, I loaded up the boys, hoping they would sleep, and headed for a gem of a second-hand store in Brandon. It didn't even really cross my mind until I'd driven almost forty minutes that they may not have a riding jacket. By then I was almost there, and I wasn't about to make it that complicated. I'd make do with almost anything to enjoy the day with Lyndon. They had to have something!

Sure enough, I left the store with a Sedici Mona black, white and a-few-red-accents-on-the-arms motor bike coat that made me feel as if God Himself had planned our upcoming date. How was it possible to have found something so perfect! Giddy, I felt pretty confident that Lyndon would find those were sixty dollars well spent!

We didn't once talk about where we planned to go for the day. I guess the freedom of being on the bike and having the kids in good care was such euphoria that it didn't matter. Either that, or we both knew that we'd be heading south, cross the border into the US and sail to Minot like we had several times during our dating days.

"You are so kickin'," Lyndon finally broke the silence about three miles past the US border crossing.

"Can't even see me," I spoke into my helmet from behind him on the bike. "But I figured you might like the coat."

"I like the lady in it," his grainy voice replied through the helmet mic. I could hear the smile in his voice.

We spent most of the next hour and a half in silence, taking in the early fall views.

Not surprisingly by now, Lyndon cruised through town to a little pizza place we'd eaten at on almost all our Minot trips. Weird, I knew. We could have had pretty much the same quality pizza anywhere, but it would taste better here, what with our attachment to the place and how it brought happy memories of our growing relationship.

Later, on the bank of the Souris River, feeling, for lack of a less corny description, "so blessed," I opened up to Lyndon. Looking back, maybe I shouldn't have, but that was before some of the hope drained out of his world, back when he always believed that next year his temporary teaching position would turn into a full-time contract. Before the school divisions amalgamated, and two schools closed their doors meaning less teaching positions, not more. Before Ms. Krause actually returned from her maternity leave when everyone, including her, were rumouring that after baby three she would stay home with the little ones for a time rather than returning to her Phys Ed position.

Anyway, right there beside the Souris River, as unpredictable as any river, I told Lyndon again how I'd come to esteem being an electrician and despise my days as a dental hygienist. "I can't fix anything by cleaning anyone's teeth," I told him. "People who already have pretty clean teeth don't really need me, and those who don't clean their own teeth probably never will. I can clean their teeth for that day, but then it's out of my control and all up to them for another year—or ten. But when I wire something, I've given it possibilities it never had before. I get to make things powerful. I get to make things safe. People are freed to spend their energies on their passions rather than subsistence living. A problem means finding the break in the circuit and fixing it. I think I'd like to get back into being an electrician."

Lyndon smiled and pulled me close. He didn't remind me how much I hated heights, or working in the cold, or being watched by a zealous customer, which was not even as bad as having to try to work while listening to the endless chatting of a lonely one.

"Were you even listening?" I whined into Lyndon's arm.

"Of course. You love getting electricity to finish its circuit." He fingered my mess of curls. "I, on the other hand, love it when sparks fly."

I couldn't help but laugh and with that we were back in the moment, enjoying our date, a brief respite from the stresses that came with having two babies less than a year apart.

But, as much as I enjoyed snuggling against Lyndon's back on the ride home, enjoyed the light changing from a hint of long shadows, to warm gold spilling over every grove of trees, every field, every pond, to dusk's purply escort back into the street-lit familiarity of our hometown, something nagged me in my stylish leather jacket with every mile on the back of that borrowed bike. Was what Lyndon said about me true? *You love getting electricity to finish its circuit.* Did I think I enjoyed the electrical trade because I could flip a switch and control it? How many of my persuasive sentences to alert him to the fact that I was dreaming about going back to work had begun with *I get to...?* Had I not even actually said *I get to make things powerful?* Even now that one struck me as kind of funny. I don't think that one had made it into my electrical pun arsenal until now. So why was I feeling nagged by my own words? Was my recent desire to get back into my career a result of my love for the work, for helping my family? Or was it ultimately a desire, in the midst of our current uncertainties, to feel in control.

Chapter Eleven

We had reached the end of August; completed our year of procrastination. Over the last couple of weeks, tension between us was high as we'd attempted to discuss our schooling options several times. Here we were again tonight after the boys had gone to bed, sitting in lawn chairs in the middle of the yard watching the sun set.

"Ainslee, you're acting naïve." Lyndon's bluntness toward me, about me, even using my name to make sure there was no mistaking the surety of his words, caught me off-guard.

"Lyndon," I volleyed his name back, frustration showing in my tone, "I refuse to look at the world as entirely sinister. What proof do you have that the educational system started out with this evil intent by government to control the nation's children? You don't think there was anyone who envisioned a public education system for what it could do for a child's potential?"

There were things we left unspoken then. Many things that had been said before. Some of those unsaid words were ones we couldn't seem in previous conversations to get the other to comprehend, and maybe we were too weary to try. Maybe saying Lyndon's name had done its work of reminding me to not use my words to stomp on the wounded one whose job it was to husband me.

"We don't have to go back through history. I agree," Lyndon finally tried again. "We can't know with certainty the intent of people in the past. The Bible doesn't give us a commentary on what education should look like, and it seems that there have been a wide variety of educational methods used," Lyndon conceded.

Then he sighed. "Ainslee, I know you doubt me, and I can't blame you for that. I was in the school system, having a life with a teacher is what you signed up for. I get that you feel life has taken a turn you weren't prepared for."

I felt myself getting uncomfortable with Lyndon's approach. "I appreciate you trying to acknowledge how this is affecting me, Lyndon, but let's not make this about me. I thought you genuinely saw teaching as a great means for ministry: being a role model for young guys, your life being an example. I know you couldn't do Phys Ed right now, your leg being what it is, and the whole Ms. Krause debacle, but there would have been other positions, even if we'd have had to move a little further away for those as well."

Lyndon refused to be swayed from the direction he'd started. "It does seem a little too coincidental–Ken also being a teacher, and in the past, mine. My work situation, Ken's call. You seem to think I'm flippant, I'm weak, I'm giving myself over to Ken's will without making up my own mind on this. Or that it's *my* plan, not *our* plan. Ainslee, I *do* love teaching, I *do* want to use my life to show Christ to a hurting world, I *do* want to be a good role model. If you think I'm running from something, I don't think that's true."

Lyndon paused then while the sun had its last chance to speak to the day—that final sliver of white brilliance that happens before the disappearing.

"When Ken introduced me to the idea of homeschooling, I could immediately see all the things I want for someone else's kid–having a godly example, coming to know Christ, learning truth and discernment and how to live a life that really matters–were things I wanted for Brewster and Arnold. It's just that, who can I trust to give that to them? Most of my past co-workers, even if they're good teachers and decent people, can't know how to shepherd my child's heart. I don't want the boys spending their days learning evolution and having to spend the evenings trying to unlearn it. I don't want them taking hours to stand in lines and wait their turns and have no time or energy to memorize scripture. I don't want them to figure out where they're at on the gender curve. I want them to know they're boys and it's okay to have an interest in art not gym, or not like to hunt. They're boys, not partial boys. I'm not wanting to run *from* something, I'm wanting to run *to* something. And Ainslee, I trust you to help me give them all these things. I didn't know when I chose you that I'd be asking you to help homeschool our kids. Didn't know if we'd get to have kids. For sure didn't know it then, but now I want you to be the one I pursue Jesus with, and what more could I want for the boys than to learn about Jesus with you? There's lots of jobs *anyone* can do but this is one only *we* can.

"Is that just *my* plan, Ainslee? What part of that doesn't seem like *our* plan?"

Lyndon's speech moved me. I was still angry that Lyndon assumed that I'd want what he wanted. Or maybe I was angry at God about that—that I'd want what *He* wanted. Who knew. But when I looked at it like that, I had to find out. Was homeschooling what God wanted for me? For *us*? Could I submit myself to God if it was? Could I fight Lyndon if it wasn't?

Chapter Twelve

September 2009

We sat there that first day of school in our fresh school-room. Lyndon had set it up for us. He'd ordered a white board and an iPad from one of the homeschool suppliers, putting them on our already dangerously high credit card. After all, this was a need, and we did get fifteen percent off because he was staff. We somehow didn't think that by the time we paid a nineteen per cent interest rate and took fifteen months to pay all that stuff and the new curriculum off, it would become the most exorbitant priced schoolroom ever.

Colourful posters and an alphabet border adorned the walls. He'd downloaded a rendition of "Oh Canada" for us, written in a key for people with average voice ranges, one with the old-fashioned lyrics. I wasn't sure how helpful it would be for me, but since the boys were about as talented with music as I was, maybe they wouldn't notice

I

my incompetence. Our nine by ten-foot bedroom looked every bit the school room. An old-fashioned, braided carpet covered one corner with a pouf for me to sit on and a small book shelf to hold a few new books that were sure to capture the boys' imaginations.

It was September 8th, after the long weekend, and the same day all the schools in the province would be starting for the season. By 8:45 a.m. the house was getting stuffy. The temperature promised to get to 27 degrees by early afternoon. We'd left the window open overnight, though I'd closed it an hour ago in an attempt to keep the cool of the night in and the heat of the day out. Scanning the list of instructions Lyndon had left me, I read *Record start time*.

8:58 got entered in the blank space beside that.

Sing "Oh Canada". Ah yes. I should have had the music cued and ready to play on the iPad but I now scrambled to find it. Arnold was digging through his pencil case. Brewster showed me where Lyndon had put the link to the music. After I managed to convince Arnold that his pencil was as sharp as it needed to be and to put his pencil sharpener down, we muddled our way through the anthem. Both boys started out strong with a hearty "O Canada," and then filled in occasional words or sounds until we got to "God keep our land." We finished, and similarly made our way through *The Lord's Prayer*.

I did okay with the Story Time. A video introducing numbers was actually fun and they wanted to watch it a second time.

I checked the time. 9:47. I felt done for the day. How long did we have to do this?

We spent three miserable days in that perfect, little bedroom-turned-school-room. I followed Lyndon's day plan. After all, he was the expert. And, to his credit, he had spent time and effort, and according to our almost maxed credit card, a fair bit of money to try to create the perfect environment with the perfect curriculum so we could all be successful. It wasn't only that I was trying to catch Lyndon's vision. I had agreed to this move and was trying to resign myself for the life it meant for me as well. I could not have wanted to support Lyndon's success more. Even after the bumps of the last year, I loved him. I was committed to our marriage and creating a godly home for our kids, to Lyndon even when that painful leg demanded more and more compromising.

It's just that the warm, fall air beckoned. Sure, the boys and I went outside when my phone alarm alerted us to recess. We threw a ball. The boys rode their bikes around the hardpacked drive. Arnold had begged Lyndon to take off his training wheels, which Lyndon did, assuming they would need to go right back on. But to our surprise, kind of, Arnold got on that bike and rode it. I winced, thinking of the bikes. Yes, we'd gotten a great deal at a yard sale, but it had meant a cash advance on the credit card. Not allowing myself to dwell on that thought, the timer on my phone dinged telling us it was time to head back inside.

Both boys cried. Feigning cheerfulness, I stuck to Lyndon's schedule.

On the fourth morning, Friday because of the previous long weekend, I put on my dark-wash jeans and an olive green, sleeveless blouse with some light-tan embroidery cascading down the front. I'd been trying to dress a bit professional—clothes to go with the role. In spite of having mustered the courage to get myself ready for the day, I dreaded each step up to the boys' rooms to wake them that morning. *Please God. Please help me want to do this.* But I couldn't make myself want to. And neither did Brewster and Arnold. We eventually ended up in our room filled with Lyndon's loving determination, and yawned our way through "Oh Canada" at which point I opened the window to let in some late summer air. And that's when I saw the snakes. About half a dozen of them slithering out from under the shrub just to the left of the window. "Come here boys," I invited, after the briefest moment of panic at the unexpected visitors. I lifted each boy up to get a glimpse of the creatures. Arnold was already pulling his desk toward the wall under the window to get a better view. Brewster's big brown eyes looked at me, expecting me to scold Arnold, but as our eyes met, I suddenly knew what to do. "We're going outside," I announced. "Snake lesson."

And so it was. I had my iPhone in the back pocket of my jeans, so after we had watched the slithering creatures for a bit, I took a few photos and then had the boys take them, trying to catch a picture before the snakes darted away.

"They're so fast!" Arnold was thrilled.

"Will it bite me?" Brewster shied away.

"No, these are garter snakes," I reassured him. "It won't hurt you."

We followed the snakes around until they reached the southern edge of our rented acreage where the unruly old garden spot turned into a grassy interlude where a barbed-wire fence separated the yard from a dug out, which by fall now had very little water left in it.

Before we knew it, the boys were hungry and I realized it was noon. Noon! The whole morning had passed while we were outside. By then we had looked at pictures of different species of garter snakes. We had attached pine cones to branches and pulled them through the dirt to mimic the movements of the snake prints. I'd told the boys about how snakes shed their skin, and Brewster brought up the story of the very first snake talked about in the Bible. Then Arnold wanted to know if snakes could talk and why could the one in the Bible and are snakes devils. They wanted to know what snakes eat, so we looked it up and the boys remembered seeing worms in the dirt by the rose bush. They spent the next twenty minutes digging through the dirt until they'd found six worms, one for each snake they'd seen.

After a sandwich, I washed them up, hardly distressed about the amount of dirt on their new school clothes. They crawled into bed for a nap while I went back downstairs, got myself an ice cream treat from the small chest freezer in the laundry room and sat outside in the shade while they napped. What a perfect day. If only we didn't have to do school work. How would I tell Lyndon that I hadn't followed his lesson plan? We'd be a day behind and we were only four days in.

* * * * *

After the snakes had hibernated for the winter and Lyndon had stopped writing out lesson plans for us, we got into a groove which still included singing "Oh Canada" and reciting "The Lord's Prayer," but didn't require filling in start times or official recess breaks. My attempts to dress in semi-professional clothing got harder, but I did insist that the boys and I did at least get dressed in something other than our pajamas. We followed some of the beautiful new curriculum Lyndon had purchased, and other books had the boys' names on the front and perhaps some scribbles in the first nine pages. Some days I justified spending our "school" time at the library or a homeschool group activity. I had discovered Pinterest and was getting ideas of my own about how to make learning interesting for the boys. Because Lyndon interacted with so many families, he sometimes shared ideas he picked up from them. We were both realigning our expectations of what our homeschool would look like.

Complete peace about our decision still eluded me, however. There were days I remembered Lyndon's provoking speech imploring me to pursue Jesus with the boys and I was resolved to do just that wholeheartedly. And then I'd have days where I was sure it couldn't possibly take homeschooling as the only means of wholeheartedly pursuing Jesus. There must be people whose children went to public school and who were intentional about pursuing Jesus with their kids. Surely all public schoolers were not mindless about their decisions and cavalier about their faith. There had to be someone who was doing public school right. And I had to find her.

Chapter Thirteen

"Brewster, can you find Arnold and tell him it's time to go?"

"Arnold," Brewster hollered.

"I could have done that," I mumbled, picking up cushions and tossing them back on the couch. How did moms with more kids ever get them ready to go anywhere? And this was just to be a simple excursion into Lethbridge for the day.

"He's crying in his room," Brewster reported.

Suddenly empathetic, I dropped the stack of books I'd gathered to return to the library, turned left down the hallway and circled back up the stairway.

I poked my head in Arnold's room. "Hey."

"Brewster said I had to make my bed before we go or we can't get any fries. But my blanket is stuck to the wall again," he wailed.

I glanced at the train track that took up most of the floor space with a Lego village surrounding it. "Arnold, you pushed your bed right up to the wall again. Remember that it's winter now and you can't do that or the air can't move and it freezes." I gently tugged and the blanket left the wall. Pulling the twin-size bed-that-came-in-a-box away from the wall several inches meant Arnold's Lego left him no space to walk, but we'd have to deal with that later when we came home.

It wasn't a great start to trying to get a few errands done with the boys in tow. Worse, was the accident we passed on the way in to the city.

We were finishing our grocery shopping. I always saved the bakery section for last so the boys could look forward to a cookie. As we picked out our bread, a senior lady honed in on the boys.

"Not in school today?" she asked, probably innocently, but still suffering with the stress of the morning, and suddenly weary of having to answer strangers thinking themselves truancy officers, I managed a stiff smile and a simple, "Not in school today."

Trust Brewster to sweetly add, "We homeschool."

"Homeschool?" She stopped in her tracks and her face registered our little alien family.

I tried not to be angry at Brewster for his honesty.

But I couldn't help myself from shooing my boys toward the till, their winter boots shluffing across the commercial vinyl plank flooring. "We need to hasten on to our next engagement, gentlemen," I announced, nodding at the senior who still scowled in our direction.

"Can't we get a cookie?" Brewster whimpered as I tightened my grip on the shopping cart and dragged them along.

"Bought baked goods rot both your teeth and mind." I spoke louder than necessary for the sake of the disapproving senior we left standing by the muffins.

* * * * *

It struck me with a jolt when I pulled a load of towels out of the state-of-the-art, glacier-blue dryer.

As if the fancy washer and dryer could make the ugly in the laundry room go away, we'd added them to the credit card over two years ago, feeling good about it then because the price was a steal since the machines had been purchased for a home renovation that never happened. I wasn't sure now, when I made payments on that card, if we were still paying for the couch or if the current amounts were beginning to make a dent in the $1400 we paid for the appliances. Either way, I loved these machines. Every time I did laundry, I was thankful for Erin McConechy's renovation mishap. And today I knew I had to see if she had anything else for sale.

I pulled out my laptop and checked the same buy-and-sell site I'd used previously. Sure enough, Erin McConechy had five items for sale. A child's size 14 dance leotard, hardware for a hanging bed, a large painting of a zebra, a crafting armoire, and men's skates.

Hmmm. I started by easily eliminating the dance thing and the craft cabinet. Men's skates? Pretty sure Lyndon's leg was too sore for skating. The hanging bed was cool but the boys' attic rooms were so small and had angled ceilings that made me unsure if I could make it work. That left the zebra painting. I didn't love it, but there was a large empty section of wall beside the TV, and I didn't hate it either. Lyndon and I were pretty committed to not having things in our home we didn't need or didn't love, but I was about to make an exception because I'd been so impacted by my interaction with Erin and her children. It would be too weird to call her up out of the blue and say, "Hey Erin, it's me, Ainslee. I uh stole, well bought, your washer and dryer and I have some things I'd really like to talk to you about cuz I think you might be an awesome person who can help me figure something big out..." Yeah, that felt a whole lot weirder to me than buying a zebra painting in hopes that she'd invite my whole family for a pizza pop supper like she had last time. Her public-schooled, teenage children had sat at the table with us, holding our hands while each one offered a short sentence-prayer before the meal. Their prayers included a troubled friend, their grandma's health, and a missionary in Japan. While we passed around a platter of baked, gooey pizza pops and carrot sticks, we discussed why the 'theory' of evolution could at best be a 'hypothesis' of evolution according to the rules of science itself.

So I messaged her, "Hi Erin. I'd like to buy your zebra painting."

* * * * *

Mrs. Nelson was new to Tracey. So new, in fact, that had her husband not been our new pastor she would have had to wait out the three-month attendance period before beginning to teach Sunday School. As it was, Arnold met her before we did. Having been without a pastor for almost four years, four *long* years of enduring guest speakers and local, sincere men, some of whom had passion, some who even had talent in preaching, but none with either formal pastoral training or much time to invest in sermon preparation—when the Nelsons arrived for a weekend visit, the congregation fell in love! And apparently the feeling was mutual, though I did find out later that both Charles and Mathilda, the Nelsons eighteen-year-old twins were enrolled at Augustana University less than an hour from Tracey so I wondered if perhaps their desire to live in the community had less to do with being drawn to Tracey Community Church and more of a draw to stay close to their young adult kids. Regardless, Lyndon and I had managed to slip away for our anniversary that weekend and missed out on all the love expressed by and to the church. At the time, we didn't think we'd missed out. It was our anniversary after all, and Dr. June Thiessen had offered to keep the boys. Had insisted that her son Conan would be heart-broken without their company.

I wanted a new pastor as much as anyone. Granted, the last two years of herding boys to church and trying to soak an oft-time mediocre sermon-blessing into a brain that either pinged with all the responsibilities of my homeschool, stay-at-home-mom, help-my-husband-more-than-most-wives-need-to life, or fought sleep if I had a few minutes to sit down, I likely hadn't been in the best place to learn scriptural knowledge anyway. But I wanted to. And it seemed like both boys had reached a new level of maturity over the summer. So much so, that I'd actually been able to form a thought during the week about getting back into the habit of taking notes during the sermon. I'd pulled out a hard-covered, coil-bound notebook, placed it in the cubby by the door, and actually remembered to bring it along to church this morning. What with the new pastor and new school year, it seemed the perfect new beginning.

During Sunday School, Pastor Nelson did not focus on a rambling introduction of himself and his family, and his hopes for our church, but rather immediately engaged us in an overview of scripture itself. We got the beautiful story of God choosing and loving a people, a nation, so that all people in all generations could know what faithful love looks like and be drawn to that Faithful Lover. I immediately knew that this man would shepherd us toward desiring to know and understand both the whole of scripture and the whole of its Author. I definitely understood the church's love.

Almost in a daze, I made it to the church basement to pick up the boys from their classes. Habit, I supposed, realizing that both boys were old enough now to make their way up on their own. *Next week*, I promised myself. Children started emerging from behind the four doors and one curtained-off area we'd figured out to make our increased Sunday School enrolment work for the coming season. Suddenly I tuned in to Arnold's voice, it sounded like he was reading: "God made me. God made a-an-an--"

And then the teacher's voice interrupted, "Animals."

"Oh, yeah, animals."

"Good job, Arnold. Good reading. What else do you learn in homeschool? Do you know what shape this is?" By now I had inched my way to the classroom door and could see only the teacher with her back to me and Arnold left in the room. She held up her Bible. "Yep. It's like an electrical box. Not the junction ones, just like a one-kind switch box."

"A rectangle!" She cooed. "Can you say rectangle? It sounds like your dad might be an electrician."

She turned around then, Arnold's new teacher. And instead of meeting the gaze of a mom pleased that she'd be spending extra time encouraging a student, she met my stony stare. Oh I've felt awful about it ever since then, always wishing I'd been able to master my emotions in that moment. Berating myself for allowing one of my biggest pet peeves to keep me from instantly loving Mrs. Nelson as much as I instantly loved her husband. And I'm sure she was not able to instantly love me either, as much as they both continued to affirm their deep bond with our congregation. But in that moment I was so weary of "the test." What made homeschool-ignorant people think it was their job to give my kids a quick pop quiz to make sure they had a brain? That they weren't too far behind the schooled kids, whatever that would look like.

"Time to go, Arnold. Tell your teacher thank you," I stated firmly.

"And, no, his *Dad* is not an electrician," I muttered under my breath once we were out of earshot.

It took several days before I recalled the first fall home-school barbeque, thinking of how awkward I felt that day arriving as wife to Lyndon in his role as the new home-school co-ordinator's assistant. Knowing I was being subtly critiqued even though he had already been hired. I did feel compassion then for Mrs. Nelson. I used to not know a thing about homeschooling either. Maybe my judgmental curiosity came off with as much offense to others as I'd taken from the new pastor's wife. In fact, recalling multiple instances in a flash—Susanna's denim skirts, Keller's large singing family, Karalee's innocent wedding—yeah, no doubt I'd been an offense.

Chapter Fourteen

September 2012

It was the time of year where I needed to write my educational plan. I looked back at my value statement from the previous years. Vague. It didn't convince even me that I knew why I valued educating my kids at home, or even if I did. It certainly didn't convey how we would attempt to reach our objectives and what our learning styles would be. How could I plan for the year with confidence if I couldn't answer those basic foundational questions?

I considered how much the boys learned when I just let them play and discover. I got excited about the science videos I'd come across online that had helped each of them understand some pretty advanced electrical concepts. Arnold's spelling had really improved after I'd been diligent with the systematic curriculum Lyndon had brought home for us to try. And I was impressed with how the boys worked together to create a little business venture when we ended up with a batch of kittens that spring. Brewster made sure they and their mama were safe and cared for. Arnold asked me for photos and got Lyndon to help him advertise them on our local buy-and-sell sites. Brewster built simple cat houses from fruit crates to send the kittens home with their new owners. Brewster would have been happy to see the kittens go to loving homes, but at Arnold's insistence the kittens were sold for $30 each, giving the boys a total of $120 to split and one kitten to share since she was shy and hid whenever prospective buyers came.

Our purpose in homeschooling was relatively easy on the basis of elimination. It wasn't because we lived far from a local school. It wasn't because our kids had allergies or disabilities, or were genius, or had been bullied. Of course, I couldn't write down that I kind of had to because my husband wouldn't look very successful in his work if his own children weren't being homeschooled when he was the facilitator. And besides, I truly had come to a place where I wanted us to be the ones to have the greatest responsibility and the greatest joy in their learning process. As long as we both had reasonably good health, Lyndon could bring in the majority of our income needs which was something that mattered deeply to him, our little rented acreage made our cost of living extremely low, we could do this.

So, why not? How would I write *because we can* in the documents and have it sound like it came from a semi-intelligent adult? I'd have to give the wording some thought, not that Lyndon or Ken Berry would be questioning me on whatever the papers said anyway.

The harder question now regarded our methods.

"I've spent several years now selling people curriculum," Lyndon stated. "I've had a chance to see Ken's reports on the results he sees from these programs. I've got my personal opinions based on my years in the public school system."

I tried to remember which programs Lyndon spoke most highly of. I knew he wasn't a fan of having the boys sit, read paragraphs, and fill in blanks for hours on end.

"So?" I waited.

"Just let them live."

"Like, don't pick something where I'll want to kill them?"

He laughed then. A big, roaring laugh where he threw his head back and slapped his knees. Then he got up from his chair and went to look out the west window, tried to say something and laughed again, wiping his eyes on his sleeve.

Finally, he tried speaking. "That's good, Ainslee. Best advice ever. I'm sure gonna use that line. *Just don't pick something that'll make you want to kill them.*"

Still giggling, he said, "Yeah, basically. Just live a happy life with them. They'll learn. Be here for them. That whole kitten thing this spring, you were amazing. It was perfect."

I took a moment to appreciate his praise and felt a mutual admiration. That was one of our best parenting moves to date, I agreed. Team Lyndon-and-Ainslee. Mission accomplished with no tears, no cajoling or fussing or threats.

"Besides, curriculum is so expensive. And a lot of it is put out by parents who are working personally and as families to put out a product, all the while touting the praises of being home and engaged with their kids. Really? Just not sure I want to support that."

I'd never heard Lyndon say that. There was the brief moment in which I recognized the incongruity of his current sentiment with the stacks of first-grade curriculum and posters that still took up space in our school room. Moving on, it sure made sense, though. Moms writing books and blogs about not being a working mom and focusing on their kids, as if books and blogs write themselves.

"I need some time, Lyndon. I've never considered what you just said. But you're advocating that we unschool? Don't use any curriculum at all? Or what?"

"Not really. If they have questions and the answers are in a book, pull out the books. If the answers are on a website, then explore the internet. If what they need to know is at the museum, or the local lumberyard, well, you get the picture."

Obviously, Lyndon was either speaking off the cuff or he'd done a one-eighty since we nearly suffocated singing

Oh Canada along with the iPad, surrounded by colourful posters and the smell of new Crayola crayons.

By the next day I'd thought through Lyndon's proposal. It sounded amazingly simple. And profound. And so common sense.

* * * * *

"We're going to be using curriculum, Lyndon. If you have an opinion, I'd love to hear it before I make the order," I announced.

"Okayyy…" He wasn't shocked, entirely. I think secretly he loved knowing that his passion could be matched when needed with my pragmatism.

I was tempted to not explain myself to him. Instead, I said, "I love your theory. But that's exactly what it is, a theory. And I don't think the whole 'let them live' thing is going to work for us. It has too many false assumptions. It assumes that we will almost always be at our best. That the boys will each have healthy and natural curiosities that will be met with us having the time and patience and resources to rise to the occasion and help them discover knowledge and truth in a timely manner. It assumes that the weather will perfectly co-operate so we can get to where we need to go, or that I'll never be in the middle of a chore that has to be completed before I can pay attention to their needs.

"It assumes that they will be self-motivated, co-operative with us and with each other, that they will not be lazy or manipulative.

"Even worse, Lyndon, it assumes *I* will be all those things!

"And as far as supporting families who are entrepreneurial while advocating homeschool, I'm not going to live my life being their police or their conscience. After all, you just encouraged me about the boys' kitten sales. Families do what they have to do to make life work.

"Let them live," I grinned cheekily in conclusion. "So, I'm going to buy some curriculum. It's going to be my helper. I'm not the teacher Lyndon, you are, and you're not here full-time. Teaching is not my gift, it's yours. I need some external motivation to help keep the boys and myself on track. I will try to let it be our tool, not our master."

Lyndon suppressed a smile then. He pulled me close and wrapped me up in his big arms. We stood leaning against the scratched kitchen counter. We held each other until my mind forgot curriculum and stopped rehearsing the arguments I'd prepared. Until I noticed the smell of Lyndon's shampoo, heard the ticking of the kitchen clock and how it almost matched the beating of Lyndon's heart. It was a long, hard-fought unity, like meeting up on a mountain plateau after having taken different trails up to the summit. We held the embrace, savouring that we'd made it to this place together. This place of mutual passion and shared vision.

Chapter Fifteen

Before we'd moved to Tracey, back when Lyndon was hopeful that the maternity leave position he'd taken would turn into a full-time teaching contract, back when we'd adjusted to the surprise of having two sons one right after the other and we were beginning to implement the concept of living for Jesus, which was something neither of us had done well up to that point, we were part of a Sunday School class that challenged us to be alive, growing Christians. Something happened to us then that gave us a hunger for God's Word in a way neither of us had had before. It was our before-and-after moment. The move to Tracey defined our 'before' lives of wanting-to-live-good-lives-not-bad, and our 'after' lives of I-cannot-believe-the-Bible-is-my-personal-love-letter-from-God. We had an appetite for scripture that made us both search its pages for knowledge and wisdom.

One of the things that happened with homeschooling is it gave me time to explore Bible stories with the boys, and since I'd had a rather elementary knowledge, the things I was learning excited me, intrigued me, sometimes confused me.

Take the day we learned about the nation of Israel asking God for a king. An earthly king.

"Why did God not want them to have a king?" Brewster asked.

"Why did the Israelites want a king?" I responded.

"I don't know," he whined.

"You read the verses this time," I told Brewster. "Look carefully at 1 Samuel chapter 8, verse 5."

"I can't read it," Brewster pushed his Bible away.

"Brewster, remember that every 'I can't' means I will respond with an 'I can't'. Yesterday we had to drive right by McDonald's because I couldn't make left turns."

"Yeah, but you really can make left turns, you just said you couldn't," Brewster protested.

"Hmmm. And you really can read the verse, right?"

Brewster pulled his Bible a little closer and silently looked at the page.

I allowed him some time to decide whether he would attempt to read or continue his habit of sulking the moment things became difficult.

"They said to him, 'You're old, and your sons don't live as you do. Give us a king to rule over us like all the other nat…nat,"

"Nations," I finished. "So, this is the nation of Israel talking to Samuel the prophet and judge. What were they asking Samuel for?"

"A king," Brewster responded, his sullenness already forgotten.

"Why?" We had circled back around to the original question. "Look at the second half of the verse," I prompted.

"Give us a king to rule over us like all the other nations." This time Brewster read fluently.

"So... they wanted a king because..." I prodded.

"Cuz all the other nations had one." Brewster answered.

"That's right. An earthly king was not God's plan for his people. God Himself wanted to be their king. Samuel was sad that the people would rather have a king than have another leader like himself. But God told him, 'Samuel, the people are not rejecting you, they are rejecting me. They do not want to have to obey Me. They are trying to find a way to do things their way rather than My way.'

"And so, in the end, here's the way God asked Samuel to respond when the Israelites did not want to obey God. He said, 'Listen to the people, warn them that they will wish they had obeyed, and then give them a king.'"

I could tell Brewster was getting bored, and we needed to be done. And, he had probably learned the most valuable lesson he needed to learn today. After all, he had submitted himself to reading out loud when he'd started with his usual 'I can't' routine.

"Okay, Brewster, you can put your books and other things away and then be done for the day. Arnold might be finished stacking those pieces of two-by-four from Mr. Neudorf by now and then you boys can go biking or find a really good tree for your tree fort."

"Yay," he cheered, making a quick escape before I could come up with anything else.

I closed the Bible History lesson book and put it on the top shelf to the right of the window. I heard the front door slam and cringed. Lyndon hated them slamming that door.

I recognized that at this stage in my boys' lives they would not be spiritually touched by the same lessons that I was. I could handle knowing that, for now, the chapter we had read was information for Brewster. Someday, it may mean transformation. However, as I tried to do after every time I looked into God's Word, I took a moment to reflect. Should it scare me that sometimes God allowed Himself to be talked into giving us what was not necessarily in our best interests? Giving us things that we could use to self-destruct?

* * * * *

"I have got to get this curriculum thing figured out," I lamented to Ken's wife, Helen Berry. I stacked the game pieces and put them back in the box while I talked.

"Oh?" She responded.

"I told Lyndon I need to use curriculum with the boys. Some of the stuff he picked originally is alright but some just isn't working for me. There's so much out there and I keep changing my mind about what to use and it's such a waste of everything to keep trying stuff."

"Yeah?"

"Mom, do we have more toothpaste?" Brewster called from the bathroom.

I groaned. "I think I forgot to buy more and we are seriously out," I told Helen.

"Mom?" Brewster repeated.

"Use baking soda," Helen suggested.

"That's a thing?" I asked. "Just a second, Brewster," I called back.

"Sure. Or coconut oil."

"I don't have any of that but I should have some baking soda," I rummaged through my meager baking supplies, finding a container.

"That's powder, Ainslee. You need the soda for teeth."

"Oh, right. Good eye," I complimented her, returning the plastic container to the shelf and pulling out the box. If I baked more, I would know this like I knew that a 100-amp sub-panel requires #4 copper wires.

"Do you not learn about baking soda when you take a dental hygienist course?" Helen asked.

"I have no idea anymore what I learned as a hygienist, Helen."

I headed toward the bathroom, then turned around. "Okay, and how does this go on the brush?" I whispered.

"Wet brush and dip," she made hand motions to go along with her instructions.

"Okay, yeah, makes sense."

I spent a couple of minutes showing the boys what to do and convincing them to try a new method. "If you're ever in another country or in the bush and you forgot your toothpaste, now you know that baking soda works," I encouraged enthusiastically.

"Mom, if I was in the bush, why would I be carrying baking soda?" Brewster challenged.

"Because it's explosive," I told him conspiratorially.

Arnold's eyes lit up, almost convinced.

"But why are we going to put it in our mouth then?" Brewster asked.

I thought fast. "Well, you see Brewster, it's not explosive until we add vinegar."

He stared dubiously at the white powder I'd poured on the blue counter for them to dip their toothbrushes in.

"I'm going to see if it explodes without vinegar," Arnold announced, coating his brush in the soda.

He went for it, transferring soda from counter to brush to mouth, carefully watching the mirror, while Brewster carefully watched Arnold.

"Tomorrow morning, boys, we add vinegar, okay?" I winked at them. "Not in our mouths, of course, but we will do a safe experiment."

By now Brewster was cautiously following Arnold's example. After a moment he shrugged. "Not bad. Thanks, Mom."

"Finish up here and come for a drink before you go to bed," I instructed before returning to the kitchen.

"You're so good with them, Ainslee," Helen encouraged me.

I stopped in my tracks. "I sure don't feel like it."

"I wish you could see what I see in you, dear Ainslee. You are kind and thoughtful, and resourceful. You're energetic and such a loyal friend."

I couldn't remember the last time anyone had praised me like this. I swallowed my emotions but knew I would savour her words later. Would pull them back out and treasure this gift. For now, I plugged in the kettle and poured some nuts in a dish to share with Helen while we waited for Ken and Lyndon to return from their home visit which was in the local area and likely wouldn't go very late tonight.

"So, yeah, I just think it's a waste to keep trying new curriculum," I continued our earlier conversation as though there'd been no interruption.

"Yeah?" She asked for the second time.

"How is it not?" I asked her. I hated when she didn't say what she thought, but just made me think about what I'd already said.

I passed the pajama-clad boys each a cup of water and hugged them tight before sending them up the steep staircase.

"It's stupid financially for one thing, even if we're buying used books. And it's unsettling for both me and the boys to keep trying to switch our methods. I feel like we have a hard time sticking with any one program long enough to have the satisfaction of finishing it and that's discouraging for all of us."

"You're looking for the fulcrum, huh?"

"Um, fancy word for balance?" I laughed.

Helen's gentle laugh never failed to make me smile. "You want to find the thing that's going to make this schooling journey smooth sailing?"

"I do. Once I settle on a curriculum the boys can just focus on learning."

"So, then what keeps you from picking something and sticking with it even if there may be other good stuff out there?" Her eyes were on mine until I looked away. "You're not online a lot, trying to find a system more perfect than what you've already decided on, are you, Ainslee?"

"Maybe that's exactly it, Helen!" How could she have put her finger on what hadn't occurred to me until just now. "Maybe I can't work with what I have because I keep wondering if there might be something that's even better. Something that will make the boys, and me, want to do school, do it well. Do life well...

"But it feels like just when we get into a good system, whether that's how we structure our days, or the material they're studying, or which subjects Lyndon teaches, things change. It's like we're always out-growing something about our methods. Either Lyndon leaves on a trip, or someone gets sick, or they just need a break from bookwork even if it's a great course."

"What part of life isn't like that?" Helen prodded. "How long does life ever feel balanced on that fulcrum? Aren't things always changing? Isn't there always some desire that makes us want to spend some time chasing it even when it wasn't in the schedule? Or a dullness of routine that makes us need to shift to something exciting to spice life up a bit? Or unexpected circumstances that make us long for the certainty of a fill-in-the-blank workbook?"

She paused to let me think while I scribbled mindlessly on the scorecard from our earlier evening Yahtzee game with the boys.

"You're right, Ainslee, about every reason you gave for finding a good program and sticking with it. But life will never be predictable. Enjoy the tame seasons when you need them, find adventure when you or the boys need to be rejuvenated, put the demands of books aside when life brings more important things your way. Don't expect to dictate your life, dear Ainslee. Try to find a rhythm rather than a system."

Chapter Sixteen

"*I bought an ice* cream for Brewster and Arnold and myself to share today," I told Lyndon confidently when he came home from the Boundless Home School Board office.

"Nice. You didn't each want your own?" he asked, setting his boots in the closet-without-a-door in the short front hall.

"No, you don't get it," I tried again.

"I bought an ice cream for Brewster. I bought an ice cream for Arnold. I bought an ice cream for myself."

"Sorry, I thought you shared one ice cream which is fine but a bit weird and even weirder considering its almost winter."

"Okay, no, no. Let me try again." I searched my mind for a fresh example.

"Alright. Here we go. Excuse my singing voice."

"Who has made the flowers that grow, the fish that swim, the birds that fly, Who has made both you and *me*,

God in heaven above." I croaked out the children's song we sang with the kids in Sunday School.

"Get it? Who has made both you and *me? Me.* Not *I.*"

Lyndon smiled knowingly. I'd been doing this kind of thing a lot lately.

"So, this has nothing to do with ice cream. Grammar lesson finally made sense to you, huh?" he laughed.

"Yes! It's crazy. Why did I not know these things? Why did it never make sense to me before? Did I have such a hard time learning these things, or did we seriously never learn them? I mean, it makes so much sense. I bought an ice cream for Brewster, I bought an ice cream for Arnold, I bought an ice cream for myself. I bought an ice cream for Brewster and Arnold and myself to share today. And why have we been singing this song wrong forever? Did no one think to stop the composer from messing with kids' minds for absolute decades? Who has made you? Who has made I? Who has made both you and I? Ridiculous. And now that I know better, I don't know if I can ever sing that song again. Which was maybe the point, for people with my singing ability to quit singing."

Lyndon laughed. "So, you're enjoying learning all the things you didn't learn the first time around? I wish I could spend more time doing lessons with the boys. There's so much I need to learn as well. I suppose I've got the advantage of being able to evaluate curriculum at work. Sometimes it's so engaging that I find myself caught up in the lessons for my own interest and I forget all about whether I think the store should carry it. When I catch myself doing that, I know it's a keeper."

* * * * *

November 2012

I felt settled that fall, for the first time in a long time. After Lyndon and I had agreed on which curriculum to order, and I'd forced myself to come up with words to fill in my educational plan that gave me a reason to believe in what we were doing, life took on a rhythm. The boys and I enjoyed learning through exploring and yet we had a loose routine. I had stopped demanding that God reveal to me sufficient reasons why He would ask us to homeschool the boys, and had just embraced the reality that we were in the privileged position that we could.

I had been to four years' worth of monthly homeschool moms support group meetings. After the first time I'd attended, when it was in Charlotte's designer sea-can house, the only time Annaliese had not been in charge, we had most often met in Annaliese's two-storey on its large lot at the outer edge of Tracey. It would have been a grand house when it was built in the 1920's. A very old house considering the history of western Canada. Western Canadian houses, as we all knew, had not been built to last the way brick and stone houses in Upper Canada had been. Still, it was amazing that Annaliese's house not only stood fairly straight, but had received enough updates over the years to have all the modern amenities we were accustomed to including a dishwasher, a luxury Lyndon and I had learned to live without in our small 1950's farm house. So, though Annaliese's house would have been intimidating in its day, it wasn't anymore. It was as drafty and creaky as our rental, though much larger. The group had met in Susanna's small living room which had new windows and flooring and trims and light fixture due to her husband Peter's good hand at carpentry. We had been to Misty's twenty-year-old split level where she'd had her Indian neighbours cater a traditional meal of curried chicken and lamb, and chick pea stew, and naan bread which I loved, and all the wonderful smells would have made me forget entirely what her house was like except I'd also been there many times for our church small-group Bible study.

So, I spontaneously offered one day to have the meeting at our house the following month. Lyndon and I hadn't invited many people over since Ken and Helen Berry had picnicked in our empty dining area with us before we'd cleaned the dead flies off the window ledges or even had one sleep in that house. I'd thought we would begin to invite others into our home. We had even talked about our conviction concerning our lack of hospitality. I remembered noting when we moved in that there would be enough space for guests at our harvest table placed in front of the pale green bench left sitting on the longest kitchen wall. I'm not sure why we didn't invite people to join us, other than I wasn't a confident cook by any means, and Lyndon's days and often evenings were filled with work. Helen had been a welcome guest on many occasions and our church small-group friends sat on our leather couch for study and coffee as frequently as we sat on theirs, but that had become a comfortable routine where Lyndon faithfully baked a pan of brownies and I made a pot of coffee and cleaned the bathroom.

But this year, when my inner turmoil about the schooling decision had been put to rest, by early November the dark corner in the living room had been filled with the Christmas tree, and Lyndon and I had hopes of inviting people to our home. I had sat there several nights after the kids had gone to bed and felt so cheered by the beauty of that tree. The shiny, white ornaments and sparkly, gold ribbons reflecting strings of warm light reminded me of a bride prepared. Wasn't that how Christmas should encourage us: that as Jesus Christ fulfilled His promise of a first coming, we could be assured of His promise of a second coming? How would I endure the cold, dark, prairie winter without tangible signs reminding me that the Light of the World *had come*, and that He *would* come again?

I was so thankful I'd not only gotten the new electrical plug in the far corner installed, but the tree put in place before the meeting. Sure, it was a bit early in the season, but was it possible to reflect too often or too long on our Christmas hope? Would anyone else feel what I felt when I sat in the cozy gliding rocker—the rocker where I'd held my infant sons? That because of a baby in a manger I could feel comfort, hope, and praise that I was part of "the bride" Christ was coming back for?

As the women arrived and found room for their boots in the open closet beside the front door, I took their winter coats and laid them on Lyndon's and my bed. I brought the dining chair that I used in the school room through the doorway into the living room and everyone shuffled over to accommodate a final arrival. Annaliese had seated herself in the back corner of the living room, right next to my glowing tree. The thought hit me then that the Christmas tree took up space in the small room we could have used for seating. I consoled myself remembering that we'd had similar close quarters in many of the homes we'd been in over the last few years. It didn't take an open-concept, like Charlotte's beautiful home, to enjoy good fellowship.

Annaliese then began her homeschool encouragement to us that evening with a history of Christmas. She sat beside my tree as if she'd known beforehand of its presence, and informed us of our modern Christmas: that pagan festival which simply became the convenient time to celebrate the birth of our Saviour. It should have never happened! And now, on top of it all, commercialism has taken over. Since we are educating our children in truth, and not according to the culture, how can we allow décor and gifts, and Santa to dominate a holy day, especially the *wrong* day?? Our children these days don't really have needs, and shouldn't we be giving to a charity if we have extra to give, think of all the children who have nothing!

I wanted to hide my beautiful tree the same desperate way I'd wanted to cover Brewster's ears when Aunt Bonnie compared them to Uncle Nick's. I wanted to reassure that tree that it meant something wonderful to me. I wanted to kick Annaliese for stealing my moments of wonder over the beautiful bride of Christ.

Would I be able to sit in the chair tonight after everyone had gone to bed and rejoice that light casts out the dark? I resented her as she ate the baking I'd put out–not that she ate the store-bought Christmas-tree-shaped sugar cookies, mind you, *that* I found too amusing to resent. But the Twix bar squares with so much fat even I could not justify eating them more than once a year. And a butter tart with its perfect old-fashioned, homemade crust that took four tries and seven YouTube videos to get just right and Lyndon loved. How dare she eat my "Christmas baking"? How dare she rob my precious, long-awaited joy?

Chapter Seventeen

Spring 2013

It was a homeschool arts-and-crafts day at the community centre. Arts-and-crafts that were funded by the government for underprivileged children. Apparently, that's what homeschoolers were. A day Brewster loved and Arnold looked forward to because several of the other boys his age would also rather play cops-and-robbers than craft, even if they routinely got scolded by one of the moms for being too rambunctious. I stood behind my boys where they sat at the long tables, and recognized Janeice beside me. I'd seen her very little since the very first homeschool barbeque over four years ago where I'd been stunned to realize her four-year-olds were nursing. Even today, it was all I could do to make eye contact as I introduced myself to her once more.

"Oh, I remember you," Janeice spoke softly. "Lyndon has come to do home visits several times."

"Of course," I acknowledged, feeling a touch of old resentments rising. Lyndon spent periods of his life traveling around the province meeting the large variety of homeschool families who had registered with the Christian Boundless Home School Board while I did the day-to-day grind of actually trying to educate the boys, which included, unfortunately for me on this balmy spring day, arts-and-crafts.

"I do remember meeting you a few years ago at the homeschool barbeque," I tried, hoping Janeice would feel that she mattered. And that she wouldn't ask what I remembered about her.

"I don't come to a lot of the meetings and activities," Janeice explained. "It's hard to pack up all the kids and find something they're all kind of interested in. Kendall is three-and-a-half now so it's getting easier to get out."

"I understand," I responded. "You have a bit of a drive to come into Tracey as well, if I remember,"

"Yeah, we do," Janeice affirmed. "Winter driving scares me. Today was sunny and it's getting warm. When it's cold and snowy I'm afraid of getting in an accident with the kids."

"Oh. Yeah, that is scary, I guess," I responded. Actually, until that moment I'd never really considered that very real possibility. Not even after the day we'd been delayed by an accident on our drive to shop in Lethbridge when Granny Truancy Officer had added to my stress in the bakery section. I'd have to put together an emergency kit to keep in the vehicle.

"We live close to town so I don't usually have far to go," I pondered, feeling sympathy for Janeice's concerns.

"My auntie and uncle lived in your house for a few years when I was growing up," Janeice told me. "That was before the new house was there obviously." I looked at Janeice's long fingers threading string on a large crafting needle. Her auntie's hands had contributed to the fingernail grooves in my cupboard doors. I didn't consider myself nostalgic, yet I was feeling a connection now.

"My cousins and I played hide and seek there, except I didn't really play, I was too shy. Besides, I fell down those wooden stairs once and that was enough to make me not really want to go back up there."

I grimaced. "Yeah, those stairs are pretty steep and I think we've all fallen down them at least once." I hadn't thought in months about the fact that Lyndon rarely went upstairs to the boys' rooms anymore. It hurt his leg to climb the stairs and the weight he'd gained over the last couple of years didn't make it any easier. "I did sprain my ankle once coming down with a hamper of dirty laundry," I reflected, "so now I get the boys to throw their clothes in the hamper in the laundry room and I just have to carry the bedding down occasionally."

"I don't know how you can sleep with your kids in those bedrooms up there," Janeice mused. "I don't like two stories."

"Oh?" I questioned.

"Well, what if there was ever a fire at night. How would they get out?"

I was stumped. I'd never really considered that. What kind of parents were Lyndon and I? I'd have to talk to him about a family fire escape plan. In just a few minutes, Janeice had given me all kinds of things to worry about.

Janeice's son returned, tugging at her shirt. She handed him a teddy bear and blushed slightly. "He's done with that so we're uh, expecting."

"Oh ok," I responded dumbly. The memory of her nursing his older siblings at the Barbeque made me blush as well. "Congratulations," I managed with a smile before returning my attention to the art project we were making.

I busied myself by mindlessly added beads to Arnold's abandoned project. He'd run off. Had no patience for crafts whereas Brewster sat and carefully produced his project. Suddenly what Janeice said hit me.

"Idiot!" I scolded myself silently.

Not once had I ever entertained the thought of using nursing as a form of birth control. Obviously with sons less than a year apart, if that had been our strategy, which it wasn't because we hadn't had one, it wouldn't have worked for us. I don't even know how it came to mind now, except I must have read about it at some point. I felt ignorant. Ignorant and stupid. Ignorant, because I knew a lot about the electrical cycle and very little about my own. Stupid, because in one conversation she'd revealed almost a handful of my inadequacies while making me kind of glad to be homeschooling. If I, who loved these boys more than anyone else could, was failing to have an adequate plan to keep them safe, imagine handing them over to the care of twenty-three-year-old Ms. Mufford every day. It was, after all, a big scary world out there.

* * * * *

Janeice's new babies had arrived and not even I was unfeeling enough to not marvel at these little boys' arrival. New life was a wonder. How could these little people not exist and now be here and so perfectly formed. That a mother's body was made to be able to stretch and carry and nurture in this way...miraculous.

"Poor Kendall is going to wonder what's wrong with him that he doesn't get a twin," Susanna, who was sitting beside me observed.

She turned to me. "Janeice and Harvey have twin boys who are eleven, the boy-girl twins who are nine, Kendall who's three and now Noah and Elijah."

I tried wrapping my mind around that. "So, two sets of twins, then Kendall, and now another set of twins," Susanna reiterated.

"Wow," I managed. And it sunk in. Once again, I could've kicked myself for being so stupidly judgmental. I supposed if I'd had five children, four of them twins, and I was in my early thirties and believed who-knew-what regarding birth control, well, nursing a four-year-old kind of made sense.

"Children are a blessing from the Lord, Janeice," Annaliese smiled, sending a warning glance my way.

"Yes, they are, Annaliese," Misty jumped in, oblivious to Annaliese's silent warning. "And so is sanity. Which is why we stopped after four. Two for each parent to keep track of was the right number for us." Misty kept her chin up and her tone light but I suspected this conversation had been had before between these two women.

"Well, you all know that I think scripture encourages a couple to have as many children as the Lord blesses them with. Children are the fruit of a healthy marriage and, as Christian families, they are our gift to the world. If we accept our duty to raise them in the fear and admonition of the Lord, there is nothing greater we can do for God's Kingdom," Annaliese stated.

"If we accept our duty to raise them in the fear and admonition of the Lord, there's sometimes no energy or money left to do anything *else* for God's Kingdom, never mind anything *greater*," Misty shot back.

"Why is it that the cost of raising children, whether that's financial or a matter of time constraints, or the cost of giving up on our personal pursuits always enters this conversation, Misty? Discipleship should never be too great an expense. Maybe your expectations are too much like what the world wants to offer their kids..."

By now, tension filled the room. I didn't know where to look. I felt the need for a deep breath but didn't dare take it for fear that the spotlight would somehow change to me.

But Misty charged ahead. "It is true, Annaliese, that many people don't have children or don't have more children, for selfish reasons. Children will get in the way of their career, or their lifestyle, or their vacations," she paused here, glancing at a photo on the wall of Annaliese and her family on the beach, "but that's not everyone's story. Some of us choose to save some of our energy for missions, for caring for people already in the world not adding more souls that will need saving."

"If you raise them right, you will multiply your evangelistic efforts, Misty."

"A soul that is born in my home is in no less need of being evangelized than any other soul."

"Misty, children are a gift from God," Annaliese pleaded. "If God were to give you an extra $20,000 would you refuse it? No thanks, God, I don't want this gift?"

"I've heard that line before, Annaliese. And what you always forget when you use it is that God does not usually plop a huge amount of money in your bank account as a gift. Usually, God gives us the opportunity to work for that 'gift'." Here Misty used her fingers to air quote the word. "Then we wisely evaluate how important it is to us to have the gift of that money. Is it worth accepting the extra work it will require to get it when we consider that same work takes away from the energy and time we can give to the things we are already working at? How is it any different with children? Sure, they are a gift. But the more children we have the less time and energy we have to give to other things in our life that also matter."

There was silence. And then Misty moved in for the kill.

"And interesting isn't it, Annaliese, that those who generally most push having as many kids as the Lord gives them, didn't."

I snuck a look back at the old beach photo on the wall. There was a much younger Annaliese, her husband Carl, and three children.

"Misty," Annaliese's eyes filled with tears. "Just be careful you're not so set on saving the world that you lose yours."

Neither woman spoke more. But Misty seemed unmoved by Annaliese's apparent sorrow.

Suddenly one of Janeice's babies cried. We all breathed.

"I brought some banana bread," Susanna offered lamely.

"Ooh, that sounds amazing," Misty seemed sincere. "I'll grab a slice on my way out. I've got to get to my class. I'm taking a course on teaching English as a second language. We've had so many immigrants move to the area in the last couple of years and I cannot believe that God is bringing this mission field to us." She waved goodbye cheerily, a slice of banana bread in each hand, and left us focussing on the needs of the crying twins.

As I tried to choke down a piece of the bread, which I assumed was delicious, after all, it came from Susanna's kitchen, I couldn't shake the unanswered question. Why did Annaliese, whose life revolved around homeschooling even when her own children were done high school, and who apparently esteemed large families, only have three children?

Chapter Eighteen

July 2013

"Girls' Weekend," Misty texted. "You in?"

Women's soccer season had ended three weeks ago. The boys and I had been diligent with school work and we'd had a week straight of cloud.

"Details?" I typed back.

"Mineral pool at Watrous. Inviting gals from the soccer team. Just saw a 50 % off deal online for this weekend."

"I'll check with Lyndon and get back to you."

"Need to know pretty quick," Misty texted.

I checked the time. 1:13. Wednesday afternoon. I groaned. Lyndon was supposed to be in a meeting with the Home School Legal Defense Council this afternoon. It could be a couple of hours before he checked his phone.

Next I googled *mineral pool at watrous*. I had no idea what Misty was talking about but the search quickly informed me of a couple of things. One was that this spa pool in the middle of Saskatchewan had water so unique it compared only to two other known places in the world. One was in the Czech Republic and the other was Israel's Dead Sea! In Nowhere, Saskatchewan! Who knew? I was beyond intrigued, and by the time I checked google maps which informed me that it was more than a six hour drive, I didn't care about the distance. It was a lot closer than either the Czech Republic or Israel!

A girls' weekend. I hadn't done anything like that since my bridal shower. *Lyndon*! I picked my phone up, willing it to show me that he'd read my message.

I checked my schedule for the weekend. *Potluck after church. Bring casserole and dessert.* Otherwise the time slots were blissfully empty. This invite couldn't have come at a better time. Lyndon made a great hashbrown casserole and brownies. I did not have to feel one bit guilty about leaving him for the weekend. Did I?

Depending what time Misty was thinking of leaving, it was possible for Arnold and Brewster to play at the Boundless Home School Board office for a few hours while Lyndon worked. We tried not to ever abuse that option, but again, it was possible.

Brewster was at my side in the kitchen before I heard him come down the steps. "Mom," he tugged on my arm, "can we have some of those like, um, boxes for our town?"

I put my phone down and looked at him, trying to repeat to myself what I'd heard him say. "Can we have any?" he repeated.

"You mean milk cartons, the ones with the roofs?"

"Yeah." Brewster nodded up and down eagerly.

"Are you playing Lego?" I asked, trying to think if I'd remembered to save any milk cartons. "Yeah, but Arnold needs a store to fix his motorbikes." Brewster informed me, following me back down the hall to the laundry room. I opened the paneled closet where I generally kept a few extra boxes for things like wrapping gifts. I heard my phone ding back in the kitchen and felt my heart rate increase but I glimpsed the pink colour of a milk carton through the open handle part of a box we'd purchased navel oranges in and pulled it out to appease Brewster and get back to making my weekend plans.

"Oh, look at that, Brewster. There's two. One for each of you," I sent him back upstairs with a smile. "Thanks for playing so nice."

"You're welcome," he responded, the clean milk cartons tucked under his arms, already clomping back up the wooden steps.

I rushed back to the kitchen where I'd left my phone on the table, hoping Lyndon didn't have some plans for the weekend I wasn't aware of.

I pushed the home button and saw Misty's message. "Ainslee?"

I knew I'd run out of time.

"Count me in," I texted.

* * * * *

Three and a half hours after Lyndon had kissed me goodbye and assured me he and the boys would enjoy a guys' weekend as much as I was looking forward to experiencing the Dead Sea of Canada, Misty and I, along with two other gals I knew only from our soccer team, stopped at the Tim Horton's in Swift Current for coffees and a sandwich supper. We had laughed away the endless vistas of flat prairie, and again when we detoured a couple of miles to see the lone tree at Swift Current, an odd attraction Cassandra found online. Misty drove, with Cassandra sitting in the front passenger seat. I enjoyed getting to know Kelsie riding beside me in the back, though I found it a challenge to mentally filter her potty mouth and focus on what she was saying. I hadn't been surrounded with language like that since I'd been a third-year electrician's apprentice and my fellow apprentice was recently released from active military duty. Anyway, that was in my want-to-live-a-good-life-not-bad, before I knew what it was to listen like Jesus was in the room. Part of me was offended and wearied by Kelsie's foul language and the other part deeply admired Misty for loving Kelsie enough to tarnish her mind for the sake of someone else's soul.

In spite of the long summer days, it was dark when we arrived and parked on the sloped road beside the lake in front of the hotel and mineral spa.

"Do you think we could see Northern Lights?" I proposed, excited by the thought.

"Don't you have to be north to see Northern Lights?" Cassandra scoffed.

"We are north!" I rebutted.

"Honey, this isn't north," Cassandra educated me. "Even if we see some, it's not going to be what you've seen on pictures."

"Oh. Well that's sad. I've never been this far north so I hoped..."

"You sound like you've been as sheltered as our sweet Misty here," Cassandra teased.

"We'll get you both enlightened yet," Kelsie promised ominously.

"Enlightened," I laughed off the threat. "Just when I thought I had all the electrical puns I needed. But seriously," I stated stubbornly. "I'm going for a walk, just in case I came all this way and miss seeing the Northern Lights."

"Well, you're not going alone at midnight," Misty responded protectively. "We'll all go for a walk. It'll be good for us after the long drive anyway." With that, Misty put herself back in charge of our group.

* * * * *

On the dot of 9:00 a.m. when the pool opened, our little group trouped from our hotel room down the stairs in our fluffy, white hotel bathrobes.

We were downright giddy. Last night had only given me the pleasure of a midnight walk, and not that of observing Northern Lights as all the other women previously had.

However, today we acted like silly school girls and co-ordinated our first steps into the buoyant waters together. The brownish water made my nose burn slightly from the smell of sulphur. When I went to itch it, I splashed the mineral-rich water in my eye and learned not to make that mistake again.

Before long, we had moved from sitting in the shallow end on underwater benches, letting the jets massage our backs, to coaxing Kelsie to the deep end where we were assured we would float.

"You don't understand," she protested. "Y'all might float but I've got enough ink on my body to suck me under!" The snake on her arm seemed alive as she flapped her arm in protest. This time we all got the sting of the water in our eyes. Kelsie swore.

I decided not to wait for her. I doggy-paddled my way across the pool, my body floating so that when I wanted to change position I had to fight to get my feet underneath me. Shortly, Cassandra gave up on Kelsie as well and joined me in treading water. Misty continued to patiently cajole Kelsie. Her persistence amazed me. As Kelsie scared all the old people out of her path with her profanity-laced protests and the colourful ink on her arms, Misty gradually got her to where she was effortlessly treading water with us. At that point I marvelled at the healing qualities of the mineral pool. Kelsie had toned down about ten notches and I could listen to her without my ears ringing.

We stayed like that, chatting and laughing and recounting soccer replays for over two hours. My curls were stiff from the minerals and I needed a drink of fresh water. We all got out then, taking a break on the lounge chairs beside the pool. I couldn't help but be envious of Misty's tanned skin and gorgeous seafoam green swimsuit with its crocheted midriff. I couldn't remember the last time I'd found a one-piece to fit my long torso. The swim shorts I wore were a practical choice and covered my legs almost down to where the freckles started. A frill on the boat neckline of my eggplant-coloured swim top helped balance my upper half with my wide hips. It was a nice look. A flattering look even. But it didn't compare. Not to Misty's perfect shape in her perfectly feminine suit, not to Kelsie's body covered in tattoos and not much else, and not even to Cassandra in her modest athletic suit with the bright stripes standing out against the black of her glowing skin. I wondered if anyone observing would guess that what drew the four of us to be here together was a shared love of soccer. This much I was sure of, that if observers were given a multiple choice as to my identity, dental hygienist, electrician, or homeschool mom, I looked every part the homeschool mom. Mrs. Homeschool would've suited me.

Shortly before noon, the seniors started clearing out of the pool. I hadn't noticed the pool attendant until then, but I watched the way he helped old ladies out of the pool, humouring them as he did so. Before long he was filling our group in on the poolside lunch available. He parked himself on a chair next to where Misty lounged, and though he attempted to address us all, it was quite evident that she was the focus of his sales pitch. No wonder. People were drawn to Misty's warm personality as quickly as she was to snacks. They bantered back and forth while the rest of us looked on stupidly until Kelsie took an exaggerated look at the clock, swore loudly, and declared her need for lunch and some time outside.

After veggie burgers, we agreed to meet back at the pool at 4:00. Cassandra and I planned a walk around the small town. Kelsie insisted on going in a different direction alone. Misty decided to stay in the room and nap.

I felt refreshed when we met back up late in the afternoon. Misty was already in the pool area when the rest of us arrived. She'd changed her swimwear to a two-piece that drew attention. Like, honestly, just drew attention. Specifically, the pool attendant's. Though I understood getting back into wet swimwear was unpleasant, her demeanor seemed as different as her skimpy outfit and it appeared she'd been down here chatting with him for some time already.

Confrontation wasn't my style, so I stayed quiet. Uncomfortably quiet.

Kelsie didn't though.

After a brief observation, Kelsie joined Misty's conversation with the man. It didn't take long before I heard her swear.

"Did you get a chance to call your husband this afternoon?" she asked Misty.

"Why? Was I supposed to?" Misty responded with a note of alarm.

"Oh, I don't know if you were *supposed* to," Kelsie sighed, "I just thought if I had a man as hot as he is, I'd be calling to check in on him. Making sure he didn't have babes all over him while I was gone. But that's just me, pining for a man as good as the one you've already got…"

Misty actually blushed. Kelsie didn't skip a beat. She jumped in making awkward conversation with the handsome pool guy until he excused himself to attend to a ventilation fan on the far side of the room.

"You're a good missionary, Misty," Kelsie laughed when he left. "You gonna tell me he was just drawn to Jesus in you? You were just caring for his soul, right? Didn't even notice those gorgeous brown eyes!" she teased.

"Oh, please, Kelsie, I can look, I just can't touch!"

Drawn to Jesus in you. So, Kelsie knew what Misty was all about. She'd heard Misty's witness herself. This was a good thing, right?

So why did I feel uneasy?

* * * * *

"I told you I can look, I just can't touch!" Misty giggled.

"And I never have," Misty continued, sobering. "Never even had eyes for anyone other than Kyle even before we were married, unlike some other people I know."

"Are you still mad about that chick Kyle used to go out with?" Cassandra asked, ignoring the dubious statement about not having eyes for anyone else when Misty herself had just said she could look, just couldn't touch.

"Didn't you meet Kyle at church?" Cassandra said. "I've never met anyone who changed like Kyle did after he started the whole church thing. He almost makes me believe there's something good about religion."

"Not *religion*," Kelsie interrupted. "*Meeting Jesus.*" She used air quotes. "I sat beside him one day a few years ago at the ball diamond, probably during the Tracey town festival. He kept telling me *it's not religion*. But whatever, he's been a different guy, that's for sure."

Cassandra interrupted Kelsie's memory. "Misty, you were always such a good girl. What made you go for him? Even if he's a good guy now, he sure had quite the history!"

Misty shifted on the bed, playing with one of the pizza crusts left on her disposable paper plate. She got a faraway look. "Oh, I know about Kyle's history, trust me. And I knew it then. You're right, I knew about him but never got to know him until he was a youth worker at church. And by then, that whole meeting Jesus thing? It was so real for him. I mean, I grew up being homeschooled, and back then it was a pretty novel concept, not like now. Our family stood out as just being weird. I hated the looks we girls got for our modest hair and clothing styles. I was just one of the Braun girls. I wanted more than our mold. I wanted to do big things, world-changing things. We girls knew our future. We would live under our father's roof until we became wives and then moms, and obviously I wanted to be a wife and mom someday, but just not have to do it under the umbrella of all these expectations. When Kyle paid attention to me, I couldn't believe it. I mean, he was hot. I was, well, not. And after growing up with all these rules and expectations, as I got to know Kyle, I was so drawn to the realness of his spiritual life. Like, he seriously just loved Jesus. I'd never met anyone like him, who sinned, and was so sorry for his sin, but didn't need a bunch of rules to keep him on the straight and narrow."

She shook her head. "But I might have been wrong about him not needing a bunch of rules," Misty ruminated. "He wanted kids pretty quick after we got married, and I understood that, I mean he is seven years older than I am. I guess I thought life with him would be an exciting time but he's gotten pretty boring."

"Well, you're wrong about one other thing, Misty," Kelsie broke the awkward silence. "You are definitely hot. Underneath those long skirts you used to wear and all that hair, was one beautiful swan!"

"Thankfully he thinks so," Misty grinned. "Got to compete somehow with all the girls he loved before..." she crooned the last of her sentence like the old country song.

"Sounds like he's the kind of guy who's trying to forget about all that," Cassandra assured Misty.

"That's what he says too," Misty responded. "But it's kind of true that I don't want him to feel like he's had to settle for the moon when he's seen the stars."

"Trust us, you're a star."

"Besides, you've seen some of those girls he used to be with. Time has not been so kind," Cassandra smirked. "You're still young and pretty and fit, and by now most of them are old."

"Yeah, like didn't he used to have a thing with Annaliese?" Kelsie added.

My ears perked up. "Like, Mrs. Homeschool Annaliese who runs the homeschool moms group?" I clarified, looking at Misty.

She looked uncomfortable but gave me a brief nod.

"Oh my! Didn't she make Kyle look like a saint long before he ever was!" Kelsie hooted. "And look at her now. Pious as a preacher's wife."

"But she's full of the whole *loving Jesus* thing now too! Ironic that those two started up the same way and are ending up the same way." Cassandra observed.

"Whoa. What are you saying," Misty's defenses were palpable. "What are you saying, they should have just stayed together?"

"No Misty. Come on. Obviously, you're perfect for Kyle and she seems happy living her homeschool life with Carl."

The sudden silence was deafening.

And even though I was still in shock from what I'd heard, all that bounced around in my brain was that last comment: *she seems happy living her homeschool life with Carl.* Because not only did Annaliese live a happy homeschool life, so did Misty. And it amplified Misty's last question about her husband Kyle and Annaliese's former relationship: *What are you saying, they should have just stayed together?*

None of us made eye contact then. Misty tucked her pajama-clad legs under a blanket. Insecurity radiated from her but I saw her lift her chin then and the stubborn set of her jaw as if she had a point to prove.

"More pizza anyone?" she offered lamely.

Chapter Nineteen

Fall 2013

Lyndon and I had sensed for some time that Arnold was a hands-on learner and found that the actual book study part of homeschooling stressed him. Truthfully, we had probably known this about him almost from the beginning. And as much as we thought we were gearing the homeschool process toward his learning style, we were also driven by our own expectations of having some actual paper work to prove that he'd been through the right procedures.

Meanwhile, Arnold procrastinated. He got hungry. He watched another YouTube video on motorbikes. He built yet another ramp. Nothing thrilled him more than the day Lyndon hired a bobcat and operator to come build a small jump. It wasn't a dream motocross track. Just a simple jump. And the only reason it worked at all on our small, rented piece of land was because of the long driveway coming south past the imposing landlord's house before curving to the left onto our yard. By continuing straight off the south of the drive, Arnold could get enough speed to complete a jump, veer to the left behind our garden spot and loop back around onto the parking space before heading back down the drive and starting the whole process again.

It bothered Lyndon that he was limited by his injury, and also that he was losing the fight to keep his weight from making physical activity harder.

I didn't know how to help either Arnold or Lyndon.

Still, I now firmly believed that God had orchestrated the timing of Lyndon's injury, which persisted inexplicably, Ms. Krause's change of plans in returning to her Phys Ed position, and Ken Berry's unique job proposal to Lyndon. I could see the blessing of keeping our kids out of the public system and under our loving, watchful care.

At one of our monthly meetings, Annaliese schooled us on the practical benefits of teaching our kids at home. "Ladies, your kids will get more sleep and better nutrition," she started.

"Excuse me," someone interrupted, "Can you explain that?"

"Basically, they can sleep until they're not tired, and they're not eating bread and processed meat for lunches."

"Well, mine are," I offered so spontaneously that it surprised even me. I generally didn't have a lot to say in group settings.

Annaliese looked at me.

"Whoops," I shrugged, a little embarrassed then.

"Mine even eat baloney, Ainslee," Susanna comforted. She was a kind friend. "And my Anna still needs naps a few times a week though she is thirteen now so I am very thankful that she can do her workbooks in the morning when she feels fresh, and then rest for a while in the afternoons."

"That's a good point, Susanna," Annaliese put herself back in the driver's seat. "Also, when they don't feel well, they aren't missing things by taking a day off. Sometimes they wouldn't be well enough to go to school but they can still get some work done at home. In fact, when they *are* doing well there is nothing keeping them from moving ahead in the seasons of high learning especially since they're not spending time on the bus or waiting in lines or waiting for the teacher's help. Does anyone else have ideas about the practical things our kids gain by being educated at home?" she concluded.

"Chasyn gets to spend a lot of time with his pets," Brenna answered. "Dogs are not bullies so that's a plus as well."

Everyone laughed.

"Speaking of bullies though," Misty said, "I do make sure about once a week I shove my kids against a wall and steal their lunch just so they don't feel like they're missing out entirely by not going to school."

There was a mixture of nervous giggles and hearty chuckles.

"Do you dare them to eat Tide pods too, Misty?" Charlotte smiled, shaking her head.

"Haven't yet. We're still trying to get up the nerve to jab each other with pencils." I was pretty sure we all knew Misty was being dramatic but I snuck a look around the room just in case.

"Horrible things kids do to each other," Charlotte grimaced along with everyone's shocked inhales. "But I guess we needn't bad-mouth school. Kids can be mean anywhere and we never know when we'll be in a circumstance that requires us to put our kids in school."

Yeah right, I thought. *I have no plans to ever need the public school system.*

Annaliese cleared her throat. "We have to remember that the reason we are here is to support each other in our choice to homeschool. Public school has many flaws and that is the reality, and we've chosen a different path. Today we talked about many opportunities we have because we homeschool that the public school can never offer us and our kids."

It was a good reminder. A reminder to focus on opportunities not on flaws. Only later did I mull over my inner response to Charlotte's defense of public school. Had I really come so far in confidence or conviction that I planned to educate our boys entirely without the public school system? What was happening to me?

* * * * *

Brewster and Arnold sat one on each end of the leather couch where the sun from the window behind them warmed their shoulders and streamed onto their books. Lyndon and I had instituted a half-hour mandatory reading time each afternoon. Brewster didn't resist the idea and especially looked forward to adventures set during the world wars. Arnold knew now that he needed to follow the program, and he was engaged as long as the book had a lot of motorbike pictures. Occasionally he would switch to another topic for a brief reprieve, such as heavy-duty machinery. I tried to coax him to expand his selection from the library to books with words, not simply photos of machines, but often I was just happy to have him comply in principle if not exactly with the spirit with which we had set the goal, which was to increase reading ability and desire.

Truth be told, I had to force myself to set an example for the boys by sitting in the glider rocker and reading next to them each afternoon. Most every day I would rather have been doing other things—mowing the grass, vacuuming the vehicle, taking clean jeans out of the beautiful glacier-blue, frontload washer the credit card cash advance had covered shortly after we'd moved into this house, and hanging them on the clothes line right out the small laundry room's back door. Pinterest, with its pictures and short captions, was a delightful discovery. I'd even gone so far as to consider crocheting while I sat there. If people could crochet and watch TV at the same time, surely I could crochet and read at the same time, right?

But my conscience never let me do any of those things. Sometimes I used the time to read my Bible. Especially when I'd come across a story in the boys' school work that I'd never read, or forgotten was in the Bible. I wasn't big on fiction but I had read a few of the Amish books that were all the rage these days. The English characters who found their lives intertwined with the Amish and learned to appreciate a simpler country life reminded me of Lyndon and myself. Here we were, by happenstance on our little acreage. I would've made a perfect character for an Amish story of an Englischer girl in distress, broken down on the edge of a Pennsylvanian Amish community, being taken in and taught how to bake bread and wash our clothes to a gleaming white using a scrub board. As it was, my adaptation to country living had looked more like me trying to take care of the old lawn mower which had come with the quirky old house and run-down garage, and putting some seeds in the newly tilled ground. Maybe if Lyndon grew his circle beard for a few weeks he could take on the character of the Amish widower who'd rescued me from the hectic, meaningless life of city folk. I laughed to myself. Reality was, I actually *had* learned some housekeeping tips from this fiction as a perk while I tried to give my sons the opportunity to learn to enjoy books.

Lately I'd been reading books about missionaries and missions. I started with Elisabeth Elliot. It seemed lame to relate my circumstance of losing part of the man I married to the pain in his leg, to her losing her husband to murder by the very people with whom they had come to share the gospel. Yet I felt so drawn to her. Her strength of character in her distress comforted me and gave me courage.

Then there was my current selection: *Death by Suburb* written by David Goetz. I got to page 101 and read, "move from the pursuit of significance in your life to simple obedience to the things of God. One feeds the self, the other starves it. One promises self-fulfillment, the other actually delivers it, but not in the way you expect."

This day while the sun shone on my boys' shoulders, their sock feet on the couch, Arnold alternating between biting on the finger in his mouth and turning pages, I read page 101 again. What did it mean? "Move from the pursuit of significance in your life to simple obedience to the things of God." I immediately thought of Misty. *I wanted more than our mold. I wanted to do big things, world-changing things.* That sounded like pursuit. When I'd heard her say it while we shared pizza in the hotel room it had sounded good. It had sounded godly. Shouldn't we all want to do world-changing things? Shouldn't we have a desire to see our lives matter for the sake of God's Kingdom?

My evaluation turned a bit closer to home then. Suddenly it was easier to see in myself that one of the reasons I found it so hard to homeschool the boys was because, in the scheme of what the culture values and esteems, this wasn't it. I did want to be significant. And even a dental hygienist position would have given me more significance than staying home with my boys the majority of my days.

Chapter Twenty

"Why did you choose to be a dental hygienist, Ainslee?" Helen prodded while we sat outside in pool chairs at Legacy Water Park.

"It just seemed like the right decision at the time. I didn't quite know what I wanted, but oddly, despite saying I didn't like kids, I think in the back of my mind I hoped to be a mom someday so the regular hours and four-day weeks were attractive. I had a friend going and the school was within an hour of where we lived so we could carpool. It was a good education that paid fairly well with not too much time or money invested. It seemed a bit prestigious too, I guess."

"So then why switch to electrician?"

I paused. I refused to explain even to Helen the loss that led to my rash change in direction.

"It seemed more necessary," was all I settled on revealing. "I never felt that cleaning people's teeth really mattered in the long run. It felt like maintenance, and I needed to have more ability to effect outcomes, I guess."

She let silence rule.

Let me reflect on my own words.

Meanwhile, we watched as the boys splashed off the slides into the pools of water on the last day the outdoor pool would be open for the season.

"What is God putting on your heart now, Ainslee? What is the *more necessary* for this season of your life? What outcomes matter most?" I didn't answer. Obviously, I didn't know the answer, and Helen appeared to not expect one. She was content to sit with me and watch Brewster and Arnold play games in the outdoor swimming pool.

Finally, she broke the silence.

"When it comes to our lives, I love the word 'expending' rather than spending because it reminds me that we are using something up, something is expiring. Our days on earth are coming to an end. God isn't asking the same specific thing of all of us, other than that we *expend* our lives for His glory and not our own.

"So I can't tell you what to pursue, Ainslee—other than to live for His glory. To do the things you know you should, like honour your husband and your marriage, train up your children to know that they are sinners who need a Saviour.

"If you can honour God more by working as an electrician than by focussing solely on homeschooling, homemaking, then have that conversation with Lyndon. Maybe there's a way you can do both."

* * * * *

There were two things from my conversation with Helen that wouldn't leave me alone. That dogged my thoughts when I made our bed and washed the dishes, when I took the boys to taekwondo class, and when I sat up watching History channel after they'd gone to bed. One was that crazy word she'd used—*expending*. Along with it, I could hear her say 'something is expiring'. Never before had it weighed so heavily on me that time with my young sons was slipping away. Lyndon had tried to tell me long ago that this gospel he longed to share by being a teacher was the same gospel that his own children needed. He'd implored me to share his passion. Had really honoured me by saying I was the one he'd like to share with in the shepherding of their hearts.

Maybe I'd been so focussed on this stupid evaluating of which schooling methods made most sense for the life I thought made sense, rather than taking seriously Lyndon's concern for teaching our kids the gospel. What would happen if I started expending my energy on making certain that my kids understood they were sinners in need of a Saviour? I knew full well their days in a public-school setting would not focus on that. Was I taking seriously the condition of my own heart so that I did not hinder their understanding of the gospel?

The other thing that nagged me again was the conversation Lyndon and I had on the banks of the Souris River after sharing pizza in Minot. I had talked about my personal desires and needs to feel like I was contributing to the world. To feel like I was, well, somebody. Honestly, I kind of liked the slight shock factor I provoked when I met someone new and told them I was an electrician. It was unexpected. It was a little daring, and unconventional. It set me apart.

So then, for whose glory was I living? Had anything changed in my motivations since then? Even when I had self-evaluated my own words about feeling powerful, was I moved to repent of being self-absorbed? Self-driven? If so, was I continually coming back to re-evaluate whether I was veering away from living for God's glory and being silently drawn toward my own? What, other than the pursuit of my own glory, would it be that left me unsatisfied in my role as a homeschooling mom? What, other than my wish to be more significant than that. Because if I really felt that going back to work as an electrician would bring God more glory, would be a more useful way to expend my days, then I had better do it. I had better pray that God would help me to find the courage to pursue being an electrician.

But when I got to the end of my thinking, I couldn't do it. I couldn't honestly pray that God would provide an electrician job for me. Not yet anyway. I could only pray for my children to know what it was like to have their hearts exposed to the Saviour who was faithfully exposing mine.

Chapter Twenty-One

Winter 2013

As I made the short drive in to Tracey, the sun glistened off a fresh layer of snow and reflected off the holiday décor that had been fastened to the town's streetlight poles. "Brewster, don't forget to be gentle with your brother when you hand him over to the Midianites. And Arnold, you cannot *spit* at him."

"But Emily did make that coat for me and then he ripped it!"

"It was supposed to be ripped!" Brewster protested. "I just forgot we were going to rip a different one."

"Boys, you forgave each other remember? Just try to do a really good job for the old people today okay." I could feel a headache coming on.

Erin McConechy came to open the front door of the senior's lodge for us.

"Hi guys," she greeted Brewster and Arnold. "Emily is just getting everyone's costumes on in the room around the corner there, okay." She directed them into a wide hall on the right.

"I'm so glad you could bring them today, Ainslee," Erin smiled. She was one of the few women I didn't have to look down at in order to make eye contact.

"This is such a great idea, Erin," I responded, remembering guiltily my agreement with the young adults who had criticized Karalee the night before her wedding for her suggestion that the youth group may want to visit the seniors' home.

"We've been coming monthly for a couple of years now," Erin said, waving back across the room at a hunched-over woman who was being wheeled into the common room.

"She looks glad to see you. Someone you know?"

"Oh, I know her now," Erin laughed.

"Right. You just said you've been coming monthly. For a couple of years. Wow. That's a lot."

"It's mostly delightful. The hardest part is getting others to join us."

"So, your kids miss school for this?"

"Absolutely!"

She left my side for a moment then, picked up a matted teddy bear that had fallen from an older woman's arms and handed it back to her before it got run over by a man in his electric scooter.

"Ainslee, you do realize that public school is just one of the tools we're using to give our kids an education, right?" There was a slight bit of hurt in her tone, but she didn't linger beside me, kept going into the hall where the kids were getting dressed for their little play about Joseph and the Coat of Many Colours. Erin's daughter, Emily, loved making costumes, and it showed as the kids came out then and admirably led a well-prepared short program focussing on Joseph's forgiveness of his brothers for selling him into slavery.

The seniors loved it. Some even cried. They clapped. So did I.

I did feel chastised though. I hadn't come so far as to feel smug or self-righteous about the homeschooling thing, did I? The very reason I'd pursued a relationship with Erin, had bought an unnecessary zebra painting to spend time with her family, was because I felt sure there must be parents who had chosen the public school system and were still being intentional with their children's hearts. And she'd proved in so many ways that it was possible to have kids in the system and yet not be controlled by it.

We ate birthday cake with the seniors then. I found myself feeding pureed cake and ice cream to an older man in a broda wheelchair and enjoying it. This quiet way of serving him felt like a good fit for me. In this moment, I wondered why I thought I hadn't enjoyed being a dental hygienist.

When he finished his cake with a smile, I wiped his chin, squeezed his hand and realized I had no idea where Brewster and Arnold had gone.

Arnold was easy enough to find. He was sitting beside an older man at a memory stimulation station and they worked together at the simple electrical circuit. Arnold was patiently explaining until the senior got the light to come on.

Brewster, however, had to be hunted down, and when I found him in a senior's room, he had a book in his lap and his head bowed. It took me a second to realize that the senior was praying with Brewster. Praying for him. I stepped back out of the room and just listened to the voice of this elder.

"Lord, help this young man to know that his strength is in the Lord and help him to be a valiant soldier for you. Amen."

"Amen," Brewster's young voice agreed. "Thanks for showing me your book and for praying with me."

"You live for Jesus now, alright."

"Yep, I will," my son answered. "Can I borrow your book and bring it back next time?"

"You can have that one," the old man responded. "Just come back and tell me what you thought of it."

I stepped further back and waited until Brewster entered the hall. "Hey mom, I just asked Jesus into my heart," he glowed.

"Did you?" I smiled.

"Yep. George wrote a book about being in the Korean War." He held the copy in front of me.

"Yeah?"

"Yep. And then he asked me if I was a soldier for God, so, yeah. Now I am." His voice cracked and he cleared his throat.

"Me too," I reminded Brewster, draping my arm across his shoulder. "I wish someone had told me about being a soldier for God when I was your age."

He looked up at me. "That's too bad. But you do love God now, right?" I hoped he wasn't asking because it wasn't obvious, but simply because he needed in this moment to hear me say so.

"Sure do, Brewster," I assured him. It baffled me then that having this new identity as a soldier in God's Kingdom of light could both simplify and complicate life. It made life simple because it gave a clear direction. But at the same time, sometimes I hated how this new life revealed things in me that were shrouded in darkness before. That I didn't have to face before. It made me see how even when I was trying so hard to do what was right, I still wanted it to be all about me.

Chapter Twenty-Two

Early 2014

The perfect opportunity came up for me. One that I knew
Lyndon would never refuse. Our church was doing a modest
addition to their building, intending to have it completed by
the end of August when our fall programs were to start back
up. I submitted a bid for the work and got the contract,
along with the new sense of respect I'd been craving from
all those who didn't know I was a certified electrician, or
who hadn't taken me seriously. My part of the work started
in late March after the framers were done. There was the
initial push to pull all the wires. Most days my boys were
thrilled to come play in the dirt piles far enough away from
the building to not be in danger from any other construction
that may be happening. They played with Tonka toys and
built roads. They ate peanut butter sandwiches and potato
chips and licorice to their hearts' content. I did have to stop
my work occasionally to remind them that we were in town

and to use the port-a-potty supplied during the renovation period rather than the backside of the dirt pile.

At the end of August, when I did the final plugs and switches, the boys helped screw on the covers until Arnold had scratched multiple spots in the freshly painted walls with his ten-year-old carelessness and I had to get him to pick up the garbage instead. It had been a happy experience. We stood back and felt so proud of ourselves, like a good team. I looked at their tanned, dirty bodies and was so pleased that this electrical job had been part of our summer.

So in our discussions later, perhaps with my modest cheque from the church lying in front of us, neither Lyndon nor I could think of any reasonable objections to continuing with me working some. My self-esteem had soared, the boys had thrived. We had a sense of purpose to our days, knowing that during the days or weeks even that we weren't required to be at the church, we needed to use our time wisely to get other things done. I felt like I'd had this part of the person of me rediscovered which inspired me to be more patient with the kids. It was an all-around win.

When Garry Richards called to ask if I'd help him, I don't know that Lyndon and I had to really think about it. He was an older contractor, a retired pastor who worked by the hour at all kinds of smaller jobs that busy, mainstream contractors didn't really want to take on. Not all his jobs would require electrical work, but when they did, could I fill that role? Perfect! Or so it seemed in theory. In practice though, it didn't quite work out that way. Garry would be remodeling a bedroom and master bath when he discovered a couple of plugs that didn't work. That led to finding that squirrels had been in the attic and chewed main wires. Or finishing a basement only to discover that the septic system would have to have an alarm placed in the septic tank. Stupid, dangerous work that needed to be done in the middle of winter so that Garry could continue with his job. In the meantime, the boys went with Lyndon to the Boundless Home School office and curriculum store. It was hard to plan ahead for my work. When Garry reached the point where he needed my time I kind of needed to be available to not hold him up too long.

After several months of this loose work arrangement, things began to unravel. Lyndon and I were having a hard time keeping up with the boys' actual schooling. I couldn't bring them with me anymore as we were mostly working either in other people's homes, or outside in the winter months. Lyndon felt the stress of not being able to focus on his work, and with the amount we were spending in groceries and eating out, babysitters, and new tools, we were wondering if the extra income was really making a difference.

I could hardly admit to Lyndon that the feeling of being someone was wearing off.

I didn't know which would have been better. In some ways I thought if the electrical work wasn't there I would have had to submit myself to it not being God's plan. With the career success, I felt like I was beginning to fail with the boys.

Chapter Twenty-Three

2015

Annaliese was still leading our monthly homeschool co-op meetings. She now had two grandchildren and two more on the way. Every once in a while, I got the feeling that she needed desperately to convince herself that her role in encouraging lives committed to homeschooling was going to change the world. Or perhaps it was just to validate what she'd committed her life to. Maybe Misty and I weren't the only ones in pursuit of significance. It had also become apparent in our support group meetings that I wasn't the only one who had seasons of questioning homeschooling as a lifestyle, but not Annaliese. I didn't know what it would feel like to so doggedly and confidently pursue a single passion.

To Annaliese's credit, she graciously moderated the conversation that day so that by the end we had heard several women share about their homeschool methods and what made them arrive at those conclusions. I had found valid points in all their reasons and, though I thought Lyndon and I had been in a good groove for the last couple of years, after hearing the benefits of alternate methods, I once again wondered if we should reconsider.

But wasn't the beauty of homeschooling this very thing—that parents get to choose how they want to approach their methods? It can vary for each child, for different seasons of life, with the changing circumstances of life, different financial or other resources available. If Annaliese would choose a child-led learning approach, and Connie Harper did whatever she could to give her kids life skills, and Susanna felt most comfortable using a tried-and-true curriculum, and Charlotte aspired to a classical literature style, then so be it. I could spend years trying each one of these with my boys and have them reach adulthood having experimented with many ideas. But I had better re-evaluate soon what really mattered to me and Lyndon. What were we hoping to offer our boys by taking on the responsibility of their education outside of the public system? Along with every other homeschool parent out there, we had better come to our own conclusions on that and then find a way to confidently incorporate our values into a daily plan. But I marvelled again that this is the delight of parenting—we get to choose. And the fearsome part is, then to be responsible, in light of our life's circumstances, to do that well.

* * * * *

I woke up to sounds of water running in the bathroom. Concern for the boys filled my mind first, but in my groggy rush to the back of the house, I spotted Lyndon's suitcase in the short hall by the front door.

"It's you," I managed, surprised to see him standing in front of the blue sink.

"I'm so sorry, I didn't want to wake you," Lyndon put his toothbrush down and gave his hands a quick wipe on the ragged towel as he reached for me.

"Why didn't you text?" I mumbled against the side of his neck.

"Didn't want to wake you." He repeated, holding me close. "Ken and I got done in Vermilion this morning. We went to Provost for a couple of meetings there, but got some really bad news…"

"Bad news? What happened?" I pulled away to look at Lyndon's face.

"Buchholz's daughter passed away. Of course, we couldn't keep any of the appointments there, and we're not scheduled to be in Cardston area until Monday so…"

I was trying to think of the homeschool families I'd met from the Provost area. "Passed away? What happened?"

"Looks like suicide."

My stomach dropped. "But aren't their kids still pretty little?"

"Yeah. Thirteen."

"Thirteen? Lyndon that's horrible."

"Yes. Yes, it is."

We both paused. Sometimes there just are no words.

"You need anything to eat before you get to bed?" I asked finally while we both stood in our little bathroom grieving for a family we barely knew. Grieving at the idea of a child's ignorant desperation.

"No, too tired to eat. And besides, I just brushed my teeth. But I'm just going to head up and say goodnight to the boys, maybe I can do it without waking them."

"Yeah, for sure." I moved aside to let Lyndon pass through the narrow bathroom door opening and with difficulty take the stairs up to Arnold and Brewster's bedrooms.

I didn't follow him. I sensed he needed a moment alone with his sleeping sons and I needed a moment to thank the Lord for answering my prayer even though it came at a time of what would be for someone else, crushing pain.

Hadn't it been just that evening after the boys and I had done our first cleaning of the garage since winter, and I'd shared a snack with them and sent them off to bed that I'd sat in our bed and resented Lyndon for leaving me to homeschool our boys, while he who had the dream and vision left with Ken Berry to check on the needs and progress of other families? Hadn't I begged the Lord for Lyndon to see that his boys were missing him, and missing time with him? Hadn't I resented Ken Berry for presenting Lyndon with this lifestyle option that sounded great in theory but seemed to benefit other families more than it benefitted us, not to mention that it stole Lyndon from me and put him in the arms of Ken. Ken who had all the time in the world for preaching his passion of homeschooling, but in reality had often left the actual work of it to Helen while he inspired other families. Ken, who seemed to have first dibs on my husband's heart. Brewster and Arnold were still young and adored any attention Lyndon gave them, and he was a good dad, but I often wondered how their hearts would handle continually getting the leftovers of his energy.

Chapter Twenty-Four

Fall 2015

Seven years had passed since the very first time I'd been to a homeschool mom's meeting. Somehow over those seven years I'd not only been willing to identify as a homeschool mom but it had become so much a part of me, that I realized at the mineral spa in Saskatchewan I even *looked* the part. Ken Berry had called Annaliese *Mrs. Homeschool* the day I'd met her. If I wasn't careful, someone might actually call *me* that!

Throughout those years we generally met at Annaliese's historic home. It was a cozy fit, but could still hold our growing group. However, just like that winter night seven years ago, Annaliese was not available and Charlotte was willing once again to host us in her open-concept, shipping-container home. She waved off all our comments about the changes in her furniture and home décor. "All that talk designers do about choosing things that are timeless? It's not true. We have to instigate change or we are out of work. But it's okay," Charlotte continued thoughtfully, "pretty much all of life is about adapting to change, isn't it? Every time I miss my saddle-worn leather couch I try to remind myself of all the things I don't have the power to hold on to anyway."

I felt emotional after that.

I loved being an electrician because it seemed to give me power to control things with the flip of a switch.

Charlotte could not have said it any more effectively for my sake. I didn't dare think of Lyndon's declining health, among all the other things I wanted to hold on to. It really struck me that even the star of *Training Designers* had things beyond her control.

We listened to Helen then. We heard a part of her story that in all the years I'd known her now, I'd never heard. Maybe I'd been too selfish to think about Helen being a person with needs. She'd always been the giver in our relationship. She loved and served Ken over and above what I thought he deserved, but I knew that I resented Ken because I felt like he'd stolen a piece of Lyndon from me. I had a hard time appreciating all the ways he'd helped Lyndon to grow as a Christian man, which he really had. Why did I think sometimes that I would rather have just had Lyndon the way he was, than have his growth come at the cost of his devotion to what Ken had led him to believe was a ministry and calling? It had also come with great cost to our little family.

I had always wondered if the Charlotte I saw on TV was the real her, or if it was just her camera personality. But now, with the same intense, genuine curiosity as she exuded on the show, she urged Helen to expand on what she'd shared.

"Helen," she asked, "if I'm hearing you correctly, your husband was teaching in the public school system almost the whole time your children were growing up and meanwhile you were homeschooling them. Are you able to share with us why you chose to homeschool them rather than having them in the school while he was teaching?"

Helen smiled. "I wasn't sure if I should bring that subject up."

Charlotte seemed uncomfortable. "I'm sorry, Helen. If it's something you don't want to talk about then I regret asking."

"No Charlotte. The regrets are ours. And very much need to be shared." Helen paused a moment to collect her thoughts. "I'm going to start a little further back in our story. When I was a very young teenager, I went to a summer Bible camp. This was where I heard what we call the gospel for the first time. I guess by *gospel* I mean the good news that, though each of us is a sinner, God gave his own son, Jesus, to stand as the perfect acceptable sacrifice on my behalf, should I choose to accept this good news," she clarified. "And I did. That week I knew my sin problem had been covered on my behalf by this God-man named Jesus. It felt like very good news.

"The problem was that I had very little teaching after that. Basically, that one week each summer throughout my teens. I learned about the importance of the Bible, that God loved me unconditionally, that I should obey God and confess my sins when I failed.

"When I met Ken in Winnipeg, he was older than me by almost eight years. He already had a teaching position. He was a good man. He asked me to go to church with him, he sang in the services, he carried a Bible. Even though I had never grown very much in my spiritual life, I wanted to spend my life with someone who loved God and who wanted to live a good life. Ken's family was also church-going and they were so good to me.

"I had so many questions about the Bible, and Ken had answers. But his explanations, starting from Creation, which I had learned a bit about at Bible camp, were so different. According to Ken, the Bible's Creation story was an allegory not to be taken literally. The story was a picture but not actual truth."

At this point Helen changed gears. She sighed and laughed her gentle tinkling laugh. "Oh, the funny thing about teachers is that they often most intimately see the flaws in the public education system. So, once we had children, Ken was a touch leery of handing them over to spend their days with Ms. Greenspan. So, two significant things happened in a relatively short period of time. One, I was invited to a neighbourhood Bible study group. Over the next winter I began to actually read the Bible. It became life to me, and I came to see it as truth in its every word.

"Secondly, Ken's younger brother, Clay, also came to see scripture in a new light. Clay had many conversations with me and Ken about the change in his perspective and what he called his new life in Jesus." Again, that gentle, tinkling laugh.

"Anyway, Ken wasn't buying it. We kept going to the same church, but Ken seemed restless and agitated. Whereas initially, when the girls would first have been ready to start school and Ken liked the idea of keeping them home, he later became, not openly hostile toward me, but certainly distant and even somewhat sarcastic." She said this last quietly. Seeming to get lost in a moment, in the remembering. "He went to many church functions; he did a lot of reading. He felt distant. But there was regular communication from his younger brother Clay talking to Ken about spiritual and Biblical things.

"At that time, we lived close enough to the school Ken taught at so he could ride his bike. And it was so utterly simple. A dead deer changed Ken's life, changed all of our lives." One more delightful laugh. I couldn't help but smile along with her.

"One day there was a dead deer beside the bike path. By the end of the week, it was almost gone. The vultures had feasted, coyotes or dogs had come and scattered or dragged off the bones. And there went Ken's belief in an old earth. He suddenly saw that slow, natural processes could not possibly have preserved fossils to the degree that they are found. The crazy idea of a catastrophic flood burying creatures in an instant and pressure treating them became not only plausible, but more likely than a slow covering by layers over a long period of time.

"And really, just like that, it was as though all Ken's brooding, his studying, his resisting, and Clay's persistent friendship, combined to lead to real conversion for Ken. He believed the Book, he valued and adored Jesus, he really began to seek out other like-minded people. Ken looked for kids he could mentor, kids who were thinkers. Later on, he embraced on a new level the virtues of homeschooling and teaching our kids truth right from the start. So, where he had always been a very devoted teacher, he became a completely devoted Christ-follower. By the time he decided to leave the public system and encourage families to home-school, our oldest daughter was almost fifteen. Though he was leery of the public school system, he'd never truly embraced the heart of homeschooling. It had always been my life with the girls rather than our life with the girls."

"Did you feel alone?" Charlotte asked, tentative.

"Oh, Charlotte," Helen answered, "of course I wanted Ken to share my reasons for being passionate about home-schooling. I wanted him to give up on the religious life we were living and find joy in knowing Jesus. So, on the one hand, when we share life so intimately with someone and yet there's a chasm between us, it's the deepest loneliness we can feel. On the other hand, my dear, I had Jesus. But Ken...really it was he who was lonely."

Chapter Twenty-Five

Winter 2015-2016

I had pulled apart the blower motor on the Toyota Rav4 we were driving. I'd actually replaced the old motor with a new one myself on a reasonably warm winter day last week, but there was this need to know that made me lay the old one out on newspaper on the kitchen table. If I could figure this out, it would be an opportunity to teach the boys more about a vehicle's electrical components.

I had just opened the unit up when my phone dinged on the table beside me. Without even picking it up I read, *"Yep agreed. Also, Ains would look so much better if she did something with those eyebrows."*

Weird.

I read it again.

Seriously? My eyebrows?? The one thing a redhead should not have to worry about! And all this time I'd been worried about my nose! Well, that and my hair. Oh, and my figure.

A text sent by Misty. Like, Misty with whom I had played soccer for years. Who showed up with her husband at our church small-group study evening when she wasn't out meeting with people who needed Jesus. Gorgeous Misty who had seemingly flaunted her beauty to a complete stranger at the mineral pool at Watrous.

For whom was this text intended? Obviously not for me.

I felt sick.

I felt mad.

Ains!!

I had always known I wasn't gorgeous. Every once in a while, Lyndon almost made me believe I was. Forever I'd told myself he hadn't chosen me for my looks, he'd chosen me for my adventurous spirit. Let other women be beautiful. I'd be interesting. I'd be daring. I'd be fun.

And I would *not* in this moment go run to the mirror and examine my eyebrows. *I would not!* I'd keep telling myself Lyndon found me to be enough of what he needed.

But was I? This whole mothering thing had sucked a lot of the adventurous spirit out of me. I had kept those boys fed and clothed and alive—perhaps my biggest achievement of them all—and what had happened to being Lyndon's sidekick, his friend?

My eyebrows?? I pushed on my home button again waiting for the dots in the speech bubble. I expected some explanation, some apology, some...What?

What did I want her to say after that? *Oh Ains.*

Ains!! *Grrr*. How hard was it to say Ainslee!

I'm so sorry. I didn't mean it. You're so beautiful. That text wasn't meant for you.

Uh, maybe not meant for me. But no. No, I'm not beautiful. I'm strong. I'm capable. I'm Lyndon's, FYI. And I thought I was your friend.

* * * * *

I woke up on the couch in the living room, though our bed was mere feet away. Brewster and Arnold snored on an air mattress they'd inflated in place of the coffee table. Hearing rustling in the kitchen I woke up enough to recognize the sound of a bread bag coming out of the cupboard, the fridge door opening, a gentle clatter from the cutlery drawer. Lyndon was home. I smiled and rolled off the couch, trying not to bump the mattress and wake the boys.

"You came home hungry," I whispered to Lyndon as I entered the nearly dark kitchen and pulled the dark stained door to the living room closed behind me, leaving the large zebra painting to watch over my sleeping sons.

Lyndon turned toward me, setting down his toast now spread with jam. "Sure did," he sighed, pulling me close.

"Oh *please*. I meant hungry for food."

"You have no idea how good it is to come home to you," Lyndon continued, arms wrapping me. I let him snuggle.

"Movie night?" He questioned, pulling away enough to gesture toward the living room.

"Cesar Millan marathon," I answered.

"They're not giving up on the dog idea," Lyndon smiled.

I groaned. "I just can't see how we'd manage a dog no matter how convinced they are that with Cesar Millan's techniques they have all the tools to train one just right."

"Ah." My husband paused, then whispered, "So you're softening."

"No, I don't think I am." I whispered back.

"You just find Cesar that handsome? That entertaining?" he teased.

"Can I not let the boys dream about having a dog? If we're not going to get one, they should at least be allowed to pretend on occasion." Even I could hear a slight whine of defensiveness in my hushed voice.

Lyndon let go of me, popped another slice of bread in the toaster and took a large bite of the one spread with jam on the plate on the counter.

"So, what are we naming it, Ainslee?" He swallowed the toast and planted a greasy kiss on my cheek.

"Not happening," I held firm in spite of his wink and teasing grin.

"I'm so glad you're here, Ainslee." Lyndon once again wrapped an arm around my shoulder and held me close while he finished the second piece of toast in a few bites. I tried to pull my curly hair away from his face so he didn't end up with hair in his food.

"Thanks for watching Cesar Millan with the boys. For letting them sleep in the living room with you. It's so cozy coming home to this. This is what I love about home-schooling. You're here doing what they're interested in." He winked and squeezed my shoulder. "Seriously though. Thanks, Ainslee. I love not having to wonder where you are when I'm gone."

We quietly tidied the kitchen then, putting the margarine and jam back in the fridge, the bread in the cupboard, leaving the plate and cutlery in the sink along with some other dishes I'd left for morning duties. Leaving the boys undisturbed and my pillow on the couch, Lyndon and I headed to bed.

He was tired from the road trip and fell asleep quickly, while I had a hard time drifting off. I told myself it was because I'd already been asleep on the couch, and also, I needed my own pillow which was on the couch, rather than the spare I'd pulled out of the armoire in our room. And while those details played a part, my mind replayed our whispered conversation from earlier. The part where he'd said *I love not having to wonder where you are when I'm gone.*

Is this how Lyndon felt? That he needed to encourage me to stay home and homeschool so that he would know where I was? His words had been *I love not having to wonder where you are when I'm gone.* But if that was his heart, encouraging me to homeschool to deal with his fear of what I might do if I had choices with my time and energy, he had to realize that he was missing two things. A woman with an impure heart will never be controlled.

Second, a man who has to control a woman's every move so he thinks he will not lose her is missing out on who she could be and what she could do if she were motivated by love.

Chapter Twenty-Six

Early Summer 2016

This soccer game was the grand finale of our season. We hadn't made it to finals despite impressive growth on our team. I was feeling fit and healthy and even vibrant. It reminded me of the way I'd felt when Lyndon and I met, and what I perceived drew him to me.

I'd actually had a professional makeover once. A gift that had come during my dental hygienist training, it was comprised of everything from teeth whitening to a new outfit from a downtown Winnipeg boutique, and included makeup and a new hair colour. It was fun. It garnered me some attention. It showed me that with enough money and effort I'd be considered somewhat pretty in a conventional sense. Still, that makeover pleased me no more than my college graduations had. Oh, both were confirmations for me, but neither compared to just this simple victory of feeling my strong legs do what they were made to do. I wished Lyndon could've been here tonight.

It was a cold evening, which hadn't mattered while we were kicking the ball around the field, but by the time we'd stood around and rehashed the game for a while the cool air was sending chills over my sweaty body.

I looked around to spot Misty chatting with the referee. Her body was beautiful even in soccer shorts and bright red uniformed shirt. For a brief moment envy filled me once more. She was several inches shorter than I, 5'6" maybe, slimmer, with the most perfect hourglass shape. Strong and sinewy. Maybe not the most gorgeous face, but definitely attractive. And as she laughed and teased the ref, even from this distance I could tell he thought so too.

"Ainslee," Misty called as she headed toward my end of the field, "do you mind if we grab a coffee to warm up before we head home? There's a couple of other women who are going as well."

"Yeah, sure we can do that. You don't need to get home to your family though?"

She waved off my concern. "They're fine. Kyle is working night shift at the barn close to home so if they need anything, he's right there." It always bothered me how little I knew about Misty's children. They were all teenagers, a bit older than mine. They often went along to the farm where Kyle worked. I got the picture they were capable kids, running the farm equipment and canning the green beans. Rarely did they come to church on Sunday mornings, as they babysat their disabled cousin, or sat and watched TV church with Kyle's elderly aunt, or stayed home to finish cooking lunch for the immigrant families Misty and Kyle hosted. The few times I had seen them, they seemed happy and well-adjusted. Lyndon and I had not encouraged our boys to have such practical servant hearts. Kyle and Misty had an ability in that area that we certainly lacked.

Since Misty and I had driven with the teammate who owned the biggest van, and each passenger was happy to spend a bit of time relaxing as teammates one last time, I readily agreed to end the evening with a coffee. Misty had been making attempts to witness all season and I didn't want to keep her from the interaction she enjoyed.

I hadn't for a second thought that the only place open after nine in a little hick town like this would be the local bar. I hadn't been in a bar since my third year of college. Not even for a coffee which is all I'd had that long ago night as well. I'd promised myself then that I wouldn't go in one again, but this seemed like the wrong time to create a scene. The circumstances were different: it was the only place open. And I didn't want to keep Misty from her desire to connect.

In the end, it wasn't so much the fact of having compromised by having a coffee in the bar that bothered me about my actions that evening. Nor was it Misty's Shirley Temple, though that seemed odd too, given that she suggested warm drinks. It wasn't really that some of the other women chose to drink a low alcoholic beer, it seemed clear that the driver was sticking to coffee. No, when I thought about it later, what seemed the most odd was that Misty's attention seemed more focussed on a man across the room than on us.

✳ ✳ ✳ ✳ ✳

It was rare that Lyndon and I watched TV together, but it was a rainy, uncharacteristically blustery Saturday evening in April and the boys were enjoying Nintendo games together. Lyndon turned the TV on and History channel was just beginning new programming.

"In the early years of homeschooling, it was not only a fight to have it considered a legally viable option, but also a bit of a social experiment. We've now had it as part of our society long enough to face some results: including the beginning of third generation homeschool students, and backlash from kids who were homeschooled and deem their lives ruined." For the next hour we tuned in to the featured documentary focussing on Canadian homeschooling.

How could I have grown up in the Prairie Provinces and not really ever heard of homeschooling? Apparently, it had been a thing for much longer than I realized.

Oh, I'd heard the word at some point, but because I had no way to relate it to my reality, and obviously no curiosity about the subject, it had really only crossed my path once Lyndon began his initial communication with Ken Berry. But seriously, homeschooling had been a thing long enough in Canada that kids who had been homeschooled were now well into home-educating their own families.

Either that, or they were well into educating the world on the failures and hypocrisies of the homeschool movement. And that was another thing that I was ignorant about. The Homeschool Movement. I honestly was beginning to think I'd spent my prairie life under a sea shell.

"Lyndon, I can't shake it, this feeling of being too close to the edge of a cult," I told Lyndon after we'd turned the TV off.

"Hearing about systems like *Earls and Pearls?*"

I nodded weakly. "And I actually had been reading some blogs just earlier this week written by, well adults now, but kids who were raised as Christian homeschoolers and have either so bought into the homeschool system that they're blind to what a relationship with Jesus really means, or they've completely turned their backs on homeschooling and Jesus."

"So, sinners homeschool, huh? And sometimes they raise sinners who practically worship homeschool and sometimes they raise sinners who resent homeschooling." I pondered that for a while, but I wasn't quite sure how Lyndon was relating it to the present conversation.

"Ainslee, don't forget that I'm a teacher. And when I hear too much about the system of public schooling, I am so afraid for each person involved in that system as well. Does that system have an agenda? Sure it does. And at its worst, at its most sinful, sinister core, is a desire to have children conform to a way of thinking that completely denies God. So, we have these two different systems, homeschool and public school, and we see the devil desiring to destroy souls using either one. In general, public school destroys our kids through apathy and conformity to worldly thinking. And yes, homeschool has the potential to destroy our kids' souls through legalism, making them believe they are good. Both systems have the potential to turn them away from seeing their need of a Saviour.

"Ainslee, you've been focussed on the worst possible outcomes of homeschooling and suddenly see the best outcomes of public school. That's not real. Kids are not products of their environment. They're products of their heart."

Why did Lyndon always have to make so much sense? I hated that I could be so easily distracted and confused about the central issues.

He continued, "So the question then changes focus from which system has the greater list of weaknesses, to which system has the greatest potential to address the needs of their heart?"

Chapter Twenty-Seven

May 2016

The latest hot potato in the homeschool community around Tracey was vaccinations. Had I heard of this topic earlier in my homeschool journey, it may have unnerved me more. As it was, I'd come to lay aside some of the triggers, and listen more to what wasn't being said. But also, as it was, Annaliese, who to her dubious credit had kept many of us dutifully homeschooling out of fear for our children's spiritual well-being, had versed herself in innumerable internet facts and anecdotes for the occasion of our September meeting. We heard of all the cover-up attempts regarding vaccinations' links to autism and the horrible ingredients used in the vaccinations themselves. We heard the statistics of drastic decrease in communicable diseases being intentionally skewed in favour of vaccinations. We heard the disgust in tone of the news reports being written about "anti-vaxxers" as though they were all a cult of herb-worshiping child neglecters. Of course, we also heard of the micro-chips being secretly implanted in our children during vaccinations that would make them easily identifiable in the near-future, end-of-world events.

I can't say that I merely listened with interest or, on the other hand, a genuine desire to learn more about the subject. After Annaliese had sat in my living room those many Christmas seasons ago and, with complete oblivion I hoped, diminished the glory of celebrating Emmanuel–God with Us–I vacillated between tuning her out and having my radar on high alert when she spoke. I didn't consider myself a highly intuitive or sensitive person, I was a little too practical for that, so when I could sense fear or indignation in a room I assumed it had been building for a while. It seemed Annaliese delighted in bringing up subjects that heightened anxiety, especially in the new moms. And today, when Karalee Gardiner started packing up her four-month-old in the very brief silence that ensued Annaliese's lesson, I decided to help her find little Toby and Jarrett and get them buckled for their forty-five-minute drive home from Tracey. I had some gummy fruit snacks in my purse, my young teen sons still enjoyed them, and gave Karalee's boys each a pack before I thought about the animated conversation at our June meeting regarding gelatin. I couldn't remember which side of that fence Karalee had landed on, or even if she'd given an opinion. Oh well, I couldn't very well back out of this now that the boys had started opening the treats. Maybe Karalee wouldn't even notice, given how distressed she seemed.

"I just had her first vaccination done last week," Karalee spoke, looking straight ahead, having put the baby in the vehicle and then come around to the driver's side and buckled herself in. She adjusted the rear-view mirror slightly to get a view of the baby in her car seat.

I flashed back seven years or so to the weekend I'd helped with the sound system at Karalee's wedding in our small church. Now with three babies, she was still so young, and I'd come to feel protective over her. Protective as if she were a little sister.

I shook my head and refused to go there. Refused to dwell on the little sister part and see her instead today as a woman who was wise, and virtuous, and desiring intensely to do what was right.

"You know it's not a moral issue," I responded, trying my clumsiest best to reassure her.

"Did you?" she asked.

"Yes."

"And they don't have autism, right?"

"No."

"Do you ever wish you hadn't?" Karalee continued. I assumed she still meant vaccinations.

"We make the best decisions we know how with the information we have at the time," I responded.

Silence. Her processing that, I guess.

"Karalee, I'm not a scientist. I'm not a doctor. I'm not in the inner chambers of government. I'm left to trust someone's information on the subject."

"Yeah. Me too." She tucked her long bangs behind her ears. "But what if I've trusted the wrong source?"

"It's not a moral issue," I repeated. "There's only one thing about which we dare not be wrong."

"You do mean Jesus, right?" She grinned, just a little.

"Sunday School answer," I smiled back. "John 14:6. 'Jesus said, I am the Way, the Truth, and the Life. No one comes to the Father except through me.'" Thanks to Susanna's example, I'd challenged myself to memorize one new Bible verse every month.

I could actually see Karalee relax just a little.

"Karalee," I sighed, "there's a billion things we don't know. We can't see into the future. Our frail humanity has never yet kept God from being God."

She breathed deep.

"Yeah, I know. I still hope I haven't hurt my kids."

"You better get them home," I smiled.

"Ainslee, thanks," she said before putting the vehicle in drive and pulling away.

I had some opinions on vaccinations which I mulled over briefly as I stood next to the sidewalk on Annaliese's street. Not strong ones anymore I realized. Because if there was one thing I agreed with Annaliese on it was this: vaccinations should not be the government's choice to make on behalf of my child. God entrusted Arnold and Brewster to Lyndon and me. We may make decisions that we would have made differently had we been able to see from a different perspective, if we'd been given more time, or had different influences. I felt then something I hadn't felt in too long: an incredible gratefulness for God's mercy. An intense gratitude that He knows I'm as hopeless as a good dental cleaning is without routine maintenance. He sees my heart. He is committed to helping those who cry to Him for wisdom and mercy.

* * * * *

Summer 2016

Arnold was twelve and Brewster thirteen the first time we took the kids on an international vacation-with-a-purpose. Finally, both boys were old enough to work with Habitat for Humanity's building project and we were all excited. Lyndon had come across a homeopathic pain patch which had helped ease his discomfort enough that we felt confident to make our plans. We knew that between the kids' inexperience and Lyndon's disability we wouldn't be a huge asset to the organization, but it still weighed on our hearts to give the kids a broader perspective in life than what they saw from the comforts of our Canadian home.

"Don't you have to get special immunizations to travel to those kinds of places?" Annaliese asked when she overheard Misty ask me about our upcoming trip at the homeschool support group meeting. I cringed inside. *Not the immunization thing again.* And the way she tensed her face when she said *those kinds of places* made me wish I'd stayed home. "I'm sure our peculiar ways are no news to you anymore, Annaliese," I said, trying to keep the sarcasm from taking over.

I quickly scanned the room then though, and it did bother me once again how un-diverse a group we were considering the face of Canada. No wonder homeschooling had a reputation for drawing the middle class. By its very nature, it basically excluded single parent families, or those with extenuating circumstances. Every once in a while, when I stopped to think about it, I was so upset by being part of this uppity side of culture that I almost insisted to Lyndon that we move far away and forget we'd ever heard of homeschool.

"Doesn't it cost a lot, Ainslee? I've heard that short-term mission trips are super expensive. And if we go then we can't give to those who really need it, right?"

"It is expensive, Susanna," I conceded. "And we do struggle with that as well. I guess we figure a lot of people go on vacation. This is our first big trip as a family. If we're going to spend our money, for us we'd rather have our boys' eyes opened to real needs within countries than simply head to tourist meccas."

Truthfully, I was proud of how much we'd saved ahead of time to cover the cost of this trip. Now seemed like the right time to go. If we prolonged the trip another half a year until we had saved the full amount, perhaps circumstances would prevent us from ever moving forward with the idea. And it really did matter to us.

"Besides," I added, "it's hard for our kids to have their heart stirred to the needs in our world and feel like they can do something about it if we never expose them to these opportunities."

"But what can you actually accomplish in such a short time anyway? Isn't it better to support ministries for local people or long-term missionaries?"

"It might be." Lyndon and I had discussed this on multiple occasions. "That's a question I've often had myself. What has given me the most confidence is what I read in scripture about the apostles' ministry and Jesus himself staying places for only a few days. If the Bible mentions it, it has to be significant. Maybe it doesn't take a long time for God to use us when He's led us to the right place at the right time. And besides, since this is something Lyndon and I can do for our boys, we feel the need to expose them to global concerns. God has put it on our hearts. We'd be foolish to not follow through when we are able."

* * * * *

The pain patch was working. We'd spent a week on Habitat's build site hammering and carrying and painting. It helped take the edge off Lyndon's constant discomfort. After years of refusing to take pain killers for fear of getting addicted, Lyndon was excited about the patch and, without hesitation as soon as we returned, signed up for a father-son canoeing trip with our sons. It was supposed to be a break for me, to have Lyndon gone with Arnold and Brewster. And I couldn't be happier for them, although I was envious.

One of my goals for their absence was to evaluate what our rental house needed in repairs. I started by wandering around the yard. Trying to have a critical eye, I sauntered north up the driveway, then turned around and came back toward the yard. At this point I couldn't see the little house behind the tall row of trees that separated us from our landlord's grand three-car-garage, two-storey. What I noticed was the motorcycle jump Lyndon had had built for the boys and they still loved to use, in spite of their increasing freedom to roam further around the countryside with their friends. I walked past a row of five Saskatoon berry trees we'd planted one of our first years on the yard. Trees whose fruit I'd painstakingly learned to use in making piro-zhki: little pies with a fancy sounding name. I noticed that, although I'd already tilled the dirt around the Saskatoons in spring, there was a new crop of weeds sprouting. If I tilled again soon, the weeds should stay under control for a good part of the summer. With my mind on dirt and weeds, I headed on to the garden spot at the south edge of the acre-sized yard. I think I had come to terms with my reasons for putting seeds in that soil faithfully every spring. In spite of how neglected we sometimes left the garden patch, it was my consolation that I was helping to provide for our family. The root cellar in the house was a perfect spot to store the carrots and potatoes that lasted right till the following summer. Sure, I'd been influenced by all the talk in our homeschool circles of organic eating and heirloom seeds, not consuming genetically modified foods or supporting mass food production, of gardening for its low-environmental footprint. And it was a connecting point among the families, something most of us shared in common and could talk about. And then there was definitely the status symbol that had swung from before my childhood days where buying your produce meant you had arrived and were able to do better things with your life than slave in the dirt, to the current exaltation of providing much better tasting carrots for your children than anything you could find in a store and the children would now live longer and more productive lives.

Debatable.

But Susanna had done the math with me and I knew that garden saved us at least $1000 each year.

In the south east corner of the yard between the newer shed Arnold and Brewster had built with Lyndon, and the original garage with its new siding, roof, and overhead door which had been mostly my project with them, was the boys' work and storage area. It was where they stored old lawn mowers and wheel barrows until ideas sprouted.

From where I stood between the garden and the garage, I took in the front of the house. Not much had changed since that very first day we'd driven onto this yard. We had replaced the light fixture Arnold broke with a zealous swat at a flying bat one evening. The house had new windows thanks to the landlord. Other than an occasional power wash, the bottle-glass stucco remained the same. A new roof had been put on the same year as the windows got done. Probably when the landlords realized we may not be going anywhere.

And why hadn't we? I couldn't have imagined initially that we would be here eight years later, but I still had no desire to leave. Sometimes Lyndon and I thought something must be wrong with us to be content renting here for so many years. But every time we'd had the conversation, we couldn't think of a good reason to buy this place or anywhere else. Our rent had not changed since 2008: $400 per month–of course the utility bills were higher now than they'd been back then. The ability we had to put money into travel rather than a home was attractive to us. We couldn't explain why neither of us felt the need to own, but we didn't. The landlord had stopped talking about demolishing the house, and the new roof and windows seemed to be proof of that. We never felt too insecure in our future there from scrutinizing the landlord's end of our conversations. We weren't a big family and continued to live by our minimalist mindset, so other than the single stretch of scratched kitchen counter, the house mostly felt plenty spacious for us in our day-to-day living. I had long ago come to terms with most of the quirks of the 1950's kitchen, had replaced things such as the drawer slides which drove me crazy, and still found myself fascinated with the chips in the ancient countertops and fingernail grooves under the door handles. Whose hands besides Janiece's auntie's, whose work, contributed to this wear?

So, other than feeling the need to put in a new insulated dryer vent and recaulking the tub surround, perhaps replacing a few boards on the exterior step I used to reach the clothesline, I couldn't think of things I felt needed change.

Chapter Twenty-Eight

A few weeks later, this time with the boys at Bible camp, after lunch I did what I had disciplined myself to do. I picked up a book. Even without the boys around, or maybe, *especially* without them around, as had been the case quite frequently this summer, on the days I was home I read in the shade beside the clothesline. Beside the newly repaired set of steps that allowed me to hang things out in the sun. *Another way I'd been influenced by Susanna,* I sighed, grinning to myself. Left to my own methods, I would have put our queen size blanket in the beautiful, shimmery blue washer and dryer that dominated the narrow laundry room. Susanna, however, managed to convince me that the sun is a natural disinfectant and I should consider both the cost savings of not using the electrical appliances for every cleaning, and how much longer our bedding and clothes would last if they did not get tumbled in the washer and dryer more often than absolutely necessary. I would have been content to remember the fantastic price I'd paid for the set when Erin changed her mind mid-renovation, and then washed and dried to my heart's content. Not Susanna. She never failed to increase in efficiency and economizing.

Turning my attention back to the book, I was thankful that Lyndon's desire to expose the boys to a love of reading had also brought me to the point where I valued the written word. My current selection made me wish I'd been interested in politics sooner. Maybe I could have defined for myself some of my inner turmoil. I'd looked for systems that were going to make it all right, make our schedule work, maximize the boys' learning and potential, give them the freedom and space to be kids while steering them to be prepared for productive adulthood and to do so without the burdens they would carry from poor choices. I wanted a formula, I wanted to work the formula, I wanted to know which methods, which path, would cause them to become what I envisioned success would look like. But according to one of our previous prime ministers, part of great leadership is being able to adapt—recognizing needs and adjusting policy to help the population achieve their own success. Parenting a homeschooler was much like good governance. Why had I never been able to make that comparison? Did I really want to dictate Brewster's and Arnold's outcomes? Did I think they should have an equal say? Or could Lyndon and I work together to create a stable environment for them to set their own goals and thrive?

* * * * *

What a weird discovery later that day when I realized that the garden had become my friend.

I remembered years ago the nervous excitement of pulling past the stately two-story with its garage doors facing north—facing rather than being sheltered from the prevailing winter winds—around the tree row, seeing our little farmhouse for the first time and finding beauty in the ugly, in the abandoned, because I determined to and because there is always some beauty in the ugly if we look for it. Oh, I knew from the first day we saw this pathetic little house that all the overgrowth needed help and, being determined to create a new home for us, we would tackle it. But I actually knew very little about gardening. I knew enough to hire a neighbour to come in and till a spot that looked like it had been a garden in a past life. Back then we were motivated by a few different things. Trying to save money by growing some things ourselves wouldn't have been at the top of my list, but dear Susanna had made sure I was aware of this benefit. And there was the phase where I'd been influenced by fellow homeschoolers and their views on all things organic, and simply the reality that local food, when we can grow it ourselves, leaves the smallest environmental foot print. There was the pressure of trying to fit in to a sub-culture where gardening formed a means of connection with other women. There was the genuine amazement that God could make seeds germinate and grow and produce even when I had to hunt for my rows among the weeds, and all the spiritual lessons this brought for the boys, not to mention giving them some chores to do. But truthfully, I had thought die-hard gardeners were rather inefficient and could be doing much better things with their time, leaving the canned corn to Green Giant who, in all honesty, did it better.

But this particular day, with the boys at camp, and Lyndon limping off to work in his office building with Ken Berry, I worked alone. I couldn't decide at first whether I was relieved to have the boys gone for the week or whether I missed them. Whether I would have preferred Lyndon's company in what had become our mutual hobby, or whether I found it freeing to not worry that he would have another sleepless night from the pain that would wake him after working his leg too hard which had happened frequently lately.

It was strange that I now knew enough to not slice off another row of cucumbers because I couldn't see the difference between those and the sunflowers that had seeded themselves around the garden. And apparently, I didn't want sunflowers sucking all the moisture away from our vegetables. I was so proud of our onions and the way they responded once we learned to plant them away from anything the sprinkler would touch. Onions didn't like to be watered. I checked the cucumbers I'd reseeded and surrounded with an inverted Styrofoam cup with the bottom pushed out to keep the cutworms away. It seemed to be working—healthy leaves pushed out the hole in the cup, reaching for the sun, even showing off a bloom. The tomato plants, which also got planted away from the sprinkler to keep water off their leaves, drooped, reminding me that I'd forgotten to carry water to their roots.

And it struck me that the garden communicated with me, responded to me and my efforts with it. Yes, it could take a lot of work, but I had found pleasure in trying to please it and then receive the satisfaction of its offerings. When I cared for it well, it produced accordingly, giving me a sense of satisfaction. Sometimes, despite the neglect of the friendship with my garden, it thrived, this incredible gift brought about by something beyond my doing. When the season brought challenges that I couldn't overcome–too much heat, tent caterpillars, more rain than our soil could drain, or uncontrollable weeds–it made me sad that I'd failed those little seeds. That I hadn't been able to provide what they needed to thrive.

Carrying the hoe and watering bucket back to the shed, I paused at the clothesline to smell the clean clothes. Frustrated, I realized that I'd reached for a white tunic with soiled hands and held it to my dirt-covered face. *That one will have to be washed again*, I chastised myself, thinking that Susanna would never have been so careless as to put an item through the washer a second time. I entered the back door through the laundry room, kicking aside a pile of dirty jeans waiting to go in the washer. Standing over the blue sink in the vintage bathroom and splashing water on my freckled, over-heated face, I caught my reflection: unkempt, dry reddish curls with the odd grey strand even more stubborn than all the rest.

When was the last time I'd had a trim? When was the last time I'd even gone anywhere where it mattered to me what my frizzy hair looked like? Here I was, at a stage of life where I did not have the constant demands of young children, where I had complete freedom to do with my day as I pleased, and I spent it in the company of a book and a garden. I had actually *chosen* the company of a garden.

And in that moment, at that stage of my life, the thought that I'd come to care so deeply about tomatoes and cucumbers grieved me. For I realized that when a garden is your friend, you are desperately lonely.

The next morning, I did what a zillion other lonely people do. I googled, *How to start a blog.* By noon, as I munched on fresh garden peas and carrots dipped in hummus, along with a tuna sandwich, I had regained a sense of optimism about life, and thought through what I may have to offer the world by blogging. I considered something about my short full-time career as an electrician or my even shorter time as a dental hygienist. Surely all those electrical puns would make for good blog material? My perfect teeth would make for a great personal photo on my blog page but other than that? Sometimes our whole view on a season of life is coloured by how the season ends, and it was impossible to forget the helplessness I felt sitting in a cold car that wouldn't start when

I knew for certain I'd plugged it in just in case that day would be the day...

I considered writing about moving to a different province and all the ways in which life had to start over with a major move, but I'd read some military wives' blogs and decided to shut up.

Being a mostly-stay-at-home mom seemed like a reasonable choice. Sure, there were a lot of SAH mommy blogs but didn't that mean there was a lot of interest in the subject?

Whoa.

I set my carrot down on the plate next to the hummus. Residue of garden dirt clung to its crevices. What about being a *homeschool* mom. Immediately I thought of the "trying to potty-train Hunter while teaching Carter to read and the preschool twins decide to surprise daddy with a cake for his birthday" blog I'd read last week. Maybe some people found it humorous. I'd simply wondered if the mom had left the blogging she wouldn't have had to clean up both a mess from another missed potty accident and a failed attempt in the kitchen, and Carter might at least be able to read, "Go, Spot, go."

Then I quickly felt bad about criticizing a complete stranger with double the number of children I had.

I kept rolling around the homeschool idea though, and by the time I was mindlessly munching on a peanut butter cookie, I realized I couldn't help the world by offering ideas or suggestions on the homeschool process. For one thing, I wasn't that great at it. For another, I was occasionally still reluctantly involved rather than being a passionate homeschool mom—a real Mrs. Homeschool. But there was something that *had* remained a constant passion since the day Lyndon and I had stood dripping wet in the lake after testifying that we trusted Jesus for our salvation, and it was this desire to grow as a Christ-follower. It was the passion that kept me homeschooling when I saw the flaws in the process but couldn't think of a better way to show Jesus to my boys. What if I blogged for moms who wanted to grow closer to Jesus but who sometimes got stuck, who just needed a reminder to be faithful in tending their spiritual garden?

Excited, I wrote a piece from my musings in the garden from the day before. Of course, I didn't admit to the part about how caring for the garden as my friend showed me how lonely I'd become as a homeschool mom. Rather, I focussed on the part about nurturing the things we want to see grow in our lives and recognizing weeds that need to be pulled when they're small before they stunt the growth we want to see.

I wasn't much of a writer but I felt good about it. Maybe hormones were making me feel very different than the day before, but rather than the weary, lonely, depressed spirit I'd had yesterday, today I had a sense of optimism and pressed ahead.

Looking at the google instructions, I saw I needed to pick a name for my blog next. Well, it should probably have the word homeschool in it. Better yet if it rhymes? I made jot notes.

> *Homeschool is Cool* – except when it's not; maybe be a bit more genuine than that

> *Homeschoolers are Fools* – Ainslee!

> *Homeschool Jewels* – If by "Jewels" I mean nuggets of wisdom...jewels might be too easily misunderstood?

> *Fools Homeschool* – Bad, bad girl, Ainslee.

> *Tools for Homeschools* – Maybe. But didn't I already decide this won't be a blog about the homeschool process??

> *Fuel for those Who Homeschool* – Hmmm. Not bad. I think this captures the gist of what I'm thinking...

Before my mood changed, I decided not to overthink it. I wouldn't be lonely every day and what were the chances of this post actually getting seen anyway? I clicked Post, closed the computer and decided to bring the tomatoes another bucket of water.

When Lyndon got home I showed him my first post.

"Wait, it has a comment!" I held my laptop in mid-air, not sure if I should let Lyndon read the post first or if I should check the comment before seeing what might be a negative response. We looked at each other. I set the computer down on the table and we leaned over, backsides in the air, elbows on the table as we read through it together.

"I don't care what the comment says, this is good, Ainslee," Lyndon affirmed before I scrolled down.

His affirmation was sufficient.

"Hey Ainslee. I'm homeschooling in Whitehorse, Yukon. I don't grow a garden up here, but your post reminded me of my childhood in the Edmonton area. I've allowed some things to grow in my life that have taken over what I used to think was important to me. So, it's sad but true that our life can get stunted by letting the wrong things take over. Thanks for warning everyone."

We stood up and Lyndon wrapped his arms around me.

"I might never do it again, Lyndon. It's just, today I was…and I know you don't think much of the whole blogging thing…" I trailed off.

"Today you were what, Ainslee?"

I froze. I hoped he wouldn't hear that part.

"Restless. Just restless I guess with the boys gone. I'm not used to long days without the boys." I laughed lightly.

"You've got a hard job, Ainslee. Hardest ever. And best. The boys will be home soon enough. I thought you had some work lined up with Garry Richards for this week?"

"You know how it goes with him. Now he's not ready until next week."

"And by then the boys will be home. Maybe you should get away for a couple of days?"

"I thought of that. Not sure if I could find someone to go with. Most of my friends don't have all their kids at summer camp this week, and it's pretty short notice."

"I'd love to take a couple days off and go with you, Ainslee, but Ken already arranged for—"

I cut Lyndon off. "Yeah, no, it's no problem. Ken needs you to keep up with all the homeschool stuff." Without hardly skipping a beat I managed, "I'm going to run out and grab some groceries to make those coconut lime truffles we like. That will give you time to work on your, uh, your stuff, and maybe we can watch the sunset with a coffee and the truffles."

"That'd be perfect," Lyndon responded. "So, I've got till about 8:30?"

"Sure. Coffee date at 8:30."

I grabbed my keys and left the house, realized as I drove the Toyota past the soccer field that the parking lot was empty so I made an impulsive turn into the lot and parked. I felt my chest heave with emotion and knew what I needed to do. I'd walk the mile and a half to the grocery store from here. I locked my vehicle and headed across the empty pitches. I would have burst into tears except that I was pleased with myself. Pleased that I hadn't resorted to pleading with Lyndon to put me and the boys first for once. Pleased that I hadn't admitted to him that I was lonely.

He was so glad to have a bit more time tonight to work on the endless task of directing homeschool families to the

resources they needed to succeed. Where was that determination when it came to our family? Why was his desire
to please Ken so much stronger than his desire to please
us? To not disappoint Ken? What about not disappointing *us*? I walked faster. Granted, Lyndon worked hard
to succeed, but the reward for him was this clamouring
for his attention. The esteem of being needed. He didn't
really care that I'd written a blog. Despite his show of
support, it was meaningless to him. Maybe he still held
to his view of several years before when he was leery of
supporting women who wrote books and blogs to contribute to their family's income, or for whatever other reason
women wrote. Maybe it wasn't important enough to him
to remember. Maybe he was too wrapped up in his own
world to care that he'd married a person.

Some of the fury had left my body and I slowed my
pace. Seeing the grocery store across the highway, I stood
at the crosswalk, resolute. I was determined to get home
and make myself the coconut lime truffles. I would enjoy
every one of them whether Lyndon was around to share
them or not. I would wonder at the sunset and enjoy an
evening coffee without the boys. I would breathe deep and
relax because next week I would need to juggle caring
for the boys while finishing the electrical job with Garry
Richards. I would not let my happiness be dependent
on Lyndon.

Chapter Twenty-Nine

August 2016

I checked my phone when I got up at 8:00 that August morning. I had a text from Karalee Gardner. "Hey Ainslee. Awkward question. I've got a massage appointment in Tracey at 11 a.m. and my sitter just cancelled. Any possibility you'd be able to watch the kids? If not, I can reschedule, so no pressure."

I checked to see what time she'd sent the message. 7:48. I'd just missed it. Which meant I suddenly felt pressure. I should welcome Karalee into my life like a younger sister the way other women had welcomed me into theirs. So why did I feel pressure? I gave my day a quick mental scan. The boys had finished the bookwork part of their schooling weeks ago, and after the mission trip with Lyndon and a week at camp, were simply enjoying their summer. I had thought of taking them to the pool in town, but we could modify that to the spray park…

"Bring them over. Maybe we can pack a picnic and take the kids to the spray park once you're done?"

"I'd love that. Thanks. See you later."

Immediately I felt old insecurities rise up. What if the baby needed her diaper changed? Or if the boys talked too much, or if I couldn't manage to engage them and they cried till their mom finished her appointment. I tried to put this in perspective. If Karalee needed someone to keep the kids alive until she came back, and then needed someone to talk to, surely, I could try to do that for her. When I thought of all that Helen had invested into my life, taking a couple of hours for someone else shouldn't be too much to offer. In fact, hadn't I just recently been feeling very alone? Maybe Karalee was actually God's provision for me.

Thankfully, Brewster and Arnold had spent a week earlier in the summer helping at Bible camp and graciously welcomed the company of Karalee's younger sons. In fact, it almost seemed like they enjoyed the excuse to get reacquainted with their sandbox Tonka toys. Karalee had left her stroller for me to take the baby for a walk down our quarter-mile drive which was a perfect way for me to bond with the little girl without overwhelming her. We looked at the overripe berries left on the Saskatoon bushes and I told her about the cirrus clouds. When we got back to the yard, she watched the boys play in the sand and pointed at the dandelions. Instead of the angst I'd felt as a younger woman around little ones, I had a few moments where I wondered why Lyndon and I had felt so contentedly done having children.

Preparing food for others had never been my forte. I often wondered what had possessed me to invite the homeschool group over years ago, going so far as to offer fancy Christmas baking. Today, I realized that I hadn't checked to see if Karalee had planned lunch for her own family or if I had unwittingly offered to prepare a picnic lunch for all of us. Oh well, worst case scenario, this is what Subway and credit cards were for...

After lunch as we gathered the paper wrappers from our Subway sandwiches, the boys ran off to play in the spray park.

"Remember, you're triple the size of most of the kids playing, so be gentle," I warned my boys as they ran off with Toby and Jarrett. It was so fun to watch them with the younger boys. My kids did not have the natural opportunity to interact with multiple age ranges, as many larger families did. I wasn't always proud of their behaviour, but today was a beautiful exception.

Baby soon fell asleep in her stroller under the shade of the large trees where Karalee and I watched the boys.

"It's nice to get away from home," Karalee sighed.

"How was your massage?" I asked.

"So nice! My neck and shoulders are always killing me, like every other mom," she huffed. "But it's such a treat to have a little break from the kids. Thanks, Ainslee."

"They were perfect," I assured her. "You don't get a lot of breaks?" I sympathized.

"Not a lot. Farming is busy for Darryl. And then in winter he mechanics for an oilfield company. I am really thankful he has work," she rushed on. "And someday it should get easier as we can afford better equipment for the farm…"

"But in the meantime, you're lonely hey?" I observed.

Tears filled her eyes. I so often felt alone in the home-school journey and assumed that everyone else had friends or family to constantly fill the void in the journey. I almost didn't know how to react to her emotions for fear that my loneliness would not only show, but overtake hers. I didn't consider myself to have great social skills, but I did know that to turn the conversation to myself when she was sharing her need would not be particularly helpful.

"I've wondered if putting the kids in school for fall might be better for them. I mean, how can I help them grow when I feel so depleted?" Karalee continued, swallowing emotion.

"The baby makes it hard to pack the boys up and take them places. And I don't want them to be handicapped socially because all they know is their quirky mom—and a depressed mom at that.

"I don't know if I have what it takes to challenge them to grow. Sometimes I feel like I'm just letting them get away with stuff because it's easier than insisting they improve. And then I look at myself, and I'm like, yeah, because I can teach them to be better? Hardly!" she humphed. "There's just so many things I know I can't teach them anyway. Like French. How are you teaching Brewster and Arnold French?" Her weepy green eyes had dried and now looked at me so sincerely I almost laughed.

Before I had the chance to respond, however, she continued. "But then, I think if I put them in school, I might be even more lonely because I would have even less reason to get out and I'd still have Baby to take with me. And if they go to school, I'll be exposed for all the things I haven't taught them yet. In school they could learn so much from the other kids. Like ideas for their art projects. But what if it costs a lot more to have them in school? See because right now, there's no pressure to buy certain kinds of things for their lunches, or certain school supplies. There's no fundraisers or birthday parties for classmates where they have to bring certain gifts."

Karalee finally trailed off and looked at me again.

I couldn't help but smile, because her verbal outburst reminded me so much of the thoughts that plagued my mind often. I didn't want to speak too quickly if all she needed was to have aired her thoughts. Maybe she wasn't actually asking for advice. On the other hand, if Baby awoke or the boys lost interest in the water, then our opportunity to talk would be over. I felt a need to say something.

"You know you can put them in school if you want, Karalee. Some moms desperately need some space and time to heal or focus on their own needs for a while. The choices we make don't have to be forever."

"I just don't know if I have what it takes to keep doing this," she almost whined.

I didn't dare tell her that she was just getting started. That the questions she had, the insecurities, would perhaps go away, only to be replaced with new questions and insecurities. I couldn't tell her how, just recently, I'd been transitioning from being overwhelmed with my boys' presence to being overwhelmed by their absence.

So, I let silence do the speaking.

I let it speak to both of us.

Until I could honestly say, "You will have a lot of good days, Karalee. God provides what we need when we need it."

Chapter Thirty

October 2016

On a cold Saturday in late October, Lyndon announced that we would all be going out to the uninsulated detached garage and cleaning up so we could park inside for the winter. Brewster and Arnold took longer than usual to finish their breakfast. It was one thing to have enthusiasm when the goal was to get an old motor running, and quite another when all the remnants needed to be sorted and stored, or even worse, for them to make the decision to give up and discard the project.

Eventually we all made it out to the garage. I was a touch irritated that Lyndon had left this project for such a cold day and had given none of us warning about it. However, I tried to be gracious enough to remind myself of the pain in his leg that had ruled his life for more years than any of us could graciously tolerate pain. The patch that made life bearable for him had certainly helped, but it wasn't a cure and we were still searching for answers. He must have woken up feeling ok to tackle this job today and decided to plunge ahead, or he was dreading getting into a frosted vehicle all winter.

"Put all the garbage into this dumpster bag," Lyndon directed, laying out and unfolding a large canvas construction dumpster.

"Whoa, this thing holds over 3000 pounds!" I stated, reading the label on the packaging Lyndon had just peeled off. "How much garbage do we have?"

Lyndon paused for a moment, bent over the mostly-unfolded bag. He spoke with irritation, slowly as if to a child. "I'm not sure, Ainslee. But I figured this was a pretty convenient way to deal with it, however much there is. Right now, there's enough to keep us from being able to park in the garage."

I bristled, hearing a condescending tone from my husband. I decided to just try to smooth the tense moment. "It's a great idea. I've never seen one of these. So, what happens when we're done with it?"

"They just come and pick it up. Easy as that." Lyndon's tone changed as he attempted to garner enthusiasm from the boys. "Who's going to get the first thing in it?"

Brewster carried a weed whacker over and dropped it in. "I couldn't get this one going," he explained.

"Awesome. That's exactly why that bag is here. You gave that weed whacker a good try, Brewster."

Soon the weed whacker was joined by a broken hoe, a rooster weather vane, a chain from an old chain saw, a pair of rubber boots with a cracked sole, a nearly complete lawn mower and blades from another, and wood scraps from building a tree fort. By now, the entire garage floor was clear and the boys were getting restless. Arnold picked up an airsoft gun from behind the winter snow shovel. "Hey isn't this Conan's?"

And just like that he pulled the trigger. The plastic pellet hit Lyndon on the arm.

"Arnold, what's wrong with you?" Lyndon levelled his gaze at Arnold. "Pretty sure you know better than to handle any kind of gun that way!"

"I didn't try to!" Arnold defended with a whine.

"Well, did you try not to?" Lyndon shot back.

Arnold narrowed his eyes and tucked in his chin.

"Put it in the van so we can take it back to Conan. We don't need any kind of a gun on the yard," Lyndon ordered, turning to pick up the broom.

I saw Arnold aim the air soft at Lyndon's butt. Then he turned on his heel and surprised Brewster with a shot that created a poof of dirt to rise at Brewster's feet.

"Idiot," Brewster muttered.

Lyndon spun around in time to realize what had happened. "Go to your room, Arnold," Lyndon ordered. "Stay there till I get there."

Arnold seemed happy to go.

"Nice way to reward him by letting him get out of finishing up here," I muttered.

Lyndon sighed.

"What else needs to go in the bag, Dad?" Brewster asked.

Lyndon didn't answer. He just kept sweeping.

"So, are you satisfied, Lyndon? Have we done enough out here for you or you can't be bothered to answer Brewster?"

"*For me*, Ainslee?" Lyndon repeated. "Do you really think I picked a miserable day to do this job for *me*? I want you to be able to park inside for the winter. But apparently I can't do enough for you."

"Why are you talking like this in front of him," I nodded my head toward Brewster.

"Brewster, you can go in as well, but you stay in the living room. Leave each other alone." At this direction, Brewster escaped our standoff.

As Brewster allowed the front door to slam behind him, Lyndon finished sweeping while I rearranged the tools hanging on the peg board. We finished at the same time and stood on opposite sides of the tidy garage, neither of us willing to be the first to concede the defeat of either leaving or continuing the argument.

"Ainslee," Lyndon finally started, "I'm not your enemy. I want what's best for you. I wish you had a proper attached, heated garage. I'm tired of worrying about how I'll be able to take care of you when, when—"

I knew he was referring to his leg. The pain that had taken over, that kept him from being active and engaging with life, with the boys. But it was more than that.

"It doesn't take a good leg to take time to play a game with the boys, Lyndon. You manage to drive all over the country whenever the homeschooling families need you. You don't need a good leg to drop whatever you're doing when Ken calls with some new idea he wants to run by you."

"I'm trying to do my utter best to provide for you and the boys. Does that not matter at all to you?" Lyndon's face had lost its soft concern.

"Stop using the providing thing as an excuse to not be here for us. As if we benefit more from a garage we can park in than we would if you could just discipline the kids properly. What kind of dad would let his son shoot an airsoft right at him..."

Lyndon's jaw dropped. "*Let* his son? *Let* him?"

I could not have been more effective in getting Lyndon to drop the gloves than if I'd been an offensive hockey player and I'd just shoved the goalie.

We fought then. Fought like we had never fought before. So many words hurled about that expressed probably years of pent-up frustrations.

"What do you want from me Ainslee?" Lyndon finally yelled. He never yelled. I was so glad the boys were inside, though thinking of them made me hope to God they had obeyed Lyndon's instruction to leave each other alone. Besides, they could probably hear Lyndon from inside.

I didn't know. I didn't say anything.

"Fine. I get it. I don't know how to be a dad, Ainslee," Lyndon finally blurted after we'd run out of old scenarios. "Neither of us knows what to expect from a dad or how to treat a dad. Neither of us does even if you think you do because you wanted one so bad. I sure have tried, Ainslee. But I guess this is just one more area in life where I won't get it right with you."

Inwardly I raged. *I wanted a dad so bad, Lyndon? I did?? What about you hanging on to Ken to fill your void? I may have wanted a dad but I'm not the one clinging to some stranger day and night!* Still silence.

Lyndon looked right at me. Waited. Then he hung his head in defeat.

"Or is that it, Ainslee? You don't want anything from me? You think our boys would be better off growing up like us, like you and me?"

I had always promised myself not to hurt Lyndon by using his soft sounding name as a weapon the way he'd heard it from his peers growing up. I had always promised myself not to take aim at his manhood. But I'd managed. I'd let my growing frustration at what I perceived as his lack of involvement in the kids' schooling build until it came out sounding like we'd be better off without him.

This—this stupid undermining silence—was worse, far worse, than any teasing he'd received.

Chapter Thirty-One

November 2016

As things often go, we were about to face a series of troubles that ran into each other until we couldn't tell apart causes and effects. Until I didn't know how far back we'd need to go to unravel our mess. Until I doubted what Lyndon and I had ever seen in a future with each other. And don't such seasons usually begin in the most random of ways.

Ken Berry died. Right there behind the sales counter in the Boundless Home School Board office. One minute he was on the phone negotiating a deal to carry a new music and art curriculum, and then he collapsed. Lyndon hadn't ever performed CPR before, even though he'd been trained and recertified repeatedly since beginning his teaching career years prior. The paramedics assured him that you can't revive someone who has had such a massive heart attack, and there was nothing wrong with his technique, but having someone go from alive to dead in a moment like that causes any observer to become introspective. Lyndon lost a co-worker, a mentor, a close friend, a man who had known him longer than I had.

The day of Ken Berry's funeral, a heavy wind blew our skiff of snow around until the poor visibility made driving dangerous and stressful. That day as he lay there in his casket, was not the first or the last day I resented Ken. Today, it was for leading us to rent this little country house which meant that even our short drive into Tracey felt treacherous. I knew that on this day my resentment was sadness that he was gone, hoping he had not taken chunks of Lyndon with him. I had always been thankful for the old farmhouse and yard that felt like ours even when it wasn't.

The week leading up to the homeschool facilitator's laying to rest had been a blur as we put our schoolwork aside and helped Lyndon answer phone calls and get out the few orders that had come in. Lyndon and I had also been sleeping on the air mattress in our school-slash-everything room, making space in our bedroom for Ken's younger brother, Clay, and sister-in-law, who had been missionaries in Rwanda for almost thirty years. They didn't seem bothered to be sharing our single bathroom, though it was the first time for us and a touch weird because of that.

The following day, Sunday, our little church group put on a potluck for Helen and all the extended family at noon. I did have to remind Brewster and Arnold to contain their exuberance under the circumstances at all the church folks' best casseroles, salads, and baking in a single meal. In fact, earlier in the week when they had been excited to find me making enchiladas, only to discover it was for a church potluck, it was all I could do to console them with the fact that I did have two pans of their favourite dish and one would go in our little freezer for a time when it was just for us. It seemed to be a universal regret that moms brought a family's most-looked-forward-to meal to church functions, leaving them to hope, desperately, they would find the right line and not be too late to at least get a sample of what they loved most.

By the time we had washed the last of the potluck meal dishes, we gathered around Helen for one more informal service of singing and remembrance. Pastor Nelson made my throat hurt as he used this final opportunity to remind us, from the apostle Paul's teaching, that feeling torn about life with Jesus, as Ken Berry now knew it, or living a life of fruitful labour on earth, is a good thing. We should have passion and longing for both, and welcome life on earth, or life in the presence of the eternal God, with equal joy as God chooses for us.

I had long forgiven our pastor's wife, Mrs. Nelson, for what I saw as her ignorant critiquing of our homeschooling choice. Day after long day her service to our congregation had been tireless. What I had seen as her testing Arnold that first day of Sunday School, in our curtained-off basement classroom, was not the only time I would perceive her blundering socially. But I had come to admire her consistent efforts. Where many pastor's wives held back from being overly involved in his ministry—the women aren't paid after all—she poured herself into serving the church, and her children in their nearby colleges, and our community, in a rhythmic balance that had caused me to marvel at her skill and commitment. I had come to find that instead of being irritated at her efforts, which occasionally came off as awkward, I found it refreshing that she wasn't perfect in her social graces, was humble enough to apologize where needed, and strong enough to not sulk about her own blunders.

Late in the afternoon, the few church people who remained stacked the last of the wooden chairs and vacuumed the bare concrete floor of the church's basement dining area. We wiped down the bathrooms. My boys seemed to have grasped the significance of the day and helped empty garbage cans and carry it outside to a small dumpster. We were all thankful that the raging wind had stopped, though leaving a temperature of -27.

We came home with just enough pieces of chocolate cake in our pan and raw vegetables on the platter to add to a supper of ham sandwiches to share with Ken's brother and his wife—Ken's brother, Clay, who had been instrumental in talking Ken through the difference between the religious life he'd been living and the life of faith which was necessary for salvation. Clay and Nancy had some work to finish that evening on a presentation they were to give at a Bible college the following week about their ministry in Rwanda, and intended to leave at 6:00 the following morning in order to arrive just in time for their first class. Lyndon found an extension cord to plug in their vehicle and managed, with the boys' help, to shovel some snow away from the house, while I cleaned up our little kitchen. I simply could not leave our breakfast and small amount of supper dishes, plus the enchilada and cake pan and vegie platter on the counter, or there would be no space to make a simple breakfast of toast and coffee. We had learned to cope with our simple stretch of counter space but, without the luxury of a dishwasher, it meant being committed to ending the day with a relatively clean slate.

After a final visit with our guests, I sank onto the air mattress at 9:30 that night. Thankfully, they wanted to go to bed early since they had an early morning and a busy week ahead. Not that the mattress in our room was exactly luxurious, but after spreading our larger bodies on this precarious, air-filled cushion for the last three nights, I looked forward to being back in our own bed.

Long after Lyndon began to snore gently, I lay awake, realizing I was completely and utterly spent. I loved Helen Berry deeply and I grieved for her. I felt concern for what lay ahead for Lyndon, for all of us. How would Ken's death impact Lyndon's work and therefore our future? What was I to do with the feelings of guilt I bore that Ken was gone and Lyndon would miss his friendship and mentorship, and I was torn between a slight pleasure that

Lyndon's mistress was no more, and fear of what or who he would turn to now. I lay there completely exhausted, yet unable to sleep for a long time, dreading that the morning would bring life as back to usual. I didn't see how I could face another day, never mind the years that lay ahead of getting up, being motivated to see to the boys' physical and spiritual and educational and social needs. I just wanted to sleep for a week. A month. The last week had been so draining...

And then it was 5:20 and our alarm was blaring. I heard the shower running and remembered immediately that Clay and Nancy needed to be on the road shortly. Lyndon also sat up and scooted his long frame slightly to the edge of the mattress that popped Lyndon forward when I rolled out. I was impressed that the old thing hadn't sprung a leak. Since we'd been storing the deflated mattress in the cellar, along with a few other camping supplies, it smelled as funky as the house had the first day we'd opened the front door with its floral oval insert. We used a spritz bottle of water to tame our hair, baby wipes to clean our faces, and each popped in a Listerine breath strip. I hated the way my nose looked with my hair all pulled back, but without access to the bathroom, it seemed the best I could do.

After Nancy and Clay let their vehicle warm up a few minutes and loaded their suitcases, I desperately longed to go back to bed. We waved goodbye from the window above the kitchen sink and, in spite of trying to put on a cheerful air that morning, I wilted back to the same grumpy exhaustion I'd felt the night before. If I'd had a clean set of sheets, I may have taken time to put them on our bed and reward my body from the four nights spent in the "schoolroom." Even lying on the couch in the living room seemed attractive–I could lie there and doze off and on all day, and since I was already dressed I could at least tell myself I hadn't stayed in my pajamas all day. But the only extra sheet set I owned, the once-white set, was tucked haphazardly on the inflated bed. One of the blessings of a small house was the need to keep a tight lid on the clutter because neither Lyndon nor I wanted the consequences of the alternative. At least that was one area we didn't have to fight to agree about.

The sheet set. I looked at the time. 6:15. In an instant my resolve returned. If I needed to remember the consequences of a small house that held more linens than we needed, I remembered Lyndon's descriptions of Connie Harper's house from his home visits there. And her kids' lack of actual teaching. If that wasn't where I wanted to end up, then I needed to choose the alternative.

Suddenly, it was much easier to choose to put my weariness aside, do a few basic exercises and then jump in the shower and deal with getting my hair out of that unflattering ponytail. If I got the laundry going once I was done in the shower, I could even get the schoolroom back in order before it was time to get going with the boys' schoolwork. I told myself I could always have a nap later in the day, but I'd do my best to start it right.

Chapter Thirty-Two

March 2017

Lyndon didn't hide from me that he felt alone and uncertain how to proceed with the work at Boundless Homeschool Board office. As in any shared effort, there are responsibilities that one partner generally takes care of, and, though the other isn't incapable of the task, they become ignorant of it. And now Lyndon didn't have the luxury of being ignorant. The stress of learning another side of the homeschool co-ordinator role was heavy. The weight of Lyndon's emotional stress was added to the actual weight his sore leg continued to bear. We kept searching for answers. It didn't seem right that a slight injury from over eight years ago could cause this level of discomfort. "Lose weight," Lyndon was told. And there was no doubt that would help, but the pain involved in exercising made that a difficult option.

Meanwhile, Brewster had discovered football. He was fourteen years old now, and over the last six months or so had been throwing around the football with friends on the school ground. Tracey High School had hired a new university graduate who was passionate about the sport, and it didn't take long for the contagion to spread among the boys at recess and spill over into after-school hours. No one had equipment of course, since the sport had not ever been offered at the school, but they learned the rules of play and scrimmaged for hours with surprisingly few injuries or intervention from school authorities. Lyndon and I saw this loose play as a good thing. Brewster was engaged in activity and interaction with the schooled kids that he'd never had opportunity for in this way. Our gentle son who was not particularly athletic had found a niche. His physical strength and mental strategy were a unique asset. But things were about to change when Brewster made an excited announcement over our supper of over-cooked pork chops.

"Mr. G's starting a real football team."

"Like, how real?" Lyndon managed, gulping down a piece of the dry meat followed by a long drink of water.

I was annoyed. "That's great news!" I smiled at Brewster and gave Lyndon the little kick under the table along with stink eyes. What a weird response.

Lyndon kind of came out of his little trance and managed to engage Brewster in telling him the scant details of a new football league with which Mr. G. was hoping to get the school registered.

When Brewster's plate was clean, he invited Arnold to come out and throw the football with him. I could tell Arnold was evaluating his chances of making it onto Mr. G.'s team as well, and he eagerly took Brewster up on the offer.

I poured Lyndon a second cup of coffee. There was no sugar-coating the fact that the meat had been too dry. If Susanna could teach me the most affordable way to buy pork chops, perhaps she could also teach me to cook them so we didn't have to wash them down.

"Wouldn't it be so fun for the boys to be able to play football?" I gushed.

Lyndon stirred some milk into his coffee.

My face twisted into a puzzled expression. I could honestly feel myself slip from excitement to annoyance.

"Why wouldn't you want them playing football, Lyndon?"

He sighed. Closed his eyes and sighed.

"It just doesn't work that way. Has nothing to do with what I want."

He rubbed a hand across his eyes and dragged it down beneath his chin.

My annoyance changed to a worried compassion. The feeling was a stranger. I'd felt little more than the duty of my vows toward my husband since we'd thrown verbal daggers at each other in the garage last fall. Even through his grief of losing Ken, I'd been no more than a loyal wife.

"What's the matter, Lyndon?"

"You just can't have students playing for a school team who aren't registered with the school. It's an insurance policy thing. This won't work."

He got up and went to the window over the kitchen sink. I could see him watching the boys. He threw his hands up and shook his head.

"I know God doesn't make us miserable on purpose but right now it sure feels like it."

"You're being a bit dramatic. There's got to be a way around that," I blurted. It wasn't like Lyndon to just give up. He was an ideas man. Surely, he'd come up with an idea.

"Oh there's a way around it alright," Lyndon conceded. "Register the boys for school and if they make the team it's a done deal."

"Lyndon, you've pushed for all kinds of policies to be changed and a lot of them have been," I reminded him matter-of-factly.

"Maybe it's time," he sighed. "I've fought for a lot of things and what difference has it made. Sports were a huge part of my life as a teen. I know how bad they want this."

I caught on then. We all have our breaking point and Lyndon had finally found his.

"Really, Lyndon? You had an answer for every downside of homeschool until this one? Just because you feel this one as if it were happening to you?"

He sank back onto the chair and looked at me.

"Football means so much to you that you'd be willing to give up everything we've sacrificed to get to where we are so they can play a game? I have searched my soul, Lyndon, to want what you wanted for them. I've turned myself inside out to share your motivations that we would give them no opportunity greater than that of wholeheartedly filling their minds and time with the things of God, and you're willing to give it all up for a *game*? A *game*, Lyndon?"

I tried to let that sink it. For both of us.

"Is homeschooling really what you see as the best way to raise our kids responsibly for God's glory, Lyndon? Or was it simply your way to gain Ken's approval? What have we been sacrificing for? Seriously, Lyndon."

I tried to make him answer me with my eyes searching his downturned face.

"I want the boys to be happy, Ainslee."

"So do I. I know that being happy is part of the way we will reach their hearts."

Every parent knew that.

"But after all these years of heading one direction, don't now switch paths for the mere sake of their happiness when our goal has been their holiness."

He squeezed his eyes shut then.

"I'm tired of the losses, Ainslee," he admitted in a whisper.

I got a lump in my throat.

I knew Ken had meant the world to him. I tended to forget that as much as I was needing to reinvent my identity, Lyndon had a health concern that had deeply changed him as well.

When Lyndon had swallowed a few times he continued, "We just need to be sure about this. Because some day when the boys are angry that they couldn't play football on the team, we need to be able to tell ourselves we chose this loss in hopes of greater gain. Even if they don't understand. We've got to be able to tell ourselves we did what we thought was right."

Chapter Thirty-Three

Lyndon came home from his trip to visit homeschool families and was riled. I could tell by his body language, his short answers, that he was introspective. The next morning, he was up making a breakfast of fried eggs, ham, and hashbrown patties as the rest of us got ready for the day. It was Arnold's turn to go look after chores at the monstrous, empty house north of our tree line while the owners spent their winter in Arizona. The unpredictable spring weather had surprised us with six inches of wet, heavy snow overnight and after about half an hour of Arnold being gone, we heard the neighbours' quad move from its usual pattern around the small farm yard—bringing a bale to the cattle—to pushing aside the fresh snow in their yard making it look like someone was home, then—on to clearing our driveway. It would not have been an entirely necessary chore, as Lyndon had upgraded our original Ford Edge with the Toyota 4-wheel-drive option several years ago, and would have been able to navigate his way off the yard. But we enjoyed seeing Arnold take advantage of the neighbours' offer to use their quad to clear our driveway as well as theirs.

Later, when Arnold came in from the dusk of the unseasonably cold morning, Lyndon took obvious pleasure in serving him a hot breakfast. Not that it was that unusual for Lyndon to cook or even to cook breakfast, but he did generally come home weary from his trips and would enjoy staying in bed a bit longer the first morning. So, I was a little thrown off by him getting up as early as he did, making breakfast for the boys and me, and then heading to the office.

And that nervous energy. I knew Lyndon well enough to perceive he was processing something which didn't get said in the quick rundown I'd gotten about his trip.

At lunch Lyndon came home. Again, not entirely unusual after being gone. But suspicious. Especially when he spent extra time at home with the boys, asking them questions about their latest projects, checking where they were at with their math.

This process of waiting for him to spill what was on his mind was totally distracting me from peacefully carrying on with our usual loose routine.

"Should we have the boys do SAT tests this year?" Lyndon asked that evening as we sat in the living room on the couch facing the zebra painting, while Arnold and Brewster had gone to youth group.

"Like standardized testing?" I slowly responded.

He looked at me innocently.

"Like the kind of standardized testing you helped get abolished as mandatory for homeschoolers?" I continued, expecting him to squirm. He didn't. More of that innocent look?

I tried a new strategy.

I waited.

But if he dared try changing the subject and moving on...

"Isn't that the part we wanted changed?" Lyndon tried to clarify.

"Isn't *what* the part we wanted changed?" I was not about to give him the satisfaction of filling in words so that he didn't have to.

"The mandatory part. Which means we can pursue getting them tested if we wanted to."

"And why would we want to?"

"Ainslee," he sighed slightly, not wanting to seem frustrated, but clearly getting there as I tried to force him to give up what was on his mind. "Don't we ask the mechanic to check the vehicle over when he does an oil change? Especially if we're going to be travelling somewhere? Isn't it just prudent to check?"

Suddenly Lyndon's extra attentiveness throughout the day to the kids schooling made sense.

"What happened?"

"Huh?"

"What happened to make you need to know their academics are on track?"

"Julie."

Now it was my turn to utter *huh*?

"Mostly Julie, but honestly Connie as well."

"Harper?"

"Yep."

"Like Connie Harper I meant."

"Yeah, I knew what you meant. You've talked about them before."

He leaned in and kissed me then. Held his cheek against my crooked nose. Brought his arm up from his side to wrap over me and tangled his fingers in my mess of curls.

Again, I waited. Despite feeling distant from Lyndon for months, I couldn't resist his tender touch.

I enjoyed having him home and close. I almost felt cherished even if I didn't have a clue yet what Julie Chen and Connie Harper had to do with Lyndon's suggestion for SAT testing for our boys.

Lyndon sat up.

"Are you ever disgusted with homeschoolers?"

"Um..."

"Like do you ever think 'homeschool.' Compound word. Loosely translated could be 'home has chosen to take responsibility for school.' Home school." He emphasized the second word.

"But then, maybe they just don't know about taking responsibility for anything. Ainslee, you should see some of these people's homes and yards and, and their hair!"

I suddenly felt self-conscious of my grey strands among tight red curls that would look especially frizzy now that Lyndon had put his fingers in it, in spite of taming it with a leave-in conditioner this morning. I didn't have time to over-evaluate that, though, before Lyndon continued spewing.

"How is it conscionable to leave a fourteen-year-old at a grade three reading level while she's having her ninth baby? Sure, her oldest son is compassionate and capable of feeding and caring for many of those younger kids. He chops wood to keep the house warm while Mr. Chen works at the mine three-weeks-in-one-week-out. I don't know when that kid has last left the yard. He can do dishes just fine, but what is with these crazy people who think it's okay to leave the schooling out of home schooling? And meanwhile, what the heck does that woman do other than talk as if she's got things under control?"

Lyndon caught himself, realizing he was ranting, and then added, "And what fools let their kids raise their other kids?"

He raised both hands in a helpless gesture as he stood up, no longer able to sit. "And somehow I'm supposed to defend homeschooling and homeschoolers."

Lyndon left the room and before long I could hear water running in the shower.

How in the world had Lyndon done it, I thought. This was only the second time ever that I'd heard him question the merits of homeschooling. The first was just recently when we realized Brewster wouldn't be able to play football with the school team.

Had Lyndon seriously never seen before that some families did a lot of home and very little schooling? How was this news to him? And why did it now suddenly become a big deal? So big a deal that he'd actually used the word *heck,* which I hadn't heard from him since someone complained to Ken Berry about Lyndon's foul mouth after that very first homeschool barbeque.

I continued to just sit on the couch.

Lyndon had talked to me. Talked to me like he used to, like we were friends and partners. I didn't feel like pulling away when he touched my hair.

Chapter Thirty-Four

I envied moms of girls for so many reasons. So many. Mind you, if my daughter had unmanageable curls like mine, my envy might be short-lived. And maybe I was seriously lousy at teaching my boys how to help me clean the house. After all, it's hard to teach things that aren't part of our personal strength set in the first place.

Lyndon was amazing at keeping clutter out of the house. Actually, with Lyndon's love of politics and travel, and since we'd said goodbye to the Kawasaki, Lyndon's interests didn't generate a ton of stuff. Maybe there was also something about the tumour in his leg that had challenged him to not go through life too weighted with things that I may someday have to sift through. He conceded to have things for the sake of Brewster and Arnold's interests, and in that lay the parts of motors, along with whatever machines they'd come off of. There were tools, not top-quality ones unless they'd been bought at garage sales, along with a shelf full of oils and filters.

Maybe it was just the people I knew. Like, going to Susanna Neudorf's house made me think if I'd had girls, I would be able to eat soup out of our bathroom sink like I could do out of hers. I didn't really notice these things at home for the most part, but coming into our house after being at hers, I saw the layers of dust on our ceiling fans, the fingerprints around each light switch.

One day when we'd been there, she was just pushing her stove back into place when we arrived, and it made me curious. What does it actually look like under my kitchen appliances?

Crazy.

It looks like a crazy ecosystem.

However, between the money and the Lego, and a valentine card I noticed Brewster sneak into his pocket rather than throw in the garbage, the ugly green appliances that wouldn't die were something the boys did move out on occasion after that day. Not that they cleaned really well before replacing them, but at least some dust got skittered out from beneath which I could then sweep up in the next kitchen cleaning.

I liked to tell myself that if I wasn't homeschooling, I'd do a better job of scrubbing the bathtub, and dusting the end tables in the living room and the tops of the baseboards, but generally, I felt successful because we didn't have knick knacks to dust around, our dishes got washed regularly, the kids hung their coats on the hooks in the hall by the front door. Would having girls mean I'd feel motivated to put in a crystal chandelier and keep it sparkling? Not likely, really. Perhaps my girls would have had to settle for knowing how and when to change the furnace filter, for being on top of oil changes and clean cabin filters in the vehicle.

So, I didn't see housecleaning in the same way that Susanna did. And although there were times I sure wished I did, I was also satisfied that it didn't drive me insane to have the kids home and not have a war with myself about my desire to deep clean.

Apparently, that was a real thing.

* * * * *

I pulled in at Helen's bungalow in Tracey just before noon. It had become a loose habit between me and Helen shortly after Ken passed away. Arnold and Brewster were enrolled in a weekly, day-long automotive class at the Lethbridge College. About twice a month I used that time to shop at Costco, headed back to Tracey in time to have lunch with Helen and divvy up the large packages into the much smaller amounts she used. Helen and I would sit at her table with the groceries in reusable shopping bags covering her kitchen counter and parts of the floor, and usually share a hot turkey sandwich and each have a cola. Then later, with the groceries repackaged, her tiny portions safely tucked in her cupboards and freezer, I would head back to Lethbridge to pick up the boys.

There was so much I loved about Helen. The cola for example. My hips and waist didn't need pop, and I'm not even sure Helen liked it–but she drank it with me and let me escape motherhood and adulthood for those moments during our lunch without ever once making me feel evaluated. Maybe, as much as there were ways in which I had admired and appreciated Ken, I did feel like he spent his whole life upholding a standard–a good standard, a godly standard–but Helen had always just loved me. Loved me without measuring me, and even more so now that she lived alone in their modest bungalow.

"Helen, your hair!" I couldn't help but stare.

She blushed and patted at her smooth, slightly-longer-than-chin-length gentle, white curls. "I went to see a new hair stylist this morning," she confessed. "I was hoping you'd give me an honest opinion..." her voice trailed off tentatively. "The girls are coming for my birthday next week."

"It's perfect."

We left so many things unsaid. I was sure she grieved not having Ken to be the one to compliment her new look.

"Do the curls look too young?" she asked, and I imagined her wondering about her daughters' response.

"No. No, it's perfect," I repeated. "You must have had a protein conditioning treatment?"

"Yes. The other stylist I went to kept pressuring me to colour my hair but I've always rebelled at that for a variety of reasons."

"This is so nice Helen. It still feels like you, but the smooth shine just makes you look so alive I guess."

She laughed a little which relieved me because I'd immediately regretted using the word *alive* when it emphasized that Ken was not.

"Let's eat!" she insisted, setting a heavy bag with meats closer to the kitchen cupboards, giving me room to pull my shoes off and pass through to her table.

After the simple meal we started dividing our portions, some cereals and dry goods first, then vegetables and fruits, then processed, and finally raw, meats.

"How did you have your hair when your girls were little," I asked Helen as we divided packages of ground beef.

"Long," she sighed. "Long and loose. Of course, it was a soft brown back then. And I grew up in the sixties and seventies, so hippy-ish, I guess. Parted down the middle; I had way too much hair for it to have that sleek, straight look that was all the rage. But I learned to do protein treatments with eggs. And Ken loved it long like that even if I felt like I could never quite tame it."

I waited a few moments, let her say Ken's name and remember.

"What made you cut it?"

"A run in with the vacuum."

"Do I get to hear the story?" I grinned.

"Pretty simple. I was vacuuming carpet on the stairs, leaning forward. The powerhead caught my long hair. The problem was, the power switch was on the vacuum cleaner itself which was at the bottom of the stairs, and I was so tangled up in the powerhead by then that I'd have fallen down the stairs if I had tried to get to it. I called Chloe to come switch it off but it took her a while to hear me over the noise of the vacuum. Then it took her a while to find the off switch. She was, after all, only three. Anyway, after this whole process I had a section that had to be cut out of the machine. And I've had it between chin and shoulder length ever since."

I had stopped packaging the meat, staring, horrified at her hair being wound tighter and tighter into the vacuum.

"The hair didn't really matter to me, Ainslee," she reassured me. "It was way too heavy anyway. I found it freeing to have it shorter. Besides, it was so much easier to take care of with all that length off. But you can imagine I made the girls put their long hair up when they got old enough to vacuum." She smiled again. "Poor Chloe. Never had to tell her twice."

I took a quick glance at Helen's new hairstyle, at her kitchen, which except for our current project tended to be tidy.

"Were you always so neat, Helen? Like your home, your hair?" I prodded.

"I learned to be more so, Ainslee. I'm a bit, well quite a bit, more free-spirited by nature," she confided, "but Ken had a need for order. He functioned best when the craft projects were relegated to the basement, when the garage held very little more than the car, when his haircuts were scheduled for every four weeks. I learned to work with his need for systems." Helen washed her hands well and then put on the kettle.

"Lyndon went out to the Harper's recently." I shared, as if I were changing the subject when I was trying to advance it without seeming desperate.

"Like Connie and Joseph's?" Helen asked.

"Right. And a few other places out that direction," I added.

"Ken always found that a hard trip," Helen mused. "Some of those families made him wonder if homeschooling was a good choice for them. And you know Ken—die-hard-homeschool advocate."

I grimaced at her use of *die-hard* but Helen seemed unfazed.

"Why do they continue if it seems like they can't quite get it done?" I was afraid my question came off as rude, but it was out.

"Oh Ainslee," she sighed. "I'll say some things, but you have to put what I'm about to share into perspective, which is that anytime we critique someone else we've silently stated that we know what the standard should be. That we know what good homeschooling should look like. That we've got it figured out." Helen poured the boiling water into the teapot.

"So Connie and her sister Julie—"

"Wait, like Julie Chen?" I interrupted.

"Yes."

"I didn't know they were sisters. Well, actually I don't really know anything about them. Forget it, carry on."

"Okay. So, Connie and her sister Julie grew up in the general area where they live now. It's far from a school for one thing so it would be a very long bus ride for those kids to go to a school. Pretty much any parent would have a hard time living out there and sending their little ones to school. Julie and Connie's parents homeschooled them as well. And when they were growing up, they definitely got the message that they must grow up to be wives and moms who homeschooled their kids. And they do. But not everyone has a gifting or a calling to teach their kids at home. Some people don't feel like they can make any other choice and still be a Christian. I think they feel if they were to forsake homeschooling, they would be forsaking Christ himself. So, they continue in the system of keeping their children out of the public education, of homesteading, of a simple, modest life, of bearing children to raise as an army for the Lord. Some of them are just overwhelmed and depressed but I think they tell themselves at least they're faithful. They'll endure until they get the victor's crown."

"Depressed," I mused.

"And, some of these women have found having another child to be the best way they know of getting positive attention. They're trying to find love through the love of their children. They'll get a few gifts and meals for the baby. Maybe a few extra days in the hospital and some extra help in their homes or with their other kids.

"As for the men, they may just as well not have the skills they need or the desire to manage a small farm but it's the only acceptable thing they can do, or it's the only thing they can do and still have an affordable place to live. I'm guessing that in Julie and Connie's family, the land was a gift. So, if they choose to leave, trying to afford a place in a more populated area with their big families becomes quite the obstacle. So, they stay. Or at least the family stays. James Chen has been trucking for years away from home. Maybe it's easier for him to be gone."

Helen got a faraway look.

"But then, maybe Ken also found it easier to be away from home as much as he was and let me figure out how to implement the ideals that he had. In spite of how personable he seemed, he struggled to connect well with our girls. And his need for order didn't always mesh well with the needs of growing children. And what if our circumstances had been different, if we'd lived physically far away from other people, if his work had not brought an adequate and stable income, if our kids had had special needs...

"Our choices, as selfless as they seem, always have something in it for us. Our good deeds are filthy rags. This good desire we have to pour ourselves into educating our kids for the glory of God can very easily become a desire for our own success story."

I didn't know what to think of the way Helen spoke about Ken. It made me uncomfortable—he was dead after all. Perhaps letting him be real even now, faults and all, made him feel close? Either way, she'd confirmed that the things I didn't like about Ken were the same things she had struggled to appreciate about him. Negative qualities are simply unpleasant, whether I'm living under the same roof as them or not.

I left Helen's house soon after that with all my smaller packages of meat and vegetables. Lugging the bags back to my vehicle helped me justify the cola we'd shared.

I thought it rather uncanny as I headed back to Lethbridge to pick up the boys, how closely Helen's thoughts echoed what went on in my head. It was like she could read my mind. Or was this battle we waged between God's glory and our own such a common struggle?

Chapter Thirty-Five

You would've thought at some point someone would have recognized the problem with Lyndon being my homeschool facilitator. This wasn't an issue until Ken Berry passed away. Thankfully, after only one evaluation with the lone, handsome facilitator, who provided me with no new tools or advice I hadn't heard before, Boundless Home School Board was able to hire additional help.

In fact, numbers were increasing to the point that we had started holding our monthly group meeting at the Mennonite church. They had a large room for the kids to play and make crafts, lots of toys for the toddlers, and a kitchen that the teens were enjoying so much they'd started making snacks for everyone. In my opinion, this was a far superior arrangement to the days of meeting in our homes. Mind you, we were a much larger group now than we'd been back when even I had hosted a November meeting in our home: the year I'd gotten the new electrical outlet put in the living room in time to put up the tree dressed in its finest white and gold. The year when Annaliese was going through her anti-Christmas phase, although I'm not sure how she resolved that. Either way, she had not publicly criticized the Christian celebration of Christmas to my knowledge again. I supposed we all were on a journey and sometimes got off on places we maybe should not have. Or maybe *I* just thought she should not have.

We were also just a group of women with our children at this particular meeting. Annaliese had decided to keep it that way in spite of a couple of men in our region who did the majority of the schooling in their homes. After Ken Berry and Lyndon had heard her reasons, they decided to invite any men in that situation to come to the Boundless Home School office for their own men's fellowship time. That seemed like a perfect solution, and after a brief hiatus from that arrangement when Ken Berry passed on, Lyndon was back to baking a pan of brownies every month to share with the guys.

Since it was October, the month of thankfulness, we started by sharing some of the ways we were thankful for how homeschooling affected our lives. This wasn't the first time we had done this exercise, but seeing as how our group kept growing, it was a benefit to all of us, especially the newer members of our group, to be reminded of the good things homeschooling offered us. Most of us felt that we spent a lot of energy defending our choice from the negative comments of others rather than appreciating what homeschool had to offer.

"So, let's just share in a sentence what we love about homeschooling," Annaliese encouraged.

Janeice started. "Our kids get to do their work with a kitten on their lap."

From there the grateful sentences flowed.

"When they hear about Slovakia, they get to research all things Slovakian until they are more interested in why noses bleed. And then they get to research noses until, well, you get it."

"Their grandparents get to teach history class."

"Astronomy lessons in sleeping bags on the trampoline way past bedtime."

"No missed lessons because of a snow storm."

"And as many days off as they want when the cousins come to visit."

"We get to spend much more time as families."

"I just keep wondering why we're so hung up on that one," Misty blurted.

There was a shocked silence in the room.

"No, I'm serious," Misty forged ahead. "I mean, we all came from a nuclear family, and then we marry and create our own, and someday our kids will do the same thing. So why are we so hung up on needing to be close as a family when it's really for such a short season of life?"

I'd never thought about it from that point of view. I mean, I'd certainly never heard anything like that on the

"Focus on the Family" radio programs I'd listened to. Maybe there was some truth to it, but to hear her say it out loud seemed almost sacrilegious.

"I'm not saying family isn't important," Misty added cautiously into the silence. "I'm just saying it seems so temporary."

Someone had the courage to rephrase what they'd heard, tell her it was good point, and the conversation continued. But I didn't hear it. Maybe if I'd never gone on that overnight trip, hadn't seen Misty appearing to flirt with a stranger, hadn't sensed this unease about her using swimwear on her attractive body to garner attention on a weekend away from her husband...

If anyone else had made the point that our families are a blessing for this life, and even then, the focus of our family shifts, or should shift as our commitments change, I would have thought it rather profound.

Coming from Misty though, it gave me a sense of foreboding.

Chapter Thirty-Six

We hadn't wanted to alarm the boys so we didn't mention the dreaded "c" word when we prepared them for Lyndon's upcoming surgery. However, there were some "what-ifs" that Lyndon and I couldn't avoid discussing between ourselves.

"I'm going to reactivate my dental hygienist license," I told Lyndon from where I sat at the table, my phone in hand. He stopped washing the pasta pot for a moment but didn't turn from where he stood at the sink to look at me. Why after all these years of marriage, did our most intimate conversations happen when we weren't looking at each other? Maybe today in light of what we were facing, I needed to be resolute. I needed not to see fear or disappointment or maybe even relief in his eyes.

"How much does it cost?" was his pragmatic response. Pragmatic. I assumed that meant he approved. Maybe even was relieved. I couldn't over-evaluate that possibility right now.

"There's room on the credit card," I answered.

"Even after we pay for the trip?" he checked, rinsing the pot and placing it on the drying rack.

"Yep. Once I pay for this there's about $3000 left on the limit so we have lots of room."

He nodded, pulling the greasy tin foil off the pan I'd lined to bake chicken pieces.

We both knew what Dave Ramsey would say about our money habits. He'd blast us for using that card and paying a revolving door of interest. We had listened to his financial peace mantra a few times, had even tried following his advice a couple of times. But honestly, we had gotten to the point where we gave ten per cent of our income and saved ten per cent into an RRSP account each pay cheque, and our financial peace came by faithfully paying the minimum balance on our card. At times, like when we got our income tax return, we'd put a large lump sum toward the amount owing. At least we kept it to one card. There should be some kudos for that. We didn't argue about money like some couples did. No, we perhaps weren't financially savvy, but there was financial peace. And when we considered booking this mission trip with the kids it was a no brainer. If there was a possibility that Lyndon's health took a serious turn for the worse, the mission experience was something we'd never regret doing together.

"You'd rather work in dental than electrical?" Lyndon queried.

"Just thinking it's wise to keep two doors open just..." I had almost said just in case. In case we had to use the life insurance policy we'd read up on a couple of weeks ago. That had been another conversation with very little conversing. Lyndon had pulled the policy out of the wood-look filing cabinet that served as his bedside table. We leaned our pillows up against the iron head board and sat next to each other on the bed examining the small print. With few words, we agreed that the coverage appeared sufficient, and he put the policy away.

Now, putting the pot in the bottom cupboard and lifting the door slightly so it would fit into place and stay closed, Lyndon cleared his throat. He started to speak then shook his head slightly and cleared his throat again. "Yeah, it's probably good to keep your options open."

* * * * *

"Ainslee," the doctor sat beside me on a chair in the waiting room while Lyndon woke up slowly in a room down the hall, "we won't know for sure until the results come back, but it seems hopeful." And within a few days we got the word.

Leiomyoma of soft tissue in left thigh. That was it. Complicated. Unusual. But probably in our past. When Lyndon's grogginess wore off and the pain meds soothed the deep incision, and he was able to shuffle along the hospital hallway, he told me to book the mission trip we'd been discussing for the following year. Though neither of us could bring ourselves to say it, we knew before the surgery that if things went well, another trip would be a celebration, and if not, well, sometimes we need to do the things with our families that are important to us in case time runs out. That set many things in motion and perhaps was part of the reason for Lyndon's easy recovery and renewed hope for our future.

* * * * *

Once Lyndon was home from the hospital and moving around enough that I felt confident to leave him, I enjoyed catching up with friends I hadn't seen in a while and wasn't even sure could still be called friends. When I came home, I told him about my adventures. He was used to being around people and missed that interaction.

I wanted to tell Lyndon what had happened earlier that day at June's house. But I was embarrassed. Would he understand? If I made myself vulnerable to him would he be able to relate or would he somehow see it as me trying to manipulate him?

I waited until we were lying beside each other in the bedroom adjacent to our living room and right off our dining space. I waited until he'd plugged in his phone and touched the lamp beside our bed and it turned off. I lay on my back. I never lay on my back to sleep. I hoped he knew this meant I wasn't ready to actually sleep.

"You tired, or is there something you want to talk about yet," Lyndon asked, turning only his head toward me without moving his leg which was still healing.

I started cautiously.

"Do you ever get embarrassed anymore?"

"Pretty sure I told you about the open pant zipper incident when the Education Minister stopped by the division office last month. So, yeah, I'm thinking that qualifies."

I giggled. Then just outright laughed. "Sorry. I guess last month is pretty fresh."

"Yep. Pretty fresh," Lyndon agreed sarcastically.

I burst out again. "Whoa. Bad word choice. That's totally not what I meant. I was just referring to timing."

Lyndon shook his head. "I'm thinking you have a good reason for bringing it up?"

"Well, for me it's more than embarrassing. Maybe more like sometimes I just can't stand myself."

"So, you're somewhere between feeling sorry for yourself and being convicted about something?"

"Maybe that's it." I took a moment to think about that.

"I said something stupid at June's today," I admitted. "In the middle of her cluttered kitchen I talked about how we try not to have too much stuff and have disciplined ourselves to wash our dishes every night.

"But it's all so dumb Lyndon, because, number one I could tell I hurt her. I mean, I didn't even know she was capable of being hurt. She's so, so successful, I guess. It's like she has everything going for her. How would I even matter enough to her that I could hurt her?

"I've been thinking about it constantly and I know it's not about the stuff. It's not about whether we're minimalist or hoarders. Somewhere in there is the real issue. It's about whether I let things or the lack of things control my relationship with God and people, or if He's really who controls and motivates me. I get that people who have a lot of clutter may be bound by their environment to where they can't obey God and minister to people. But those of us who work at having our environment controlled are sometimes so consumed by following our own rules for ourselves, or so unable to focus on anything else when we're not completely in control that we are too arrogant to hear the Lord and too self-focussed to obey or give up what matters to us if the Lord should ask us to do greater things.

"You and I happen to be on the same page with this, but what about those couples to whom extra things mean comfort and happiness? Like, I don't really like to read even though I try to do it, so I don't need a bunch of books to make me happy. And I don't want to clean any more than necessary so I'm willing to live without candles and picture frames on the end tables. But if I wasn't me, I'd want you to honour me by not just putting up with books in every room, but even buying them for me. Or bringing me a new candle just because you thought I'd like the smell of it.

"And when I judge June by calling her things left out 'clutter', I'm making a value statement. Because she doesn't value space in the same way I do, I've said my system of order supersedes her value of allowing her family space to be relaxed and herself freedom to pursue the things she enjoys and has committed herself to.

"And what is wrong with me that I'd actually say those things in front of her, in her house? I'd hate if I've ruined our friendship, and maybe I have. I hate how arrogant I sounded. As if my personality style and choices are better, instead of just are. Like, did I finally find the courage to lay down the one trump card I think I have with her? *Hey, you're a vet and a dog breeder, and know all about how money works, and a mom of five, but guess what, June?*" I knew I sounded saucy. "*I might only be an ex-dental hygienist—and not a very good one, mind you—and a very part-time wanna-be electrician. But at least I'm not a hoarder. So, take that.*"

Lyndon laughed. And then moaned when the blanket rubbed against his still-tender incision.

I was going to apologize for that too but it was too precious. This laughing together. The freedom to share my soul, my broken, ugly soul.

It had been almost three years that I'd felt our relationship being tested. Where I was quite sure that if we still were a team, we were on a bad losing streak and at least one of us was in danger of being traded. Lying here on my back beside Lyndon I don't know if I'd ever felt so glad to be known. So glad to have shared enough life with someone that parts of our history could speak for me. Maybe this would be our turning point, our comeback moment.

* * * * *

About six weeks after surgery, when the pain of the incision had mostly healed, Lyndon started physio. To his surprise, the persistent pain in his leg was gone. We had lived with that pain for so many years it had shaped both our routines and our psyches.

We should have been overjoyed when the doctor sat us down and gave us the "not malignant" conversation, but it's strange how sometimes life moves so fast that you don't have time in the moment to reflect on what could have happened, you just move forward. And that's how this was for us.

It reminded me of the time as a child I was riding my bicycle on a dry gravel road, and as a vehicle passed and raised up a cloud of dust, I steered across the road, intending to turn into a neighbour's lane. Only, I wasn't aware in that dust cloud of another vehicle's speedy approach. The driver saw me in that final second and honked a frightened warning. At the time all I could think was *Phewf*, and I carried on to play with my friend. But over the years, I'd been sick at times, thinking of the danger I was in. More than that though, was the realization of how often our lives are in danger and we have no idea of all the times

God spares us. What has He spared us for? So, when we got the results of the successful removal of this fibroid from Lyndon's thigh, we breathed a relieved '*phew*' and carried on. The magnitude of what we'd been through wouldn't hit us until much later, and that too is an incredible way God spares us.

Chapter Thirty-Seven

Early Winter 2017

Lyndon and I were driving around Tracey one evening after we'd dropped the boys off at youth. It was a beautiful late-fall evening, Lyndon's thigh muscles were healing, and quite often we'd find friends out and about to spend the boys' youth nights with. As we cruised in the downtown area, we noticed, on the same block as the Boundless Homeschool Board office, activity in front of a storefront next to Little Caesar's Pizza which had born a "For Lease" sign for most of the last year. Curious, Lyndon slowed our Toyota to observe movers carrying items into the building.

"Work out equipment?" I asked.

"I think you're right," he answered.

"Cool," I responded without giving it any further thought. "Wanna drive by Pete and Susanna's?"

Lyndon simply turned the vehicle east.

* * * * *

Christmas 2017

I sat that night in the same glider rocker I'd sat in every Christmas for the past fifteen years. The white leather, which had only become softer over the years, made me realize that we'd probably spent most of our married life making payments on our credit card for luxury items like this, and yet somehow, this moment made it all seem worthwhile. As I leaned my head back, I remembered both countless hours rocking my baby boys in this chair, and many more hours where I was so tired, I would have loved nothing more than to sit and rock, and instead hurried to keep up with their busy antics. Admiring once again the lights from the decorated Christmas tree in the darkened room, I found myself worshiping the God who would choose an earthly bride, calling her the Church, co-heirs, brothers and sisters, and give her the power to be light in a dark world. Power to radiate His beauty and glory, and promise her an eternal future with Himself. While I meditated again on the mystery that God would see value in a people so broken, would love so deeply that He could turn His face on a precious, sinless Son to redeem us while we were still sinners, I suddenly found myself focussing on my own unspoken words. Bride…brothers…sisters…Son…

Family words. And somehow that helped me. For so long now I'd been mulling over Misty's argument that family was temporary. *Why did we make such a big deal about strong family ties, and especially how homeschooling helps create a strong family, when it can really only be for this lifetime?* But here I sat, reminded that God is the one who instituted family. He gave Adam a wife. God even chose a bride for Himself. God had, within Himself, esteemed family relationships by presenting Himself as both Father and Son, showing ultimate love and ultimate submission. So yes, though the family unit of Lyndon and me and Brewster and Arnold is not eternal, it was the earthly process God chose to show us about spiritual truths. The earthly process God chose so we would know what He means when He calls us His children, and Himself: our provider, our Daddy. The earthly process we could relate to when He claims to adore the church as a bride and anticipates that she dress herself in the whiteness of His righteousness.

So, I sat here now thankful for my earthly family, for the insight these roles gave into how God wants to relate to me, with a deep sense of commitment to brothers and sisters in the church. Still somehow, holding it all loosely because, like my tree, the beauty was in what it pointed to.

* * * * *

"I signed up at the new gym today," Lyndon announced. I looked up from trimming my fingernails at the desk in our bedroom. It took a moment for that to sink in. I had gotten used to my husband's pain keeping him from an active life. It was hard to remember that he'd once been a

Phys Ed teacher, or that after all these years the desire to be fit was still there.

"So, we were right. It is a gym. That's great," I responded, aiming for the right amount of enthusiasm. I didn't want to appear so enthused that he'd be afraid of disappointing me if his body wasn't able to handle regular workouts yet, or that he'd feel he'd been a disappointment to me all these years.

"It's so close to the office, I figured I could go during my lunch break. Wanna join me?"

I didn't respond immediately. I would be playing soccer again in another two months. Maybe Lyndon wanted me to go with him so he didn't have to show up there alone?

"I'll let you go on your own for now." I wasn't sure if it would be better for Lyndon to test himself without me there as a witness.

It didn't take long for Lyndon to gain not only strength and agility, but also lose weight. His spirits were lighter than they'd been in years. So, I found it quite annoying when I changed my mind and joined him at the gym in late January, and by the end of February had seen a decrease in only three pounds on the scale. Why, in the past, had I been able to be mostly content with feeling strong, and now I felt frustrated that my size wasn't changing the way Lyndon's was? Why was my focus not entirely on his success? It was almost as if I found his success threatening.

Chapter Thirty-Eight

Spring 2018

Because of Easter break, we were able to plan a whole month to take the boys and volunteer with mission work in Honduras. We could have had no way of knowing when I renewed my dental hygienist license it would be a perfect fit for this particular trip.

We hauled our four full, battered suitcases into the airport, and each carried a bag as full as we were allowed to pack them while remaining carry-ons. In our carry-ons we'd stuffed two changes of clothes for each person, and extra shoes. Flying out of Calgary in April meant we needed the sweaters we each wore. The suitcases were filled with donations from our church family to the community in Honduras that would host us.

"Did you guys tell Mom about our adventure today?" Lyndon encouraged the boys to tell me about the happenings at their build site as we sat around the supper table at the mission complex.

"We got stuck," Brewster supplied.

What was it with guys' communication abilities?

"On the way up or down?" I asked, referring to the mountain.

"It was going down—"

"Which should have been not as bad," Arnold interrupted. "But going down is scarier cuz we were close to the edge of the mountain and close to a curve so we couldn't see if there was anyone coming."

"And then Dad had to walk all the way back up to the site to get the tractor to pull us out," Brewster smiled at Lyndon.

"Sure did," Lyndon responded.

"How far did you have to walk back, Lyndon?"

Lyndon swallowed his mouthful of curried lentils and thought a moment.

"Probably close to two miles and that doesn't sound too bad, but it was all uphill..."

I grinned at my husband. We all knew that couldn't have happened a year ago. Before the surgery that resolved the issue of his constant pain. Before the discipline of working out had helped him get down to a healthy 220 pounds.

"You rock Dad," Brewster managed as he stuffed a chunk of tortilla in his mouth and followed up with a spoon of the curry.

"Yeah, Dad," Arnold echoed.

* * * * *

Pastor and Mrs. Nelson welcomed us back with far more accolades than we deserved. I knew they were using our experience to steer the church toward not only more of a missions heart, but also a focus on our families. I had come so far in my affections toward Mrs. Nelson from our first encounter, where my insecurity about homeschooling made defensiveness my near downfall.

We ate at the Nelson's for lunch our first Sunday back. Well, Lyndon and I did. The boys had gone to Subway with a group of friends from the youth group.

"So, it sounds like the driving was an adventure," Pastor Nelson recapped after we had described hair-raising stories from the moment we'd exited the Honduran airport.

"Do you think from an economic point of view your presence there was helpful?" Pastor Nelson wondered.

I looked at Lyndon. He hesitated. "How do we know what the long-term effect is," he mused. "Were we efficient workers? Not really. I mean, most young teen kids aren't going to be super effective house builders." He gave a short laugh. "What am I saying? I work with books, I spend a lot of time on the road, I'm not great at any construction. Ainslee would've been a better help at the build site than I was." He paused to rub my shoulder and wink at me. "But she was too busy helping Dr. Grey work on people's teeth. A woman of many talents!"

His praise sure felt good. But he hadn't really answered the question so he elaborated. "I'm not smart enough to wrap my head around how short-term missions like this affects a country. So, I'll just have to leave that part of it to the fact that we were there long enough to love the community, for the boys to realize that people are people no matter where you go, and I think that's a worthwhile life-long lesson. I think no matter what economic level we're at, we all have had times in our life where we're needy. Sometimes we need a tangible, physical solution to our issue, and sometimes it's more of an emotional need that's filled by someone coming alongside. Feeling loved and cared for is always worth the price.

"On a personal level," Lyndon continued, "I, uh, well," he cleared his throat and took a sip of water, "I—working with my boys, being with my boys, it was really something."

Later, as I helped Mrs. Nelson clean up the kitchen, she continued the conversation from earlier around their well-worn oak table.

"What about for you, Ainslee? What's your personal summary?"

"It was such a great change of pace. I mean, I do love Tracey, and all, but there's something about an adventure that fuels me," I grinned.

"No issues in your house while you were gone?"

"It's the beauty of renting. Get someone to check the house, lock the door, walk away…and may I mention that this is why I don't want a dog!"

"What was it like to get back into dental work?"

"Scary. I'd forgotten how much I dislike drool and bad breath." I shuddered then.

"But actually, I quit because it felt pointless in light of the bigger things in life." I sighed. "In light of…electrical pun. So many good puns as an electrician. That I miss. But back to dentistry. It felt so temporary when I worked in the clinic and like I had such a minimal ability to impact anyone's life. In Honduras it was different. Maybe it's more that I'm different, I don't know. Here in Canada, I felt like people had all the tools they needed to take care of their mouth, they were just lazy. There, they lacked both the tools and the knowledge and it left them in pain for one thing, and mal-nourished, and self-conscious. It just felt more useful to be there."

"It must have been a bit of a surprise to find yourself helping in the clinic when you went thinking you'd be working on the build with your guys?"

"Wow, yeah for sure. I had no idea when I reactivated my license that I'd be using it in Honduras. I was expecting to be doing wiring, that's for sure." I paused.

"It's weird, because partly I really enjoyed having an outlet that was me-focussed. I enjoyed being away from the boys and hearing about their adventures at the end of the day. And then again, I missed them like crazy. I felt left out. But mostly, I guess, I envied Lyndon. When he spent a lot of time with Brewster and Arnold, they adored him. The three of them acted like best friends. When I spend pretty much my whole life with them, they just seem to think that's how it should be. I feel taken for granted.

"So, if it wasn't that I've spent quite a few years wishing Lyndon would be more engaged with the kids, I'd feel taken for granted. Under the circumstances I think I better be thankful God has answered my prayers."

I didn't tell Mrs. Nelson that my prayers had not only been for Lyndon to be more engaged with the kids, but for our marriage. I'd never let the disappointments about our marriage become so defined that I would have even thought of reaching out for help in that area. Maybe I'd thought that sacrificing our marriage on the altar of home-schooling was just par for the course.

Chapter Thirty-Nine

Summer 2018

In our ten years in Tracey, I'd come to appreciate the people I'd gotten to know. But I'd never quite found that soulmate. The girl who would've motorbiked to Vancouver Island with me, or climbed Ha Ling Peak outside of Canmore. I suppose those were dreams I had given up sharing with Lyndon. But it happened so slowly that I didn't realize that maybe some of the reasons I had felt distance from him was because we hadn't found new ways to connect when his health limited us from enjoying the adventures we'd dreamed of having.

I loved the times of playing soccer with Misty. She was energy, and just like the reasons I became an electrician, I loved that about her. Right up until the switch flipped and she'd suddenly left Kyle–or at least suddenly from my point of view–I admired the ways in which she defied convention and fought to define herself. I was often challenged by her deep compassion for people and the state of their souls. Why was it that we often fell into two camps: those who had discernment and those who had compassion. The ones with discernment tended to be aloof and critical, and the ones with compassion tended to walk too close to the edge of a cliff when they allowed themselves to care about others who were falling over that cliff.

Maybe June had come the closest to being a soulmate. Or maybe she had embodied qualities that I thought I wanted to emulate, but as I watched that play out in her life, I reconsidered. She was a vet, she was trained and accomplished in something a bit unconventional. At the same time, she'd found a way to mesh her personal interests with her desire to invest in her family by homeschooling them and running her practice from home. She diversified by getting financial training and seemed to be successful in that as well. Definitely knowledgeable. Yet, it was the very things that I admired that seemed to keep her from having time for relationships that didn't work into her career goals. I suppose if I'd had a bunch of money to invest, I may have been a bigger priority in her life. And then, as time went on, I realized that where I thought she could have it all, she apparently couldn't. She perceived Conan's needs could not be met by schooling him at home without siblings, and because of the way June had dispersed herself, perhaps she was right, and public school was the better option for him. Regardless, her busyness and a schedule that was so different from mine did put a kink in our friendship.

Helen Berry had unconsciously become over the years likely my greatest confidante. I always felt she was my ally. With her kids being grown, I didn't have to compare my kids to hers, I just always felt that she loved them and Brewster and Arnold equally felt loved by her. I wasn't there to observe the years Helen taught her children at home and she didn't share too much about her methods. She related from a place of reflecting on her successes and failures which seemed to always amount to what went on in her heart, not her methods.

One of the biggest ways Helen had influenced me was to take time to read scripture. *Go to the source.* And though I had always had an underlying resentment toward Ken Berry, he did the same for Lyndon. Not even cherished Pastor Nelson had such a great influence in us trying to make a habit of studying the Words that we would say we wanted to have shape every part of our lives.

That day as I read Luke 24, and it spoke about a time of troublesome signs that would alert us to a change in God's Kingdom, I pondered how that should influence our living. I wasn't sure what this *end of the age* meant. What came to mind were other passages about being alert and prepared for God's coming Kingdom. Was I alert? Was I teaching my boys to be prepared for what would happen in the last days? Or was I allowing myself to be lulled to sleep by philosophies that sounded right but missed the greatest truths of God's Kingdom—that to be prepared for His Kingdom I would have to genuinely let Him be king.

Chapter Forty

Summer 2018

I had just come down our worn wooden steps with arms full of laundry from stripping the boys' bedsheets when I heard my phone ding. I turned left off the stairs, dumped the load on the small section of floor in the laundry room and then came back up the hall to where I'd left my phone on the kitchen table.

"Hi Ainslee. It's June Thiessen. I got your new number from Garry Richards. Are you up for a little electrical work?"

The fact that June had used Garry Richards to get my new number told the truth about our distancing friendship.

"Perhaps," I texted back. "What do you need?"

I was still embarrassed about my end of the conversation the last time I'd sat in June's kitchen having tea. I wasn't about to commit too readily.

"Run wires for a couple of new outlets in the kennel."

"I can come have a look this afternoon if that works for you?"

"I'm here till 4:00," she responded.

I checked the time. Lyndon had brought the boys into town this morning to help at a taekwondo tournament. They were supposed to be done by mid-afternoon. "How about right after lunch?"

She sent a thumbs-up emoji.

I paused a moment before setting my phone back on the table and returning to the laundry room. I hadn't heard from June in ages. After she had made the decision to put Conan in school and she was often gone meeting clients on the weekends so we didn't see each other that often at church, our lives had just naturally drifted apart. Other than the awkward visit last fall after Lyndon's surgery, when I'd arrogantly evaluated June's 'clutter,' it had been probably three years before I'd even been on the Thiessen's yard, in spite of the fact that they lived less than six miles from us.

I could hear the dogs barking as soon as I opened the van door. A range of colourful hens wandered at will around the dusty yard. The split-level house looked even more tired than it had the last time I'd seen it. Paint peeled off both the siding and the railing around the front deck. The wind ruffled my greying red curls which shouldn't even be happening. Wasn't the one perk of red hair supposed to be that it didn't go grey? Why did I even have to think about my hair now when I could see June coming out of the barn in her black dress pants tucked into long cowboy boots, an elegant necklace with its large grouping of circles flashing against a white shirt, and mauve cardigan tying it all together.

I straightened my plaid shirt and pulled my shades down over my eyes, waving at June as I headed in her direction. My new black running shoes picked up dust with each step.

"You found your way here," June smiled.

I bit back my immediate retorts. Words like *the road is equally long both ways, June.* Or *no problem. Just followed Arnold's tracks.*

Swallowing, I managed, "It's been too long, hasn't it? The boys and I have had such happy times here with you."

Saying the words reminded me of their truth, and it was as if the act of forcing myself to deny power to my bitterness released me. "Your animals look like they're doing well," I observed with genuine appreciation.

"I just sent our first puppy to Africa; South Africa actually," June beamed. "His new family had come out to visit their relatives in Lethbridge. We had sold a pup to a doctor there and when the relatives saw her, they were intrigued. After searching for eighteen months for a similar dog, they decided they really wanted a brother to the one they'd met here."

"Wow, I didn't realize the pups you have are so unique," I responded.

"They are pretty special," she glowed, gesturing for me to follow her into the barn. "It's taken us eighteen years to feel confident about the traits we're aiming for. See the blue of this one's eyes? And his fur is easy to maintain. He doesn't need a lot of grooming."

"He's beautiful," I crooned. But in spite of the boys' pleas for a dog and the dog training videos we'd watched, I decided not to flaunt my ignorance by engaging further in the conversation. June might be offended if I had to admit that I didn't even know what breed her dogs were.

"Where are you hoping to add plugs?"

"I'm wanting to add a grooming station," June laughed. "I know I just said they don't need a lot of grooming, but we've been showing them for quite a few years now and Howard is getting tired of me bringing them in the bathroom to get them ready. He says it's one thing to explain that you're late because you're waiting for your wife to get out of the bathroom, and quite another when the explanation is that you're waiting for the *dogs* to be done in the bathroom!"

I couldn't help but laugh.

She explained where she'd like to have the station built and I took some time to follow the wires back to the breaker panel which, as she thought, had enough room to add the plug-ins that she was requesting.

"Will you want me to also run wires to install a photography light?" I asked.

June looked at me blankly.

"Like, if you're selling them using the internet you can set up a photo booth to take great shots after they've been groomed?"

"Ainslee," June grabbed my arm. "You are a genius! What a great idea!"

I didn't even know where the idea had come from. I'd seen these hardwired photography lights somewhere recently and it just seemed to fit her business.

We discussed the practicality of the idea then. I verified that this was possible with the space left on the barn's breaker panel. I was able to help her tweak her plans so she could more easily access the space to take photos of her hens as well.

And somehow in the process of dreaming together, any distance between us vanished. I had not felt as appreciated for my skills in a long time. So, when we ended up having tea together in her kitchen with its dusty-rose countertops as full as I'd always remembered them, years of divide vanished.

"I've been too busy," June lamented.

"You've had a lot of responsibility," I tried to reassure, any resentment gone.

"I've done it to myself," she brushed me off. "As my older kids got more independent, I felt I should try to prepare for the next stage of life. I didn't want to be that desperate, empty-nest mom. So, I tried a few different things; well, the dog breeding we'd been doing for years. And, of course, I've always kept up my vet license. And just when I realized I loved the financial world and could maybe make a go of that as well, we were surprised by little Conan. I wonder sometimes, though, if I've been so busy preparing for the empty-nest stage that I've left the stage I was in too soon. I think Conan has gone through things he wouldn't have needed to if I'd paid attention to the stage I was in a little longer."

Despite the first pay cheque I'd ever received from June folded in my pocket, it made me sad when I mulled this through later: that she hadn't stopped to change direction when she'd sensed her error. Even now, would it really be too late to pour a bit more effort into Conan?

* * * * *

Erin was the one I'd sought out when I needed to believe there were parents who schooled their kids intentionally and purposely, and who had actually chosen the public education system. I valued her almost as much as I valued dear Helen. I also still valued the gorgeous laundry set I'd purchased when her home renovation didn't go as planned. The zebra painting that I liked-but-didn't-love still hung beside the TV in the living room. As I'd hoped, purchasing it led to a meal of hamburger soup: my family gathered around with Erin's. And it was as true as I'd hoped, that Erin and her husband were doing all of life, including spiritual life, intentionally with their kids. Her example had kept me from arrogance when I'd felt so little to be proud of in my life, other than that I'd given up a lot to homeschool my kids. Many parents did the same—and that didn't necessarily require homeschooling.

Of course, my routine and Erin's differed so we didn't get to see a whole lot of each other. This particular day though, Erin had come to pick raspberries from my patch that had been one of the treasures we discovered on the old farmyard, and wouldn't die in spite of my ignorant neglect. Erin noticed the three lawn mowers in various stages of assembly in front of the old garage. "Let me guess. Arnold is trying to get one of the three to work?" She queried.

"Close. But better." I couldn't keep the pride out of my voice. "Arnold is building a go-kart."

"Kidding!"

"No, he really is," I bragged. "He's so good with mechanics, and Lyndon knows just enough welding to help him build a frame."

"That's awesome," Erin grinned. "Your boys are always into something. You don't mind the mess?" She asked. And I knew she wasn't being critical of the partially gutted lawn mowers and pieces of their motors lying beside them, she just couldn't imagine transferring that to her beautiful cul-de-sac.

"Not really," I responded. "It's signs of life and energy. It makes me feel like I'm doing this part of parenting right. Besides, I like seeing how things work too."

"Hmm. So, this is your 'craft room'."

I laughed. "Exactly. Probably how you felt when you saw Emily working on a costume."

"Makes sense." We shared a brief silence then, thinking of her youngest daughter Emily working as a fashion designer in far-away Toronto, leaving Erin as an empty-nester. "How is Emily managing so far from home?"

"Mostly good," Erin smiled. It faltered though, and she continued with a sigh, "I feel concerned for her, Ainslee. Her marks are excellent, she loves what she's doing, she's making some friends. I get the feeling that all that busyness and drive to succeed is keeping her from finding solid Christian companionship. If she's attending a church or a Bible study group, she never talks about it." Erin played with the handle of the empty ice cream pail she had brought to pick raspberries. "I hope she doesn't entertain doubt or arrogance or independence until those things make themselves at home in her life."

It was hard for me to know how to respond to that. If I didn't say anything after Erin shared her concern, would she think I didn't care what happened to Emily? And if I said too much, would I validate Erin's disquiet, as though I knew something that would justify her concern for her daughter?

"She's fortunate to have you as her mom," I told Erin sincerely. "I can pray for her too—that she makes it a priority to look for Christian company." It felt awkward to say. I knew how to think about spiritual things, but after all this time, I still wasn't comfortable voicing those thoughts.

"Thank you," she whispered, keeping her gaze eastward. Probably saying a silent prayer for her daughter in Toronto even as we stood here. She cleared her throat then. And brought her focus back to the scattered lawn mowers.

"Time to explore personal interests is one thing I wish I could have given my kids more of," Erin mused nodding toward Arnold's project. "I do love that homeschooling gives kids the flexibility to pursue their passions."

"I'd love for Arnold to finish his high school work at least a year early," I said.

Erin looked at me.

"*Why?*"

It didn't come out as a question asked in curiousity, or even as a polite response. Her *why* had this indignant air. Like, *what is wrong with you?*

I was obviously a bit taken aback and Erin's apology was swift. "Sorry, Ainslee. I'll listen. Why would you want Arnold to finish high school early?"

"I just think he is so good at this whole mechanicing thing he could start an apprenticeship and get a head start on a career."

"*Why?*" Her tone hadn't changed.

I stared.

"Ainslee, don't be offended. I just mean it. *Why?*"

"You just hear so many stories of kids getting into trouble in these years of finishing school but not knowing what they want next. I think if he keeps moving *toward* something it will keep him from having time to get depressed, to get into meaningless things…" I trailed off.

"I hadn't thought of that. It makes sense."

"But now I want to hear your side," I prodded.

"It's just that they grow up so fast as it is. He'll leave home and move on to the next thing soon enough. And I suppose I say that from feeling a bit lonely, missing my kids and their craft-room messes." She smiled. "But I do find, Ainslee, that sometimes it's like homeschoolers need to prove the point that their kids are knowledgeable and capable. And your kids' early accomplishments help to validate your choice to homeschool. It helps to prove that you were right to keep them out of the time-wasting, public school system. That you've raised someone who can contribute at an early age, and it's your badge of honour."

She glanced at me. I knew she was concerned about offending me.

"Just make sure your need to succeed doesn't drive you to push them faster than they're really ready to go."

We stood there then. Her in the sadness of having worked herself out of the job of parenting. Me processing her loving warning.

"Thanks, Erin." And I meant it. I knew she could see it in me—this desire to do life well—and she sincerely wanted to remind me to enjoy my boys, more than to be defined by their outcomes.

Chapter Forty-One

"Hey," I greeted Misty as I slid into the booth at the Petro-Can truck stop diner. I'd asked to meet her here because it wasn't a place I expected to run into other women having lunch.

"Ainslee, I'm going to tell you right up front, don't bother crying. Your tears will not change my mind," Misty stated, composed.

There were very few things I cried about, which was something Lyndon never thanked me for. I don't think he realized how emotional most women were. Still, I was taken aback by Misty's composed bluntness. Of course, I had hoped, and prayed, and yes, even cried, that Misty would soften her heart to her family.

And suddenly I wasn't sure why I had asked her to go for lunch. Was I really thinking that anything I had to offer her would change her mind? Did I simply need to be able to assuage my conscience in years to come, being able to reassure myself that I tried to help Misty and Kyle salvage their marriage? Or was I in my own way trying to do legacy work, making it easier on God so Misty's children wouldn't have the baggage of their parents' broken marriage around which to navigate their faith? Or did I need to know what happened so I could consider myself warned and not experience the same train wreck in my life–was I attempting to avoid pain?

At any rate, here we were, sitting across from each other with the pie case nearby full of mountainous slices of lemon meringue and chocolate cream, and I had zero desire to order any of it. Instead, I decided on a bowl of tomato orzo soup while Misty ordered a BLT and fries. Was it wrong of me to hate that she could eat that and still attract the attention of men and women alike?

"I know what you want, Ainslee," Misty said once the mature waitress had left us, had ministered to us with her soothing, gravelly smoker's voice and her mothering, which I'm sure kept the good truckers coming back.

Misty pulled her phone out, found what she was looking for, and handed it to me. "Scroll right when you're done."

I looked at the screen. Seven girls in a row, fall leaves clinging to elm trees in the background. "You and your sisters?" I looked up and she nodded. It didn't really matter which was Misty, they all looked the same in their long skirts and turtlenecks under simple cable sweaters; just slightly different heights. It looked as if Misty had taken the photo from a book. A caption underneath the photo read, "The Jacob Braun Girls, 1994." I ran my finger right across the screen. Kyle and Misty's wedding photo. I looked up. "What year was this?" I asked.

"1999." She waited while I took in her young face and Kyle's slightly more mature one. Kyle's dark tux and contrasting silvery white vest. Her dress. Her plain, straight, T-shirt style neckline wedding dress. In an era where strapless and lacy was the standard, there would have been a hundred ways to create an attractive yet modest wedding dress. Misty's was definitely modest. And even I, with my limited fashion sense, could see it wasn't particularly attractive.

"You want to know what happened to me and Kyle? Those clothes tell the story. I finally got suffocated by those turtlenecks and long skirts and all they represent. Kyle might have wanted the girl in those pictures. He might have thought she was pure or innocent. Maybe he even thought she could keep him from going back to his old way of life. But I don't want to be his purity trophy. I need to be free to be me, not only one of the *Braun girls*."

"But this was so long ago, Misty. You've had almost twenty years to make adult choices. To, to dress the way you feel expresses who you are…"

"Not really. I've had almost twenty years to live with a man who can't accept that his past is forgiven. Who needs to prove how good he can be. Meanwhile, Ainslee, I really was good. I stayed in my father's home like a good daughter. And in the end who gets the credit? Kyle. Kyle! *Isn't it amazing the good man that Kyle has become. What a miracle that Kyle is now living for the Lord."*

"What are you saying, Misty? That you didn't want to live a pure life?

"I have Ainslee. I have been true to that man!"

I swallowed and tried to ignore the obvious.

"What did you want that you weren't getting? Why did you give up?"

"I told you I don't want to be suffocated."

"So how is life with Francis any different? Life gets boring, routine, and mundane. What is going to make life better with a new man? Whose attention is going to give you the affirmation you're craving? From how many people do you need that attention? Whose stamp of approval will be enough?"

"I'm done talking about it, Ainslee."

But by this time, I felt I had nothing to lose. "Misty, what makes your need to be validated, I don't know, to be special, greater than your kids' need for security so they don't end up having to prove themselves the way you're trying to? Why is Kyle's affirmation of you not enough?"

"Maybe because he's refused to get to know me. He has this picture in his head of who he wants me to be and that's never been the real me."

"But Misty, your clothing is flattering to you, Kyle has encouraged your ministry teaching English to immigrants, he's taken on a huge part of schooling the kids to free up your time. What's missing? If you needed to prove the point that you're not that dowdy girl any more, you've proved it. If you wanted to get back at Kyle for living a promiscuous life while you were keeping yourself for him, you've now done that too. When you feel like Francis doesn't know you anymore, because we're always changing, all of us, where will you run then?

"You can see truth and flaws in other peoples' lives Misty. Kyle may have hurt you deeply, maybe you're even protecting him by refusing to expose what's really going on. But who has invested in your life most? Who are you invested in? I still hope it's Kyle and your kids, Misty."

I looked down. My cup of coffee blurred. I couldn't believe I'd talked like this. I tended to appease. But I had one more thing to say.

"I'll pay for your lunch, Misty, but I need to run. I have simply got to get home and pluck my eyebrows."

I slid out of that booth, handed the waitress my credit card at the till, and I left.

I thought about driving to Helen's to decompress, but I was too exhausted by my unexpected blunt speech to even tell her about it in a way that made sense. Instead, I sat in the vehicle when I got home and wondered why I'd brought up the eyebrows. I'd never mentioned that bizarre text. Not once. Not to Lyndon, not even to Helen. And ultimately, I knew exactly why I'd used it today. Not because I was trying to get back at Misty. But because sometimes a forceful personality cannot hear until they are met with some force.

Misty may feel she'd been treated unfairly. *But may I remind you Misty, that there is a cruel side to you. An unfair, cruel side.* And I mentally echoed what Annaliese had told Misty: *be careful you're not so busy saving the world that you lose yours.* What had Annaliese known about Misty, or about human nature, that had necessitated those words?

Chapter Forty-Two

Many of the homeschoolers we met were, in the scheme of our culture, low income. They were mostly single-income families, larger families, families that valued time with their children more than climbing corporate ladders. But I recognized my perception was skewed based on our location in small-town Tracey. I'd read enough blogs to see that some homeschoolers were, from my perspective, unimaginably wealthy.

However, no matter how I looked at it, homeschooling seemed to be a luxury, a first-world choice. It was generally a choice for two-parent homes, homes who had not been befallen by tragedy, or other circumstances that robbed parents of their ability to apply themselves to their children's education. And then we dared to act self-righteous about it. We homeschoolers acted as though people who put their kids in public schools cared less about their kids, weren't committed parents, or weren't willing to sacrifice for the sake of their children's greater good. Sometimes those were the very families who could teach us all deep lessons about sacrifice, and loss, and stamina. They could teach us what it means to choose to follow Jesus when we've made poor choices in our past, when we are reeling from abandonment or betrayal, when we've suffered death or illness, or when dignity demands that both parents work to stay out of government systems. Sometimes when Annaliese got on her high horse about homeschooling being the only good option for families, I wished I could take her to the slums of Honduras. Could she really tell the parents picking through garbage to provide for their families that they should stay home and teach their own kids to read? Or I'd like Annaliese to look Kyle in the eye and tell him that, despite Misty's unfaithfulness and new relationship with her Filipino boyfriend, he should find a way to keep his kids out of the public school system. Oh, actually, if he'd not allowed himself and his wife to have a heart for missions in the first place, they could have avoided this mess.

* * * * *

Late Summer 2018

One of the absolute best decisions Lyndon and I had made earlier that year was an impulsive splurge on electric bicycles for each of us. The Costco sales flyer with the picture of the fat tires, wide seat, and printed-in-red $400 savings tag, made the dual purchase just slightly less than our first family van had been. But so worth it. *Built in air conditioning* we joked with each other as we pedaled down one country road after another. Oh, it wasn't a motorbike, and Lyndon had repeatedly mourned that. The thought of trading in our motorbiking days for this new mode of transportation felt similar to switching from his mustang to that first minivan. But for me, it was an unleashed freedom after years of focussing on our sons. I loved that wind-in-my-hair feeling, the brief reprieve from my responsibility, my ordinary. Several years ago, I'd felt an exhilaration at taking the lawn mower up the driveway toward the grid road and the rural McMansion behind us, elated that I was finally at a stage where I could leave the boys to play alone on the yard for the twenty or thirty minutes it took me to run the mower over the shallow grassy ditches beside our narrow gravelled drive. Now, Lyndon and I had often spent whole evenings biking to town, up and down every street, or to the gravel pits with the sun-warmed water holes just big enough to take a dip, splash at each other, and pretend we were on a beach somewhere, except so much better since we often had the place to ourselves.

I felt healthy, and happy. Alive as a person and alive in my marriage. I often brought my camera and photographed the places we toured. A blooming weed, a caved-in, old barn, and actually-for-real a fox hole with a kit curiously peeking out.

On the days we pedaled into town I loved riding the streets of acquaintances and finding them working in their yards. We had visits standing by the curb, seeing their current outdoor projects, sometimes getting invited to sit around their backyard firepits.

My personal peace and enjoyment of this season pervaded my senses. I would have thought that God would warn me, send me a foreshadowing of what was to come, whisper to my spirit to keep my eyes open.

But no.

Not once until the moment we saw Brewster vaping with a group of guys behind the health clinic as we cruised a back alley, did I suspect he was in trouble.

Not once.

Behind the health clinic! Could it get any more ironic? And how thankful I was Lyndon saw him too. Thankful and yet sick that I couldn't tell myself I hadn't seen this.

Neither of us stopped our bikes. We hardly even slowed down. We actually waved to the group, which included a couple of kids from church—kids whose vaping didn't break *our* hearts—perhaps didn't even break their own parents' hearts.

But Brewster had just been baptized this spring. Brewster had prayed to invite Jesus into his heart with the senior at the care home years ago. Brewster was compliant and submissive and generally cheerful. And with all these thoughts churning, I took the lead and pedaled toward home. I turned the power assist option off, and let my grief and rage power me toward the edge of the town of Tracey and across the gravel road to our home. I felt sick to my stomach. Empty.

Biking home the hard way, I stored my electric bike in its spot in the garage, which had become more often work space for Arnold and Brewster than a parking spot for our handsome Toyota. The overhead door I'd installed with the boys' help often simply stayed open so we could at least put the nose of the vehicle inside and keep the frost off the windshield.

The process of taking a hot bath soothed some of my nervous, angry energy. Lyndon knew better than to talk to me. Later, when I'd washed every dish in the kitchen and even paid the bills before their due date, we lay in our bed surrounded by the wood-grain paneling walls, their texture still slightly defined in the moonlight.

One of the treasures we'd discovered in the overgrown grass in those early days on our acre in the country was an old, simple, iron bedframe. It had been left leaning against the back of the ramshackle garage with other pieces of salvaged iron. Neither Lyndon nor I were particularly nostalgic, but we were so desperately looking for signs of hope, beauty in what felt like our ugly. The landlord apologized about the pile of metal after Lyndon mentioned it to him, and offered to immediately have a metal salvage company come remove it. He was taken aback that we would ask for the rusty old bedframe, but made it very clear that we were to suit ourselves. We immediately set the frame aside and were glad to see the rest of the metal safely leave the yard to be recycled. So, after a few months of recovering financially from the time we'd been without any work, and then the cost of the move, we hired an autobody shop to cut the bedframe and weld in about six inches to both the length and width of the old frame to take it from a double to a queen size. The owner took our project as a personal opportunity for creativity, rather than the tedium of his usual work—precise restoration of metal to match its former factory shape. The end result kept the bed frame simple, with a subtle, raised pattern worked over both welds spaced evenly across the ends, so that the new inserted six-inch piece was centered to look as if it had been part of the original design. Sandblasting off the rust and adding a beautiful matte black paint job created a unique piece that still wouldn't have held a lot of value to many people, but was full of meaning to us.

The old frame against the panel-board walls of our bedroom hadn't looked great, but I wasn't design savvy, so we lived with it, and slept fine. Until Charlotte, from *Training Designers,* suggested one day switching our magenta comforter for a pale blue, gently-patterned quilt. And when I purchased that, along with the crisp, white bed sheets and plush, slate-blue blanket to layer at the foot of the bed, oh, and the new glass lamps she recommended, our room transformed. It became magical rather than dowdy. How could people see things that way? My only regret had been the white bed sheets, and it didn't take long before we replace those with a silvery grey. At that point, the credit card had some room to work with, even after paying the autobody mechanic for the bed—the bed which from a financial perspective had made no sense. We were living with newfound feelings of hope, after all, so the splurge, and the interest charges they incurred, felt like a worthwhile investment.

But tonight, the bed frame, my symbol of hope in the broken, brought little comfort. The bedding, which had lost its luxuriousness several years ago, resonated more with my spirit. Worn out.

I lay on my back, my tangled curls catching the tears that rolled toward my ears.

How could Brewster have been so sneaky? What else was he into? How could I live in the same house with this child, make his meals, mark his school work, put his clean socks away, and be so blind? I mentally circled back to the night after our very first fall homeschool barbeque and scolded myself because back then I'd felt just as deceived by Lyndon. Did I simply have issues seeing truth even if it was right there in front of me? Was I crying because I couldn't trust Brewster, or because I couldn't trust myself?

"He's home," Lyndon whispered.

I lay still, listening through the open window. Sure enough, I could hear the crunch of his bicycle tires coming up the driveway.

My heart sped up while I tried to control my angry breathing.

Within a few minutes the front door opened. Because our bedroom door and windows were open, the movement of the front door created a straight path for air movement and our curtains fluttered, shifting the shadows from the moon.

I heard Brewster hang his coat on a hanger and set his shoes in the open closet area. Part of me felt like getting up and interrogating him. Part of me hoped that Lyndon would deal with his son in a way that made sure something like this would not happen again. And part of me knew we were both too blindsided to deal with Brewster reasonably.

I expected to hear the bathroom door close next, and water running. Instead, footsteps slowly, tentatively approached our bedroom door.

"I'm home," he whispered.

In the shadows I could see his young, man-body leaning against the door frame.

Just go away, I thought. In spite of the flash of a memory then, a memory of Aunt Bonnie touching Brewster's baby ears, wide smile, saying they looked just like Uncle Nick's, I held my son at a distance this night. The very thing I had thought then I would never do. Could never do.

"I'm glad you're home, Brewster," Lyndon answered without moving.

Brewster stayed there. Stayed leaning against the door frame.

"Dad?" Brewster whispered.

"Come," Lyndon responded moving toward me, making room beside him on the bed.

To my surprise, the invitation worked. The half child, half young man came and sat beside Lyndon, who wrapped his bare arms around Brewster and pulled him close. Before I knew it, the three of us lay in the bed on our backs, Brewster on top of the faded patterned quilt.

"I never did that before, honest," Brewster managed, his voice trembling.

I expected Lyndon to respond. He didn't. But I felt his shoulder move as he reached over himself to touch his son lying beside him.

"I'm sorry, Dad and Mom." And then Brewster cried. We waited. Lyndon seemed to wait with a confidence so deep, so peaceful, that I felt my heart soften. I almost wanted the anger to stay. Because if it left, I'd recognize compassion rather than being filled with this angry sense of betrayal. My tears started again, and by now I couldn't have spoken if I'd chosen to.

I felt Lyndon's shoulder moving, his hand gripping Brewster's arm.

"I love you," Lyndon reassured Brewster.

"I'm glad God brought you there, Dad. I didn't want to be there, but I didn't know how to leave," Brewster responded with his shaky voice, hands wiping at his face, muffling his words, shaking the bed slightly.

"I'm glad God brought us there too," Lyndon said.

In spite of Lyndon's gracious response, my mind raced with bitter words. *What else would you like to tell us, Brewster? How long have you really been vaping, Brewster?*

But I stayed silent. Not a word of compassion. Not a word of mercy. Not a word of empathy, and God knew that was the least I should have for my son.

Once more I could feel Lyndon reach across himself and touch Brewster. "You better get some sleep, son. We can talk about some consequences in the morning."

"Okay. Love you, Dad. Good night, Mom."

"Good night," I managed.

The bed shook as Brewster rolled out of it and padded out of our room and toward the bathroom.

Lyndon stayed lying on his back right next to me. He folded his hands across his chest and I assumed he was praying. And in a way, I was too.

"Oh God, I don't know what to believe. I just don't know what's truth. I've poured so much into this child, and don't know what to trust."

* * * * *

I slowly woke the next morning to birds chirping, and indirect light coming in our west-facing bedroom windows. I could smell fresh coffee. For a moment my world felt peaceful. All was right. Then, hearing the front door open, and what sounded like Lyndon filling a coffee cup, I remembered.

Last night.

Friday night.

A night where I'd had to face the realization that I could no longer make my child obey me. His obedience was beyond my control.

And that left me facing the condition of his heart. There was nothing I wanted more than for my son to walk in obedience to Jesus. And he had repented last night. Hadn't he?

Arggh.

Here I was. Back to the unseen condition of Brewster's heart. How could I know if he was truly sorry? Like, not sorry he'd been caught, but repentant.

I thought of Lyndon's response in comparison to mine. Lyndon had embraced his son. Had invited Brewster into an intimate place. Had said *I love you.* Lyndon had not made Brewster dread the consequences to come. I had given him precious little more than silence. I had been proud of myself for only what I had *not* allowed to come out of my mouth–that I had lay on my back rather than stomping my foot and shaking my finger. Pointing my finger.

After all the times I had prayed for other youth. Had prayed that the Lord would use me to be part of his plan for saving souls. And I couldn't offer my son one bit of grace. How would I have responded had I been dealing with someone else's child? Would I have had to muster up compassion? Would I have corralled some empathy? Or would those evangelistic feelings of mercy just have been there without having to round them up? Would I have thanked God for allowing me to be a part of His redemptive process? Would I have petitioned God that the verbally repentant would have a sincerity of heart so that sneaking and peer pressure would not lead them to a lifetime of unhealthy habits?

I wiped my eyes on the corner of my silvery-grey pillowcase.

No, I didn't actually know Brewster's heart. I had no way of knowing or controlling the direction his heart would take. That didn't abdicate Lyndon and me from persevering in creating a home and limits that would encourage a godly direction.

But to withhold myself from entering the discipleship process that I would have been so willing to enter with offspring not my own, only exposed me as a sulking fool.

Chapter Forty-Three

Fall 2018

I noticed Arnold roasting two hot dogs on his pronged, long-handled fork over the open fire at the homeschool fall barbeque. I smiled to myself. Two at a time. Of course. Why waste time? Eat lots, play hard. That was my Arnold.

How that boy had grown over the summer. We'd had to buy him new pants three times over the last two months, this last time realizing we needed to find a men's clothing store rather than relying on the larger boys' sizes at Old Navy. I observed him as he crouched in the splotchy grass beside the fire pit. His tanned summer skin and sunbleached course hair which he'd had cut by a stylist for the first time recently, rather than at the barber where Lyndon had taken him for years, made him look older than the fifteen-year-old that he was. Arnold was an even huskier build than Brewster, and was now only about half an inch shorter than his older brother. Seeing him here made me realize he wasn't really a boy anymore. He was on the verge of manhood. The sad hit me in a little wave. A stage of life had passed, and, like it always does, a new stage met my eyes before I was ready for it, before I'd had time to prepare. My youngest was almost a young man.

While I watched, he inspected the hot dogs, looking behind him as if waiting on someone. I followed the turn of his head. She gave him a thumbs-up and a beautiful smile. My heart actually skittered, stuttered. Together, they went over to the folding table where the hotdog buns and condiments were laid out. She squeezed mustard on two buns. Arnold hated mustard. He didn't stop her, didn't scrape the mustard off. Just kept smiling. Taking their paper plates with the hotdogs and potato chips and raw vegetables, he sauntered off around the corner of the gazebo where they vanished from my line of sight.

My Arnold. Sharing a picnic supper with Egypt Keller.

If I had thought I wasn't prepared for leaving childhood clothing sizes behind, I certainly wasn't prepared to see my son catering to a girl. Any girl. But Egypt? Like from the E-harmony gang, Egypt?

She was lovely. Even I, in my protective mothering role, could see that. Long, shiny dark hair that fell to her waist except for a straight bang cut just beneath her eyebrow line. She wore a long denim skirt, cute black boots, a white T-shirt and a soft orangey-red sweater that popped with the autumn foliage in the park around us. My son was not the only one who had reached a new stage.

And though I knew I couldn't trust myself in this moment, a slight panic gripped me. My son was showing interest in a girl whose life seemed defined. How could my homeschooled, Sunday-School-raised son not know that throughout scripture, Egypt meant bondage. Or at least in this case, that she came from a family who certainly appeared to represent bondage.

Even now, though Evangeline and Ezekiel were taking online courses through Liberty University, and Ethan and Eliza had married, the family singing group E-harmony still performed regularly. Only now it had thirteen performers instead of the original eleven, but the newest married members were, no joke, named Erin and Everett.

This isn't going to last, I reassured myself, thinking again of my Arnold going off to eat his one measly hotdog with Egypt. He doesn't sing. His name is Arnold. Starts with an 'A'.

Then again...neither does he eat mustard.

* * * * *

I had not grieved for anyone the way I grieved for Misty since I stood in front of the parking stall with the malfunctioning plug and couldn't get to the hospital in time to say goodbye. I didn't care what she'd done in leaving Kyle, she'd been a friend to me. A friend who'd been mean enough to send a stupid text about my eyebrows, and had not once complimented my straight, white teeth. She made us laugh, she made us think. She made us uncomfortable.

A troubled friend at times, sure, but I'd actually cared enough about her to intentionally try and hurt her feelings to get her to listen to reason. I'd never done that before or since.

It was incomprehensible for the truth to be that she'd slipped stepping out of the shower and had cracked her head on the tiled tub surround. But officials deemed it was so. No one else had been in the house, and that's where Francis found her two days later. In the bathroom where bodies are most often found.

Divine retribution. If I heard that theory spoken in hushed, holy tones once more, I feared not that I would be found silent as I was following Brewster's apology after being caught vaping, but that I would completely ruin Lyndon's reputation, and whoever had called Lyndon's mouth foul for saying *heck* would be left aghast at me.

I simply did not understand God. I couldn't reconcile the truth that He had allowed Misty's life to end, with the knowledge that He is not vengeful. I settled, finally, on telling myself that He is just. He is good. He is merciful.

Now breathe. In. Out.

Grief hadn't killed me the first time and it likely wouldn't kill me now either.

Chapter Forty-Four

Early Spring 2019

I arrived at Annaliese's historic house by 9:30 that morning. Brewster and Arnold shared a virtual physics class from ten till noon three days a week this semester. Sometimes I sat in our small spare room with them, simply because it was mentally refreshing for me to be challenged with remembering the mathematical formulas—with remembering my days as an electrical student and apprentice. It made it easier for me to help them later if I'd heard the methods their online teacher was using to explain the subject to them.

Today I used the time to follow up on a request I'd had from Annaliese to do some rewiring in a room she was hoping to change into a quilting room.

I'd been at her house probably three dozen times before our homeschool group got too large and we started meeting at the lovely Mennonite Church. Back as long as I could remember, Annaliese's children had been grown. She had to be in her late fifties by now. Almost twenty years older than I was, I figured.

She lived in a large, old house on the edge of town. A house that would have been a grand farmhouse in the early twentieth century, and had in the years since then been swallowed into the edges of Tracey. It stood tall on a street with half-acre lots, its verandas on both the main and upper floors giving views of the rolling hills and their potato crops surrounding the town.

I had never known this house with children in it. By the time I started attending the homeschool support meetings, Annaliese's children were basically grown. Still, as long as I could remember, children were welcome in her house. Today, her front yard was littered with a couple of bikes and a Little Tikes lemonade stand in the bare spot on the brown grass where the snow had melted in the heat of the early spring sun.

"Welcome to my grandma daycare," Annaliese laughed, waiting to welcome me from her front porch.

"Now if these were lawn mower parts I'd feel right at home," I responded with a smile although, in reality, Lyndon insisted the mess stay by the detached garage, and preferably in the shed he'd built with the boys.

"I'd offer you a bleeding heart," Annaliese pointed to a couple of pots lined up close to her house under the shade of the veranda, "but I don't think you love to garden, so don't feel pressure to take one. I thinned mine out in fall and these should be planted as soon as the ground thaws."

I was rescued from answering immediately by the sudden, deep barking of a dog from next door. "Patches!" Annaliese hollered. The silence was immediate. She ushered me through her decorative screen door and into the entry with its hardwood-look tile floors. I was still mulling Annaliese's comment about me not loving to garden. Often, I had felt like after all the years we'd now been acquainted, Annaliese knew nothing about me, nor did she desire to. I would have thought she judged rather than perceived. But maybe that was actually me.

"I've gotten to that age, Ainslee, where I need a quilting room," she told me, though she'd mentioned when she called that this was the reason she needed some electrical plugs moved. I followed her up the carpeted staircase into a large, light-filled, empty room.

"This was Nadine and Jenny's bedroom. But that was forever ago, and some things need to change." Her eyes got glassy then. Turning, she pulled out a computer-generated plan for the room.

"I've been dreaming," she confessed. "So, you tell me what it would take to bring this plan to life and then I'll have to decide if it's something we can afford or how many other rooms would end up being affected."

I spent the next half-hour checking things over. The house had gotten a major overhaul in the late nineties so the wiring was relatively current. As far as plugs being raised to counter height, that was a fairly simple fix. After climbing into the attic through the opening in the hall, I suggested she add pot lights to the room, and task lighting over her cutting table to extend her working time into the evenings, or gloomy winter days. Annaliese showed me a couple of the cabinetry samples she was leaning toward and asked for my recommendation about which metal accents to go with and how that would affect her light fixture choices. I did find this part of our meeting rather humourous when I thought of my own original 1950's painted kitchen cabinetry and simple hardware. Sure, I'd updated the outlets and switches to flat rather than toggle ones, but what electrician wouldn't do that. The single light fixture I had changed over the kitchen table, hadn't been a great choice—the light golden swirl pattern on each of the six shades held together by an oil rubbed bronze frame, had been a popular choice at the time, but took up too much visual space in our small house according to Charlotte, who had transformed our bedroom. So, who was I to be giving design advice?

"Honestly, Charlotte has a great eye for décor. But I'll draw up a plan and get you preliminary pricing based on what I've seen here today. I can bring your estimate to our homeschool meeting next week." It felt so good to use words like *preliminary pricing*. I realized it didn't put me in the same category as Dr. June Thiessen: vet, financial advisor, breeder of dogs and exotic chicks. Still, today I would allow myself the pleasure of saying *preliminary pricing*.

"Ainslee," Annaliese paused and looked at the carpet. "Do you have time for a coffee?"

"Uh, you know what? I do," I answered, realizing there was no good reason I couldn't stay. I followed her back down the stairs to her well-worn kitchen. I'd been in this room so many times, but generally it was filled with a lot of other women. The space, which had felt tight then, seemed spacious now. I supposed I had never appreciated Annaliese's hospitality sufficiently. Regardless her passion for all things homeschooling, at times to a fault, her efforts had created a community for me and a place to form my value system, even when my values were formed precisely *because of* the areas where I disagreed with her perspective.

I watched the Common Grackle feeding in her Mountain Ash while she made us coffee. Today, without the direct sunlight, the bird looked mostly black, though I knew that on many other days it would shimmer with blues and purples and gold in its feathers. What I really hoped to see was a Bohemian Waxwing, but none appeared to feed on the bright red berries left after a whole winter of nothing but cold and snow.

Annaliese handed me a coffee and we sat at her scuffed dining table. "So Ainslee, as far as bringing an estimate to the meeting next week, I won't be coming anymore."

No preamble.

On the one hand it made no difference. We had become a group of about sixty women meeting any given month, and Lyndon said there were now over 300 families homeschooling just in about a 200 km radius of Tracey. Of course, many of them were not registered with the Boundless Home School Board. Still, the movement had grown by leaps and bounds since the early twenty-first century when we'd been initiated.

So why did I feel stunned? I met Annaliese's eyes, waiting for her to explain. She had completely fulfilled the role of *Mrs. Homeschool.*

"I know I've preached homeschooling, along with many other things, as though it's the gospel." Her voice was thick. Tears fell. "Misty meant the world to me, Ainslee. We were both in such danger. She fought so hard to resist being held captive by systems. And I've tried to atone for my sins by creating systems."

My throat immediately felt thick at the mention of Misty's name.

"I'm sure you've heard that I had an immoral past. It's true. And probably not even exaggerated. When Proverbs speaks of Foolishness personified as a woman—that was me." She covered her face with her hands. "Kyle is several years younger than I am. It makes me sick that I aided his downfall." She resorted to using her sleeve to wipe not only her eyes, but moisture around her mouth as well.

"When things ended between us, he got saved and transformed. The Apostle Paul would've used Kyle as an example if we were living in Bible times," her red face held a shaky grin.

"A while later, I got saved too." She took a calming breath. Remembering her moment. Her Kingdom of Darkness to Kingdom of Light moment.

"I just have always struggled to remember that I need to *live* by the same grace with which Jesus saved me. I hate that, though I've hated my sin, I keep trying to make certain I never go back there. It's like I can't accept that God has promised to keep me. And, and I think I've honestly wanted to keep others from the awfulness of sin, but in the process, I make rules. And I can see that, though rules help bring some stability to my life, I keep having to change them based on the current circumstances, or my current state of mind."

While Annaliese paused and laid her forearms and palms on the table, I thought of the Apostle Paul again, this time saying in Romans 7:24, *"Oh wretched man that I am. Who will rescue me...?"*

Neither of us spoke. How does one bridge the gap of regrets? Misty had died. We would never really know the condition of her heart. We cherished the ways she challenged us, brought brightness to our days, and we deeply mourned her sin and whatever led her there.

"Misty and I have been so much alike. She lived with regret that being good made her to miss out on some party, some celebration. I've tried to atone for my own sin by controlling myself and those around me. I've done a lot of good things for a lot of bad reasons." While she paused, I reflected on the way I also kept forgetting that God's grace both saves me and keeps me. I had my own ways of trying to let good deeds keep me in God's favour.

"I'm so thankful that God gave me Carl. How he's been able to forgive me and want me is amazing. My sin had a consequence, and when the cervical cancer came followed by a hysterectomy, I felt like I deserved this disappointment."

And there it was. Said as though I should have known it all along. The missing puzzle piece as to why Annaliese had three children: cancer brought on by a promiscuous life. I was way beyond judging her in that moment. Though she shared matter-of-factly, it was obvious she would give anything to do some things over. So would I.

"Yes, I felt like I deserved not only what was happening to my body, but also that I deserved not being able to have the large family I would have wanted. But Carl didn't. Didn't think I deserved it, that is. He's never held my past against me even when my sin affected him as well." Annaliese shivered and rubbed her hands over the warm mug she held.

"Yet I had this desperate need to warn others. And there we are, back to my desire to control."

As though her next comment was deeply connected to the last, she added, "Misty was so done feeling controlled. I don't understand how Kyle couldn't convince her that he loved her...maybe he hoped what he saw as purity in her would protect him from himself."

Where had I heard that before, I mused.

"Annaliese, there was tension between you and Misty. And it makes sense, you'd been with the man she married. But there also seems to be a deep connection. What, what made you love her?"

Annaliese's face froze in surprise for a moment.

She looked at me as if I were a stranger then gave her head a slight shake.

"What made me love her, Ainslee? She—Misty is my niece."

I stared, processing what I'd heard.

The two women who had deeply opposing points of view on many subjects, yet who shared a life of homeschooling, who had a history with the same man, who would have claimed a shared faith, actually shared a family connection?

It was mind-boggling.

Annaliese explained, "My much-older brother and sister-in-law homeschooled their seven beautiful girls. While my brother and his wife were raising their lovely family and giving our parents granddaughters to be proud of, *I* was living in a pit. And that should help you understand the scandal."

I tried to take that in.

Fun-loving, mission-minded, husband-leaving Misty, married the man with whom her aunt had fornicated. *Yeah, I guess that should help me understand the scandal.*

The older woman shook her head. "And some people think small towns have no secrets…"

She walked to the door with me.

As we stood on the veranda, and I'd forgotten entirely why I'd entered her home, I saw again the hibernating plants she'd offered me.

"You're right, Annaliese, I don't much enjoy gardening. But I'd like one of your pots if you still mean it."

"Absolutely!" she responded, gesturing for me to take my pick.

So I left, fittingly taking my Bleeding Heart, hoping it would awaken with the coming spring.

Chapter Forty-Five

Fall 2019

"*I want to go* to school next year," Arnold stated. I looked up from my Sudoku book almost as if I wasn't sure who was speaking.

"All my friends are going to school," he added.

What was he going to do next? Ask for a king for Israel? A king like all the other nations had?

If only I'd known then what Helen shared with me later. That the constant tension of wondering what the next year holds is not necessarily a bad thing. That making a blanket decision about homeschooling, or not, all of my children for an indefinite period of time, is not necessarily in their best interest. That the uncertainty and the inability to see into the future and how each possibility affects each of our needs, forces me to acknowledge that I'm not enough. Wrestling with myself, with Lyndon, with spoken and unspoken needs by each one of us, forces me to cry out to the Lord. To long for things that He possesses and I don't. To need Jesus. Wasn't that what had started all this? A driving desire to know Jesus? For my boys to know Him? And if Arnold was demanding a king for Israel, at what point did I allow him to find out for himself that kings call for heavy taxes?

* * * * *

I spent the next several days feeling sick and anxious after Arnold's announcement about his desire to go to school. He had hinted at it many times over the last two years but we hadn't taken him too seriously. We had tried the distractions long before he'd ever verbalized the desire—building the motorbike ramp for one. We had tried to show him how he could invest his time in profitable ways by having him take the mechanics course, being involved with a Habitat build.

Lyndon and I had warned him about the dangers of the current school curriculum, the waste of time, the pressures that would come with spending more time with ungodly people. We had addressed the issue of pornography, knowing full well in our own minds that if that was an area our son was allowing himself to drift, he would find ways to explore in that area from the very comforts of our own home, using the technological tools we had supplied as a means for his education, in spite of the filtering software we had installed.

I was concerned for Lyndon's sake. What would it look like for his career if his own son were not in the home-school system? This had begun, after all, as Lyndon's pursuit; as his passion to leave a legacy, to be a witness to kids in general, and then had become the focus of raising his own kids.

We were so close to Brewster's graduation. So close to *one down, only one more to go.* So close to having accomplished our part of their homeschool journey. So close to *our* goal.

I thought I'd resolved this battle in my mind years ago. I mean, how was it even possible now, that after all the initial years I'd spent coming to terms with seeing the actual value in homeschooling, then learning to embrace and implement it, and setting my own life goals aside for this greater good, that now at the very end, if Arnold got his way, I'd be forced to fail. Again.

What did it mean, in this context, that Christ must become greater and I must become less? Did it mean that I must give of myself, my goals, my dreams, my desires? My personhood? I knew this process of parenthood, and in our case of homeschooling, should leave Christ exalted. So why did I feel like it might just be leaving the person of me shredded?

I knew, had known for a long time, that this home-school journey, this parenting journey, wasn't completely about me. Brewster's disobedience last summer had shown me that I wasn't in control of his heart. Even if I could now find a way to make Arnold continue to homeschool, to persuade him to not drift off course, I could not make him love Jesus. And it was this thought, finally, that made me sob. Was it not this very thing, this raising my kids to love Jesus, that had compelled me to pour myself out for their sake? To leave the prestige of having a career, a title? To learn to be a homemaker, Lyndon's helpmeet? To be a Mrs. Homeschool? And in the end, would I now have to live with the reality that I had failed at the very centre, the very crux of the mission?

The very next week, Arnold slammed the front door on his way out of the house.

I cringed.

"Where are you going?" I looked up from raking dead leaves out of the corner beside the front door where they landed. Leaves that fell from the tree row in behind the house after the north winds brought them over the roof.

Arnold carried his motorbike helmet. "Riding with Conan. Won't be home for supper. Aunt June wants us to look after the dogs and stuff."

"Where'd the Thiessens go this time?"

"I dunno. Some vet convention maybe, or money meetings?"

"Of course." I tried to keep my voice level. "Well, what time are you going to be home? I'm sure Conan has school tomorrow." And just in case resentment revealed itself in my voice I added, "And so do you, Arnold."

"Yep, won't be too late," Arnold answered without committing, or without so much as turning to look at me.

He straddled his bike then. The same bike he'd declined to ride when Lyndon and Brewster had gone for an evening ride the week before. In fairness, they were taking the electric bicycles. Arnold's motorbike afforded him possibilities that made the electric bicycles a lame option. At least he gave me a slight nod as he left the yard, and in raising my hand to wave, I scraped my arm against the bottle-glass stucco of the house. Tears came easily. Not for the scrape which, as we had known from day one, would be inevitable. But either for Arnold, or myself. I wasn't really sure.

I loved June Thiessen. I admired the same things about her I always had. Part of me understood why she had enrolled Conan in school, claiming he was too lonely being kind of an only child on the tail end of their family. So why did I feel like I hated her? In truth, I also felt like she had compromised. When I met her, it seemed she was so committed to giving Conan the same experience she'd given her other children. But as much as I felt disappointment in her, I also knew that reality dictated that homeschooling Conan wouldn't have been, couldn't have been, the same experience she'd given the other children.

I also worried that Conan would be a bad influence on Arnold. Who knew what he was picking up in school? Conan was a couple of years older. Was it really just shared interests between Arnold and Conan that created a connection when Brewster and Conan's friendship kind of drifted? Did I need to be concerned that Conan was trying to get Arnold into drugs the way I'd always suspected Conan was the reason for Brewster's vaping, and that Brewster's subsequent repentance was the reason his friendship with Conan died out?

What was my problem? Did I really continue to believe that homeschooling Brewster and Arnold was the best thing for them? Or was I becoming afraid that, after having worked so hard to first gain and then give up my identity as an electrician, if I also lost my identity as a homeschool mom there'd be nothing left of me?

Chapter Forty-Six

November 2019

In mid-November I drove Arnold to Medicine Hat for a rehearsal of *The Sound of Music*. This was a large production put on by a dedicated group of homeschoolers from quite a radius of our southeastern corner of Alberta. I almost had to pinch myself. Here I was in a theatre, because my son, my son Arnold, was involved in a theatrical production. The child who was busy, industrious, hands-on, mechanical, had put all those skills to use in building sets for the play. It had given me so much pleasure to help him think through some of the electrical required to make his ideas come to life.

Egypt Keller, who would play Liesl, had come to our acreage with some of her friends on numerous occasions to paint the finished sets. This arrangement made Brewster suddenly very helpful to Arnold and the small group of young ladies. Their presence on our yard was a consolation, as Arnold realized Egypt's role meant she would be in love with Rolf. The despicable Rolf, played by Chasyn whom I clearly remembered as the interrupting tether ball player. *Look at me, Mom. See what I did with the ball there, Mom...?*

But Chasyn had matured into quite a dashing young fellow who was using his gift of speaking to represent Creation Science Ministries across the Prairie Provinces. "You have to remember, Arnold, that Rolf irreparably betrayed Liesl," I reminded him one day, intending it to be consolation for the worry I could see nagged at him whenever he observed Egypt practicing her dance with Chasyn.

Now as I sat alone in the plush theatre seat, having walked by Chasyn and Egypt once again practicing their dance in a side room down the hall, I felt nervous for my son. I hoped the fact that Chasyn was three years older than Egypt would be a detriment to her turning her affections toward him...And then I almost laughed at my protective thoughts. Hadn't I just a couple of months ago feared what it would mean for Arnold to get involved with the Keller family? I couldn't see how he could fit into their mold and retain his sense of self, but my, my, my how his practical side had been a perfect pairing to her musical and artistic expression.

"May I join you?"

"Of course," I responded to the voice before I'd even looked up. Evelyn Keller flipped the seat beside me down and arranged herself like a lady. How could she move so gracefully? She appeared to me as an elegant queen. I pictured the beautiful, Biblical queen Esther as I took in Evelyn's olive skin, long dark hair coiled into a flattering loose roll resting on the fur collar of her long winter coat. She removed her leather gloves and managed to cross her legs in the tight space between the rows of seats, revealing knee-high leather boots under a longer silvery-grey knit dress.

"What am I thinking, I'm going to cook in this coat," Evelyn laughed at herself as she unbuttoned the pale blue, faux wool and slipped it off her shoulders. A scarf with its riot of pink and plum colours stayed tied around her neck and I had to lick some moisture onto my dry lips as I tried to brightly smile and greet her. The dark purple jeans and lilac sweater under my tailored jean jacket, which I'd felt so good in when I'd left the hotel that morning, suddenly seemed frumpy and so unladylike.

Eleven kids! She has eleven kids! I heard myself chant incredulously in my head.

"It's so lovely to have a chance to visit with you, Ainslee," the queen started.

And when I met her eyes, I forgot that she had a vested interest in getting to know me as the mother of the boy her daughter was showing interest in, and I simply believed she meant it.

"All these years we've been acquaintances now, and I've never had the opportunity to get to know you. How has life been for you in Tracey?" Her sincerity disarmed me.

I reflected on the decade since we'd made the seemingly impulsive 859-kilometer drive to our abandoned, dead-fly-filled house and started making it a home.

"I can't imagine life anywhere else," I finally answered. And it was true.

We chatted easily then. I had always seen Evelyn as aloof and rigid. Probably even seen her as demanding, vigilant that her *music machine ministry* continue to function without glitches. But that wasn't who I perceived on this day. Sitting in the plush theatre chairs, her in her elegant knit dress and coifed hair, me mostly having forgotten about my coloured jeans which would be comfortable for getting groceries when we finished here, I just saw someone who simply couldn't be less than she was. Like, it just wasn't possible for a queen to live an ordinary life. But it also wasn't possible for a queen to relate to a commoner and yet here we were sharing smiles and ideas and downright camaraderie.

"How can we live less than an hour apart and see so little of each other?" I mused aloud.

"I don't get out much," Evelyn laughed wryly. And when she looked up, I saw shiny eyes. Her unshed tears.

So many possible responses filled my mind, but I couldn't voice any of them.

The beautiful queen Evelyn fished in her faux-fur coat pocket for a tissue.

"Sorry," she laughed. "I've just spilled not only my thoughts, but now my tears as well." She dabbed at her cheeks. "This homeschooling journey can be pretty lonely for us moms. You'd think I'd be used to it after all these years but...I guess it's rare to find such a good listener. So, thank you, Ainslee."

She blew her nose then. Cleaned those nasal passages right out. I relaxed. *That* was not ladylike.

"I've genuinely tried to pour out my life so my kids can succeed and be blessings to the world and sometimes that leaves little room for me to have any relationships outside of them. It's rare to find people who genuinely cheer us on in our life journeys. It often seems like people hope we will fail—hope that our kids will have moral failures, hope our marriages fail, hope our homeschooled kids won't be able to get into colleges and have successful careers. So, it's tiring to fight against the schemes of the devil against our children and our marriages, only to be scorned by fellow believers who have, for whatever reasons, had deep disappointments and then seem to wish we would find ourselves in the same pit."

At this point, her ruminating turned to exhorting.

"Ainslee, don't be afraid of fighting to succeed. There will be many who hope you will be mediocre, who will resent your family's spiritual successes, who practically wish for you to fall. Don't give in to it, no matter how alone you feel at times. Fight to have kids who grow up to love Jesus. It's worth it."

Shopping for ground beef and toilet tissue later, I couldn't stop thinking about her impassioned plea. I knew she was partly preaching to herself—using mine to be the ears which would hold her accountable to her own words. Nevertheless, it was a message sent from God for me that day.

Yes, on the one hand, I could not make my sons love Jesus. But I needed to also refuse to be passive for fear that others would perceive me as trying to be better than them. I did not want the devil to win in his struggle for both my children's and my own heart.

"Jesus. Oh, Jesus," my mind cried.

With what other words could I bare myself to God's mercy?

* * * * *

It was with deep humility that I told Lyndon about my visit with Evelyn Keller when we got home and the boys had helped me make a pot of chili before challenging each other to a video game.

We talked about Evelyn's vulnerable admission about not only their musical ministry, but their personal life.

"Lyndon, I've been one of the very ones who has subtly wished for her demise," I acknowledged. "I didn't once try to get to know her. I've just looked at her realm and made assumptions. Maybe she's a manipulator and I was royally duped today. Then again, maybe God has blessed the Keller family with a shared love and passion for the music ministry that I simply don't understand because I can't imagine myself ever being so loyal to a cause. Maybe I'm not willing to be that kind of a team player."

All these years, their pursuit had made me uncomfortable, had made me skeptical of both their motives and their methods. What if I had not judged correctly? And what was the matter with me that I felt I had to judge their case at all?

What I didn't tell Lyndon was the way I'd felt when he began to experience the success of his healing and subsequent weight loss. I could see no benefit in divulging that his success frustrated me. As long as Lyndon had been fat, my large frame was less obvious. When he lost almost fifty pounds and received people's affirmation, as happy as I was for him, it was a little hard to take.

And that seemed to sum up pretty well that Evelyn knew what deep inside we all know: we are self-focused, self-exalting people, just trying desperately to hide that we want other people to do well—but not better than us.

Chapter Forty-Seven

2020

In January, Lyndon and I were able to slip away to Calgary for a weekend. It felt a little silly to be dressed in our rented formal evening wear, but Lyndon insisted we add the splurge to our credit card and celebrate twenty years of our marriage with steak at the top of the Calgary Tower.

"At least I bought comfortable, sensible shoes I can walk in," I told Lyndon as we stood alone in the elevator, and now that I was still, I didn't need to worry about tripping on the long skirt I wore.

He shivered slightly and wrapped an arm around the fur on my shoulders.

"We should have rented you a coat too," I sympathized, feeling bad that Lyndon had thought of my comfort but neglected his own.

"It's a short walk from the hotel," he consoled, shrugging his broad shoulders. The silk lapels on his tuxedo shimmered. "Besides, I'm warm now," he grinned down at me.

"We didn't even look this good on our wedding day," I laughed.

"I wish I gave you more opportunities to dress like a princess," Lyndon apologized.

I felt bad then. Wondering how much I'd said to him about my feelings of inadequacy being in the company of the beautiful Evelyn Keller. Wondering how much pressure he'd put on himself to provide me with an opportunity to feel elegant. When he'd suggested the formal date, I'd thought he was a little crazy. I couldn't imagine feeling anything but awkward in a long shimmering gown. But when the store associate had looked me over and immediately brought out this deep green number with its embroidered and sequined front, a dress that draped perfectly over my hips, even I could see how a well-made garment flattered features that generally felt like liabilities. I tried on a few other dresses, but she obviously knew what she was doing, and none brought the sparkle right up into my face the way the first one had.

We savoured our steaks—meat that wasn't dried out from my inept abilities in the kitchen. Some Christmas décor remained in the restaurant and added to the atmosphere of looking out over the city, twinkling lights far below us in the dark of the winter evening. It seemed a shame for us to sit across a table from each other in our fantastic clothing and admire each other only from this limited point of view while we sipped coffee and shared a chocolate-raspberry cheesecake.

After the symphony and the midnight carriage ride, during which Lyndon broke down and wore his winter parka, despite it looking shabby over the tux, after an evening out which was a far cry from our motorbike dates of days gone by, we hung up our finery. Lyndon had even arranged for its return to the store, so all we had to do was leave it in the hotel closet. We cuddled in cozy pajamas, nibbled on fruit and chocolate, and enjoyed herbal tea, and I shoved away the occasional thoughts of what this would add up to on the next credit card bill.

"You spoiled me rotten tonight, Lyndon."

"There's a first for everything," he responded.

"You've been good to me," I assured him.

"I want us to grow old together, Ainslee. To grow old and be happy together. I'm sorry I haven't shown you enough how much you matter to me."

"Sometimes life is just hard, Lyndon. I've never really thought you don't care." Even as I said it, I thought back to the times I felt Lyndon had chosen time with Ken, time with his career rather than time with us. I couldn't say it didn't hurt. However, it was almost true. Other than the big blow up in the garage where I wasn't sure how much of the venom we'd spit at each other was simply frustration that boiled over in the moment, and how much was our true feelings that we'd finally confessed in the most hurtful of ways, I hadn't doubted that Lyndon cared for me.

"Sometimes I worry that we'll have spent so much energy on the boys that there'll be nothing left of us when they grow up, Ainslee." He took my hand and rubbed his fingers over my wedding band.

"Really?" I found it hard to believe that Lyndon worried about our future.

"It should be easier now because I can do more things with you. I can do more things *for* you. You've been such a champ." He still rubbed my hand and I realized my trimmed fingernails hardly looked like those of the lady I'd tried to be tonight. "You've been so good to me and the boys."

"Thanks, Lyndon." He hadn't said that often enough. Hadn't acknowledged often enough how hard it was to put aside my personal ambitions to serve my family. Maybe I also hadn't acknowledged often enough the ways Lyndon had tried to serve us.

"Ainslee, it's a challenging season with Brewster and Arnold. I often can't tell what's going on in their hearts. I'm not always sure if Brewster is actually doing well, or if it's easier for him to make us think he's being compliant and he's still got a duplicitous heart. And Arnold? I don't know what he's trying to find. I can't tell if he's just looking for independence and has a deep need to chart his own course, or if he's looking for trouble and is about to find it."

I had wondered the same, and, ever since my talk with Evelyn Keller, I'd found myself hoping maybe Egypt would be enough inspiration for Arnold to make good choices. But that was hardly fair, was it. If he couldn't be drawn to good because he saw value in righteousness, it was a burden I dare not place on Egypt—that she should be sufficient reason for good choices on his part. It was a burden she could never bear in the long run anyway. Arnold would have to be the pilot of his own heart.

Lyndon continued, "You matter to me, Ainslee. Our marriage matters to me. We've made our share of mistakes but I want you to know that as much as I feel our boys are better off being homeschooled, I can't do that, and I can't ask you to do that, at the expense of us. So, if Arnold insists on going to school for second semester, I don't think we can stop him."

I looked at Lyndon's eyes then. I could tell it pained him to say it. As much as I had learned over time to value having the boys learn without the frailties of the public school system, Lyndon had, in one conversation with Ken Berry, been convinced of the merits and possibilities of raising children both unencumbered by a godless system, and under the care of their parents to whom their ultimate success mattered most.

"I don't think it makes sense to either of us for Arnold to keep saying he wants to take a high school shop class when he's already taken a mechanics class at the college level, but I have a feeling we had better just make peace with letting him choose."

Lyndon had obviously just made his closing statement about the matter. I agreed with him.

Still, that didn't make it easy when we got home the next day and found Arnold filling out Tracey High School forms at the kitchen table. It grated on me that this was the moment he finally chose to be self-motivated about anything involving paper. In spite of that painful jab, I was so thankful it hadn't completely blindsided me.

Chapter Forty-Eight

February 2020

As I had done so many times over the years, I turned to Helen's listening ear. Of course, even I didn't realize that's what I was doing. Her south-facing deck was the perfect shelter to soak up the late winter sun. Helen offered me a patio chair covered in red flowered cushions on her small patio. Between the chair where I sat and the one she would soon occupy was a little table with a blooming amaryllis. Both trumpet-shaped flowers were a bright poppy red which matched the seat cushions, though those had faded from the sun over several years of use.

Again, I observed Helen's back yard. She had stayed in her small family home after Ken's death a few years ago. It was a comfortable home for her. But nothing about their life spoke of luxury or extravagance. Helen enjoyed their small yard, especially the apple and cherry trees. She didn't travel much, other than to see her daughters on occasion.

She continued her part-time job with a catering company. Helen was sitting out on her patio, reading, with a blanket wrapped around her shoulders when I arrived, but she immediately set her book down on the little table beside the amaryllis. Now, while she was in the house getting us a warm drink, I observed the title. *"Hebrews: Approaching God with Confidence."*

The screen door opened and Helen stepped out with two mugs of strawberry tea she'd steeped while I sat outside. The stirring spoon clanked against the ceramic side as she passed one to me along with a couple of packets of sugar. With Helen's *I LOVE my Wife* mug set on the table between us, she pulled her sunglasses from the top of her head and tried to smooth her hair back into place. Helen had continued to splurge with a professional haircut and protein treatments, but since I'd surprised her with my visit, pieces of hair from the cowlick on the right side of her forehead stuck out at awkward angles.

"You've been reading," I observed, taking a sip of the hot, fruit-flavoured black tea.

"I always need to be reminded that Jesus is superior," Helen winked.

Helen had assured me when I showed up at her back door, parking my electric bike in front of her garage, that she had no plans for the day and was so glad I'd come. I chose to believe her, and didn't rush the conversation. Yet, I didn't have the insight to know what she meant. I hadn't read the Biblical book of Hebrews in a while and couldn't even immediately recall what it was about other than chapter eleven which spoke about heroes of the faith.

"Sorry, Helen, Jesus is superior to what?" I finally succumbed to my curiosity.

"Jesus is superior to systems."

"Ah, okay."

We watched the birds in her apple tree which had bloomed and was getting its first spring leaves.

"What's on your mind, Ainslee?"

My heavy heart could hardly think, never mind form a rational conversation.

"The boys, I guess," I managed.

"You told me about finding Brewster vaping the year before last. Is there more?" She prodded.

"No," I answered quickly. "I don't know." I sighed.

"Brewster claimed it was a one-time thing. He says he was glad we saw him. Even said he thinks God sent us down the back alley that day. I have no reason to believe either of the guys is in trouble, but then again, I didn't see that coming either."

It was hard to acknowledge my worries about the boys. Hard to put into words that all might not be turning out as I'd hoped and worked for.

"Arnold says he's going to school next year. It just makes no sense. Why? He doesn't really know that group of kids even though he claims his best friends are going to school. He's had so many opportunities to do things without being stuck in a classroom, and now he thinks he'll spend his days stuck in a desk? He won't get the credits he needs to graduate from public high school anyway..."

I couldn't help it. Tears rolled down my cheeks.

Helen took the few steps across the patio and through the screen door into her house, returning shortly with a box of tissues. She waited until I'd wiped at my cheeks and nose and was breathing evenly again.

"What are you afraid of, Ainslee?"

Afraid? I didn't think I was afraid, but so many what-ifs came to mind.

What if he got into the wrong crowd at school?

What if he hardened his heart to the Lord?

What if Lyndon and I hadn't prepared him to do well academically?

What if he met a girl who interested him more than Egypt? What if Egypt's family would disapprove of him going to school?

What if my struggle to cherish homeschooling my sons, allowing it to shape my days, my very identity, would now be deemed worthless? What if I'd put in all these years for nothing?

Because somewhere along the way, I'd changed my mind from a homeschool skeptic to embracing the opportunity to, along with Lyndon, shape and mentor our boys.

As if she could read my mind, Helen said, "Maybe you've done what you set out to do, Ainslee."

"I'm not ready for this to be done. And I can see that he's too old to control—I don't really get a say."

Helen nodded. With complete empathy, she said, "There's so many things in life we face that we're not ready for. And we can't control."

Immediately, I thought of Ken's sudden death. "I'm so sorry, Helen."

"Ainslee, this is your story, and you get to grieve your losses if that's what this will be for you."

"How did you manage your grief?"

She pointed to her book on Hebrews.

"Jesus is superior, remember? Superior to the systems which were meant to prepare us for His coming. Before I understood the gospel, I didn't know that God set up the priestly system in the Old Testament as a picture of what it would take to approach a Holy God. Once I understood that Jesus is the great High Priest and we have access into His very presence 'to receive mercy and find grace to help in time of need', I learned to approach Him with confidence. That doesn't give you control, dear Ainslee. But it sure gives comfort."

Maybe I would always battle myself. Maybe I would get to the end of my life, whenever that would be, and find that every attempt toward righteous living would eventually reveal self-righteousness. That true, Christ-centered living meant my self-sufficiency, my systems, must be broken and replaced with nothing other than this need-to-know Jesus. To know that I can come before Him with confidence to find mercy and grace.

And to trust that He can do that for my children as well.

Chapter Forty-Nine

Early March 2020

Lyndon and I had woken up early that Saturday morning. We'd enjoyed a cup of coffee and some personal time reading. Brewster and Arnold had been out late with the youth group the night before so they were still sleeping upstairs in their small attic rooms, where the play forts in the eaves had become over the years simply storage space.

The forecast was for a beautiful early spring weekend, so we had decided to invite a group of friends to join us at Sugar Valley Campsite for the first barbeque of the season. We'd have to bundle up a bit to enjoy being outside, but after a winter season, each of the other families we'd contacted had been excited to join us. We had bought a bulk amount of ground beef the evening before when we'd gone shopping while the boys were at youth group and now we worked together at mixing it up. I made a trip down to the root cellar to get the hamburger press while Lyndon started mixing the eggs, cracker crumbs, and spices into the meat. I set cookie sheets on the table and lined them with silicone baking sheets so we could form the burger patties and freeze them in layers for later. Susanna's informal financial lessons had literally paid off. Burger patties was something we'd been making ourselves for several years now.

We both sat at the kitchen table, listening to a Christian radio station, I rolled a ball of meat into the press and Lyndon formed and removed it, laying it on the pan. Our hands each had a layer of moist, raw meat.

We heard movement upstairs, and then footsteps coming down the stairs and into the bathroom as the door closed. Several burger patties later, Arnold emerged and came up the hall, carrying his backpack.

I smiled at him, "You're up earlier than I expected. What adventure do you have planned?"

Arnold didn't meet my eyes. His face didn't light up at the burgers stacked on the table. Lyndon's shoulders slumped a little. His movements with the burger press slowed.

"Mom and Dad, I'm moving out. I'm gonna go live with Conan." He opened the fridge, poured himself a glass of juice. He took one long drink and set the empty glass in the sink.

He continued to move with resolve. Walked around the wall with the stove, which was the closest point to where Lyndon and I sat, our hands covered in raw burger meat.

Arnold picked up his backpack, stepped into the front hall, stooping to grab his shoes out of the closet.

While he knelt to put them on and do up the laces, first one knee and then the other down on the carpet, I heard Lyndon's voice. "Arnold, let me know if you run into any problems with your car. Your bed is always here."

I found my voice in time to say, "Love you, Arnold. Text if you need anything."

The front door opened and closed with its usual thump, which always seemed louder than it needed to.

I pushed my chair away from the table and went to the sink, leaving little clumps of ground beef mix on the taps when I turned them on. As Arnold threw his backpack in the back seat and started his car and pulled out of the drive, I used dish soap to get the grease off my hands. I used my shoulder to wipe the tears off my freckled cheek.

Meanwhile, I could hear Lyndon in the bathroom. Water ran there as well.

After a while he came to the kitchen. Stood behind me looking out the window at the empty yard. The burgers sat unfinished and uncovered on the table. Lyndon wrapped his arms around me while we leaned against the silver-edged counter.

"Oh Lord, watch over our dear boy," he prayed, his cheeks wet.

"We don't know his heart, but You do, dear Father. Protect him from the evil one. You have shown us so much favour. That You would choose to save us, bringing people like Ken and Helen into our lives to teach us what it means to walk in faith…

"From being fatherless to knowing Your merciful love, dear Father…

"Oh God, as You've faithfully shown us Your grace, do the same for Arnold. Unchanging, merciful, faithful God, continue Your work in Arnold's heart…

Chapter Fifty

In the days after Arnold left, so did the last of our snow. Each morning I checked my phone hoping for some word from him. Lyndon would have a coffee and read his Bible. Then he'd send Arnold a brief message, a few words of love. Brewster tended to sleep in, as his evening shifts at the local Co-op Gas Bar kept him working until midnight several nights each week. So, after Lyndon left for work in the morning, I often had an hour before Brewster would be up and around the house.

It felt appropriate, actually even necessary, in those days after Arnold left, to take those first minutes of quiet to go to the short front hall where I'd last seen my son. I envisioned him putting on his shoes here, kneeling here, first one knee down on the carpet then the other. Morning after morning I knelt there too. I knelt on both my knees and asked the God who created my son, who knew his heart and loved him, to bring whatever it took into Arnold's life so that he would choose to kneel before Holy God willingly. That he would find God sufficient for his restlessness or rebellion—I didn't know which.

Then I would read my Bible and, like Elisabeth Elliot, widow of the martyred missionary, choose to not let Arnold's leaving destroy me. Though some days I thought the battle and resolve to choose, might. I tried to regard June Thiessen's regretful advice about failing to stay engaged with Conan and made it my goal to not lose time with Brewster in spite of the grief I felt over Arnold.

I also prayed to not resent Conan. That was all I could manage.

As I had for many years now, I made it my daily prayer to be moved from the pursuit of significance to the pursuit of simple obedience.

It would seem that as the boys got older, it would have been the perfect time to take on more electrical work and have them work with me, learning about the trade. However, they had each found part-time work of their own at entry level jobs that gave them the pleasure of working with their peers. So, I still did the occasional small job for Garry, but wasn't able to take on any contracts I couldn't complete by myself. Thankfully, a dentist at church had asked if I'd be open to filling a part-time maternity leave position starting in August if all went as planned for the mom-to-be. I hadn't committed yet, but as much as I didn't want to be a dental hygienist, I also needed more real-time social interaction than I was getting, now that the boys were running their own schedules.

*****

March 15, 2020

I had just gotten up from my knees on the slate-blue entry carpet when my phone dinged.

"Ainslee, did you listen to the news? The government just closed all schools."

"Because of that Covid thing?" I texted back.

"Yep. I'll come home at lunch, talk to you then."

Worry filled my gut. What would Arnold's plan be? *He has to come home. I can't make him come home. If he had just stayed the course and finished his homeschooling this wouldn't be an issue*! My worry turned to anger. Then I warned myself, "Man's anger does not bring about the righteous life God requires." As I recited the memorized scripture, I thanked God again for Susanna's example. Anyway, how would my anger help Arnold if he *did* come home. Still, I couldn't get myself to be productive. Arnold had texted briefly in the last week to let us know he was doing fine and continuing to attend school in Tracey, but if he really had been and now couldn't, what would he do?

As promised, Lyndon came home at noon. In the years since Ken had passed away, Boundless Home School Board had hired three new staff to keep up with the increasing demand of homeschooling in the province. This made it a bit easier for Lyndon to slip away at noon and have others to cover for him if necessary. Brewster joined us for lunch, although I couldn't eat more than half my toasted cheese and tomato sandwich. We talked about the news, the health crisis that had started in China and now affected every single person in our province halfway around the world.

At 12:45, Brewster went back to our school room for his online physics class which started at 1:00. Lyndon put his shoes back on, bending over with ease. Even in the midst of our current stress I couldn't help but admire and appreciate my husband's healthy, fit body. Despite my occasional envy, it was a comfort. After all the years that leg had brought increasing stress to our lives, God provided so graciously, so mercifully, that most days we forgot the pain that had ruled our days and suffocated our marriage. So now I would take this small reminder, this reminder on the very spot where Arnold made his stubborn departure, that the same God who provided mercy through every painful trial of the tumour years had not changed or removed his mercy.

Lyndon wrapped me up there in front of the door with its oval glass insert of flowers, and pulled me against his shoulder. I leaned my cheek against him, the hair on his chin tickling my nose. I reached up to rub my nose and shifted. We stood like that for several minutes. I flashed back years to the day I realized I'd forgotten about school, the day I was smacked in the face by Walmart's seasonal display and convenient school supply lists. The day Lyndon and I sat across from each other at McDonald's while the boys enjoyed the play centre in their new socks, and, despite our shortcomings, we were the best team in the league. Now here we were, once again smacked in the face. But we were a team. A team with another injury, once again with an unknown future, but with a shared trust in a God who wouldn't leave us.

"I'll let you know if I hear anything from Arnold," Lyndon promised before leaving for work.

We didn't hear from Arnold that day, but early in the evening we bundled up, pulled our electric bikes out of the garage and rode to town. We biked by Canadian Tire and saw Arnold's car parked on the vehicle service-centre side of the building where he worked in the evenings doing oil changes. We didn't go in to the store as Covid had become a crazy concern—rather, we chose to assume that if his vehicle was there, he would be working his usual shift. Some businesses had been declared essential services and were allowed to stay open despite the raging virus.

Another two weeks passed. We spent several of our evenings playing card games with Brewster. With all non-essential travel banned, the service station had cancelled most of Brewster's work shifts as there simply was no need for him. The few people who needed fuel were required to pump their own. Arnold texted both of us more than he had when he first left, so, despite the increasing unknowns of current events, we worried less than we had when he first walked out.

Still, while the plague in our world kept us from our friends, our church, I fought a different plague in my mind. Maybe if we'd given in to Arnold's request to go to school earlier, he wouldn't have walked out that day. What could we have done to keep him from kneeling in the front hall simply putting his shoes on while we watched, burger meat covering our hands, showing us how helpless we were to stop him? Showing us that when we think we are creating good family times, life is unpredictably messy. Maybe if we'd lived in a bigger house where Arnold's husky frame wasn't limited to the size of a twin bed. Maybe if I'd made enchiladas more often when there was no one else to share them with, no church potluck. Maybe if we'd done whatever it took so he and Brewster could've joined Mr. G's football team. Maybe if we'd let him get the dog he wanted. Maybe…

Maybe what? Maybe then we could have controlled his heart? Could've forced the outcome we had worked so hard to achieve? Could've seen the results of having done this parenting journey right?

I felt indignant and offended that after all the years I'd given to submit myself to both God and Lyndon, this was my reward.

Brewster flew through his school work. Without being able to spend evenings working or hanging out with friends, he rode his motorbike when he wasn't studying, and spent evenings tweaking his bike with Lyndon who was busier than ever as the weeks went by and parents gained concern about taking charge of their kids' education.

I continued to blog. *Fuel for Those Who Homeschool.* There wasn't much more I could do at this point.

Day after day, I engaged readers who had discovered my blog now that the whole world was homeschooling.

And day after day I wrestled with my grief and disappointment that I had poured myself into my kids, and they could just leave me to grapple with the unknowns.

It took me a few days to begin to resonate with readers around the world who found themselves cast into this homeschool role. At first, I couldn't respond. Condescending platitudes found their way onto my keyboard and even I could see that words like *crisis schooling is not the same as homeschooling* would benefit no one. Really, the difference was that what pandemic life required other parents to process in days, had dragged on for years in mine. And where I *felt* I didn't have a choice, they really didn't. In the past, parents like me had the luxury of mulling over their children's educational needs, experimenting with options. We knew nothing of being cast into this position with zero initiative on our part. But I suspected that once this plague ended and we again had choices, some parents would embrace an option that was initially unfamiliar and uncomfortable because they saw its merits.

The last Friday in May, I started the day by taking my electric bike out for an hour. I read my Bible alone by the pools in the gravel pits where Lyndon and I had enjoyed solace. Today, completing the book of Judges, I reflected on the Israelites' cycle of recognizing their need for God, being strengthened through His mercy, then their pride and subsequent failure. In the hardening of their hearts, their seasons of reliance on God became shallower, and their indifference greater, until the book ended with these words: *Everyone did what was right in his own eyes.*

Was that where my search, my pursuit, of significance would leave me—doing what was right in my own eyes? I could stay shattered and disappointed by Arnold's unexplained choice and what would it do to me?

Ainslee, is this the thing that is going to be the destroyer of your faith?

I am so disappointed, God, I responded. *I don't know that my son's soul is right with You. I have fought for his soul. For Arnold's and for Brewster's. How could you create these boys and not require that they give You their souls? How could that bring You glory?*

I sobbed then. Tears that were in part cries for God's mercy on my boys, part pity for myself and the vanity of all the years I'd invested with no guarantee of results. Tears that recognized despite my efforts, I had no control over the most intimate choice of their hearts.

Ainslee, is this the thing that is going to be the destroyer of your faith?

It was the same question I'd been confronted with years ago when I'd read a book that asked me to move from the pursuit of significance in life to simple obedience to the things of God. I could handle some of my failures—I had not put either my dental hygienist or electrician training to really good use—but please God, please don't let me fail as a Christian mother.

Ainslee, is this the thing that is going to be the destroyer of your faith?

I had never yet outright said *no* to the things God had asked of me. I wasn't sure I'd ever so clearly heard Him ask for my obedience. Heard Him ask for me to carry on in faith. Could I obey? Could I submit? Could I genuinely love a God who refused to guarantee outcomes and would so clearly ask me to simply walk in obedience?

I took another hour to cycle around the countryside. The growth in the potato and corn and beet fields made me smile through my tears. I pedalled until my legs hurt, until I'd thought through the cycling in the Israelites' journey of being led by judges and everyone doing what was right in their own eyes. Until I knew that, as much as I wanted to hold God to a duty to give my sons hearts that honoured Him, I couldn't. Yet He could rightfully hold *me* to such a standard—a heart that would honour Him.

Had any of the past twelve years even been about homeschooling? Or had it been about my sons' hearts? My heart? I knew that as surely as the curly, dark-green potato leaves were thriving in the summer heat, I desired to allow myself to grow in God's grace.

And I would continue in fervent prayer that my sons would do the same.

Chapter Fifty-One

Deep in thought, panting for breath, filled with the deep satisfaction of time spent in the presence of an Almighty, All-Knowing God, I pedalled around the McMansion which was looking dusty from the gravel road in spite of its mud-coloured finishes.

Arnold stood in front of the house beside his car. My handsome son whom I hadn't seen in almost three months was thinner than he'd been when he left. My son, whose wiry, strawberry-blond hair looked greasy and in need of a cut, just like the rest of us in the midst of a pandemic. Maybe I would finally have the courage to try Susanna's advice that we cut our own hair. It was weird that I suddenly wished my curly hair wasn't so disheveled from riding, and I felt embarrassed by how red my face looked when I'd been exercising. Red, and inevitably dirty as well. Thoughts I'd have if Arnold were a visitor.

I felt tongue-tied. I couldn't hug him, he was sixteen after all. So, I dismounted beside his car, smiled, and gave him a simple, "Hello, Arnold."

He met my eyes briefly. "Dad said I could move back cuz Conan and I don't really have work right now so..." he trailed off.

I knew very well that unless the Thiessens were pitching in money for the boys' rent, it was doubtful they would be able to continue making the payments themselves with the uncertainty and scarcity of work. It did surprise me though that Arnold was waiting for my permission, as if he needed me to hold out the golden sceptre.

Memories of the night Brewster sobbed in our bed and all he got from me was arrogant silence filled me with shame. God help me, I would not make the same mistake twice.

"Arnold," I waited until he looked up. "Your room is just as you left it. I hope you'll have a toasted cheese and tomato sandwich with me for lunch."

His face softened a bit.

I might never know why he wondered if he was welcome back. Maybe he didn't even know.

"Are you going to need to do some laundry?" I asked as he pulled his bag from the back seat.

"That'd be awesome, thanks."

* * * * *

"Dear Readers," my next blog post began.

"We want to give our kids what we didn't have growing up. We determine to do better than that, to make sure our kids don't lack material stuff or don't feel negative emotion. As if we have that kind of power. We offer them the gift of homeschooling so we maximize our opportunity to impact their minds with Godly values, or we give them every chance to succeed in sports so they feel like heroes, or *not* homeschooling so they don't feel like the outcast we felt like. Whatever our good intention is, it cannot give them a perfect life. It cannot keep them from scars or pain or unmet needs."

I stopped typing. My eyes blurred as I thought back to moments where I'd changed my mind: crushing on Benny Painchaud, hating pumpkin pie, leaving my work in a dentist's office—

All these years I'd been looking for reasons to settle my *mind* about homeschooling. Maybe what I'd really needed was a change of *heart*. Maybe what I'd needed all along was not so much the right information to do the right thing, but simply letting myself be transformed to Christ's likeness.

"Dear reader," I continued, using a tone Helen would use with me, "there is no formula to ensure a successful life either for ourselves or for our kids. And obedience to God doesn't come with guarantees.

"But a genuine pursuit of God does come with the comfort of His presence. Know that always, God is pursuing you. Maybe that will lead you to educate your kids at home. Maybe not. In the end, homeschooling is not our children's salvation—Jesus is."

Discussion Questions

1. Could you relate to the rural setting of Tracey, Alberta? What do you see as the benefits or challenges of homeschooling in a rural versus urban location? (Chapter 1)

2. How familiar do you consider yourself to be regarding homeschooling? Did you read this book with a pre-disposition either for or against home education? (Chapter 1)

3. Did you like Ken? Is there anyone in your spouse's life who you feel competes for their attention or commitment? Has this ever caused tension between you and your spouse? (Chapter 1, 31)

4. Are you able to pinpoint your own Kingdom of Darkness to Kingdom of Light moment? Does your spiritual story have a clearly defined *before and after* component? If so, what was your impetus for growth? If not, how do you explain the lack of

clarity about such a monumental shift? (Chapters 1, 21, 39, 44)

5. How did you feel about Ainslee and Lyndon's financial habits? Did their perspective on money challenge or reinforce your own? Would you be content without home ownership? Are you at a place of contentment regarding your finances and material possessions? (Chapters 2, 27, 37)

6. Is it healthy to have a mentor as Ainslee had with Helen? Do you have someone who mentors you? Did you seek her out or did she seek you out, or did your relationship evolve into such over time? (Chapters 4, 5, 15, 20, 24, 29, 34, 39, 48)

7. Did it bother you, or encourage you, that Ainslee had career and personal dreams that were sometimes at odds with being a stay-at-home wife and mom? (Chapter 5)

8. Did you like or dislike the Keller family who performed as *E-harmony*? Did your opinion change as the story progressed? Have you ever wondered whether certain parents were coercing their children to co-operate? Are there times you have bribed or demanded your children's co-operation? (Chapters 6, 46)

9. Dr. June Thiessen both inspires and intimidates Ainslee. Are there people who intimidate you? What did you like about June? Is it possible to successfully homeschool a single child? (Chapters 8, 40, 45)

10. Are you aware of groups or individuals who have suffered for their belief in Jesus as Susanna did in the Bolivian Mennonite colony? (Chapter 9)

11. Ainslee plays soccer on a women's league. What are you pursuing as personal interests? Is it important to have pursuits outside of your husband and children? Why or why not? (Chapter 10)

12. Are homeschool parents known for taking stances? What issues do you generally associate with things homeschool families are strongly for or against? (Chapters 12, 26, 42)

13. If it's true that homeschool families have strong opinions, how do you explain this?

14. If you are currently homeschooling, or considering it for the future of your family, what methods do you use or lean toward? Did you agree or disagree with Ainslee's reasons for choosing to use curriculum? (Chapter 14)

15. Misty intentionally pursued relationships with people for the purpose of evangelism. Is it possible to be pursuing godly passions, such as evangelism, while at the same time allowing ungodliness into our lives? If so, how do you explain this? (Chapters, 16, 17, 18, 26)

16. Janeice nursed her children for an extended period, using it as a form of birth control. Are you, like Ainslee, disgusted by this approach? Do you relate to

Janeice? Are there benefits to extended nursing you would like others to know about? (Chapter 17)

17. Are there people whom you know or perceive to homeschool because of a desire to keep their children close? Are there any issues with this approach? (Chapter 17)

18. Do we dare discuss family size? Are there any scriptures you would use either for or against limiting the size of your family? Do you feel passionately on one side or the other of this debate? (Chapter 17)

19. How did you respond to Misty's desire to be noticed? Do you find yourself longing for the affirmation of men other than your husband? (Chapters 18, 26)

20. Helen talks about her own and Ken's journey to salvation. Were you able to connect? How would you explain salvation? (Chapter 24)

21. Ainslee states to the younger Karalee that vaccines are not a moral issue. Do you believe this? Are there ever times when vaccines are a moral issue? (Chapter 27)

22. How is your husband similar to, or different than, Lyndon? What relationship advice would you give Ainslee and Lyndon? (Chapter 30)

23. Ainslee struggles with how much value to place on our earthly families. Her conclusion is that, although earthly families are temporary, families are the means by which we learn spiritual concepts. What

do you believe is the importance of earthly families? (Chapters 35, 37)

24. The pain from Lyndon's tumour began as a sports injury that wouldn't heal. Are there health concerns in your family that have shaped your decisions, the direction your family has taken, or even your personalities? (Chapter 36)

25. Have you ever dealt with a child, like Brewster, who tends to be agreeable but is sneaky? How do you know when your child's repentance is real? How does a parent discern the difference between restlessness and rebellion in their child's life? (Chapters 42, 50)

26. Annaliese interpreted her cervical cancer as a punishment for her sexual sin, although her husband did not look at it that way. Have you ever perceived a hardship in your life as a punishment for sin? Do you believe that God causes or allows difficulties in your life in response to sin? Why or why not? (Chapter 44)

27. If there is a natural bent toward legalism (like Annaliese), or liberty (like Misty) in response to our past, which would be your bent? (Chapter 44)

28. This story tells Ainslee's journey with homeschooling. It concludes with a lack of certainty about Arnold's intentions. Did you complete the book and feel that there is something other than Jesus in which you have placed your hope for your children? (Chapter 51)

Connect With the Author

To order additional copies of *Mrs. Homeschool,* or to request a bulk discount, contact Karen via e-mail or visit her website.

e-mail: authorkarenpeters@gmail.com
website: www.karenlouisepeters.ca

Printed in Canada